Mark & Anita Bubeck,

Enjoy!

Dec. 2001

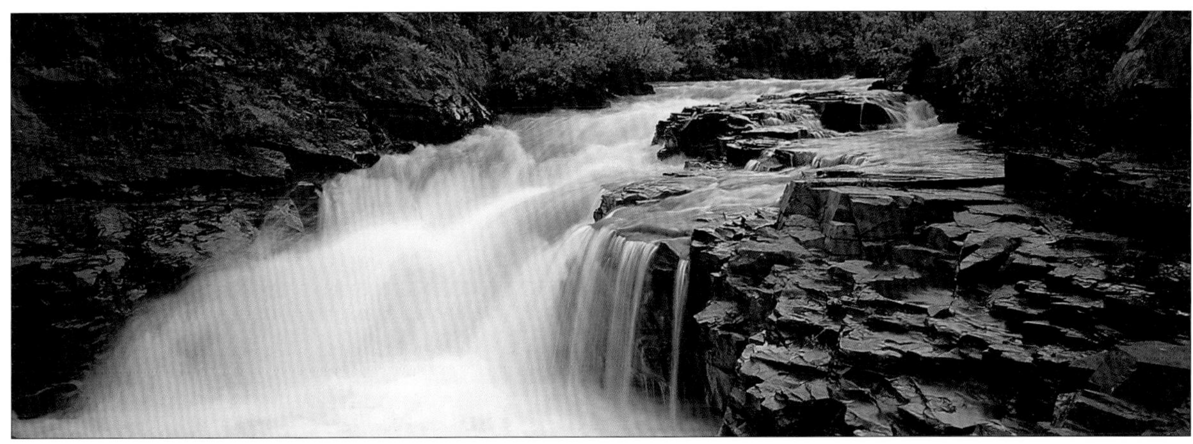

God said, "Be glad and rejoice forever in what I create."

Isaiah 65:18

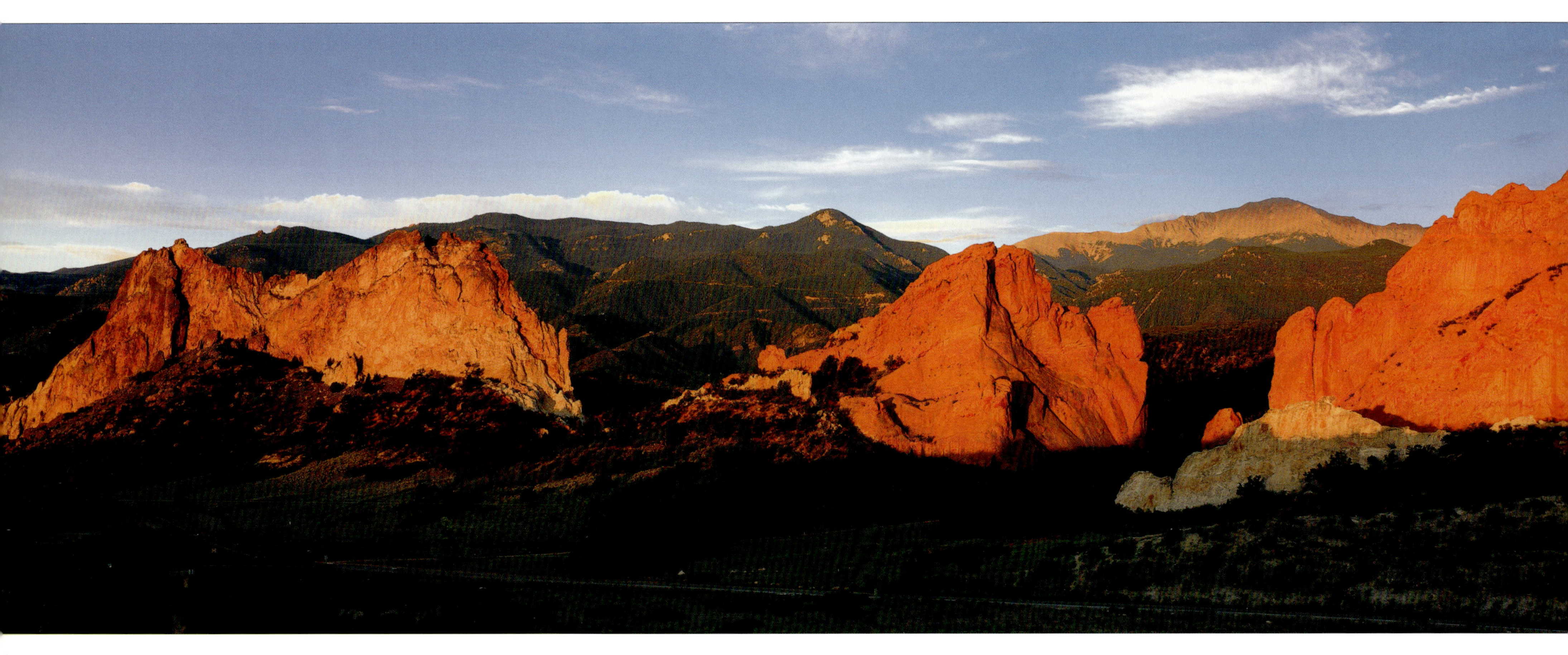

Garden of the Gods, Colorado Springs

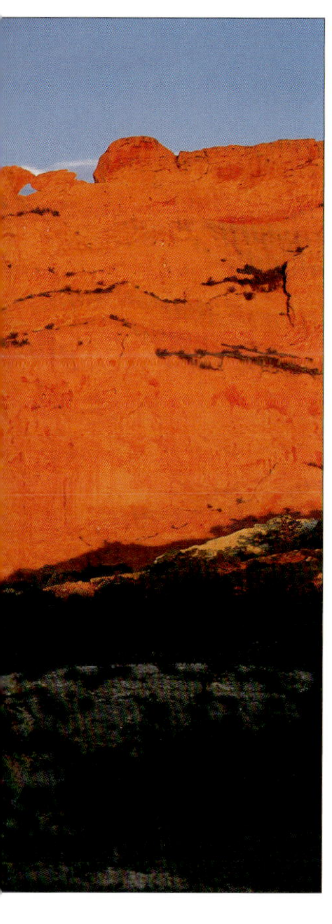

COLORADO

Rocky Mountain Wide

PANOGRAPHIC IMAGES™ BY JIM KEEN

LIBRARY OF CONGRESS CONTROL NUMBER
2001118843

1. Colorado - Pictorial Works 2. Landscape - Colorado
3. Nature Photography - Colorado

ISBN #0-9713355-0-8

Design by John Hamilton
Copy Editing by Don Pape

Cover jacket photograph of Jim Keen by Alan Feuerhaken

Special thanks to the following
for their assistance in the creation of this book:
Ken Krause
Dave Linder
Bill & Amy Stearns
Bob Tillman
Bob and Jan Vasquez
Eastern Mountain Sports
Mountain Hardware

Published by
Keen Media
www.keenmedia.com
800/363-5336
Printed in Canada

This book is dedicated to my wife

Roann,

who gave me a camera for my birthday the second year of our marriage.

Her commitment to me and personal daily encouragement has continued for more than 36 years.

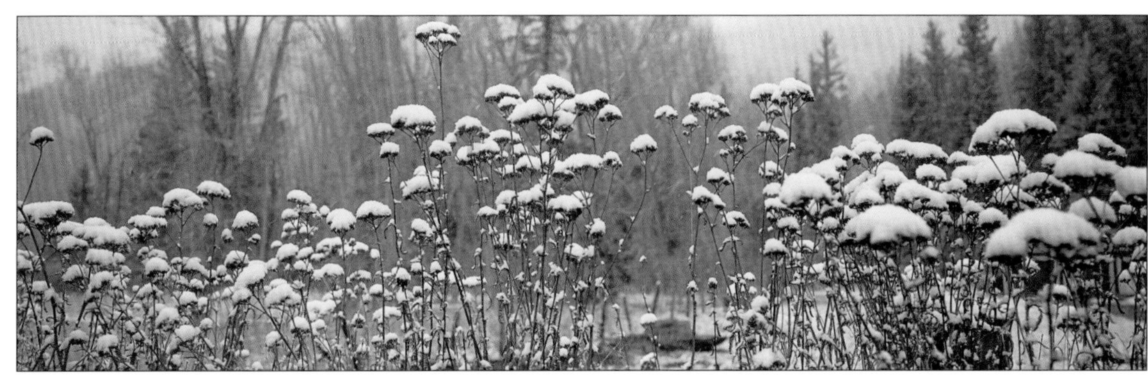

About the Cover

I had this panographic image™ of Longs Peak in my mind for several months, but for one reason or another was not able to create it. Finally my schedule cleared in early May 2001, and there was a full moon. The hike up Three Sisters is not long, but with 18 inches of fresh snow from the day before and a seventy-pound pack, it was slow going to my campsite. That night the weather cleared and the morning was numbingly cold, but the moonset was perfect and well worth the effort to create this image. As the sun began to warm everything up, I took advantage of the beauty of the Rockies and lingered, reading from the front porch of my tent before hiking back to the trailhead.

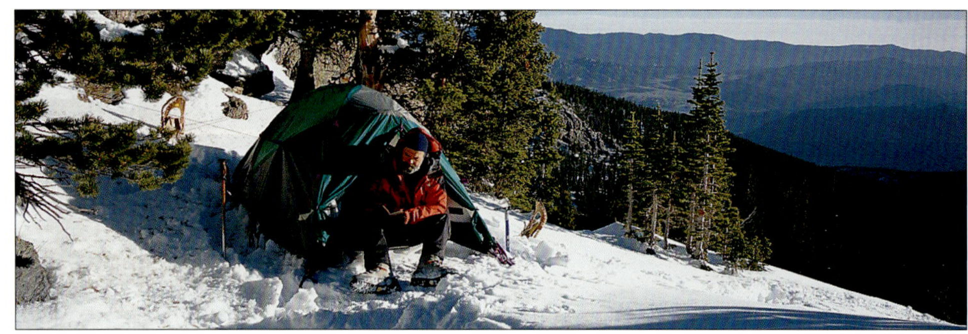

View of Longs Peak looking west from the Three Sisters

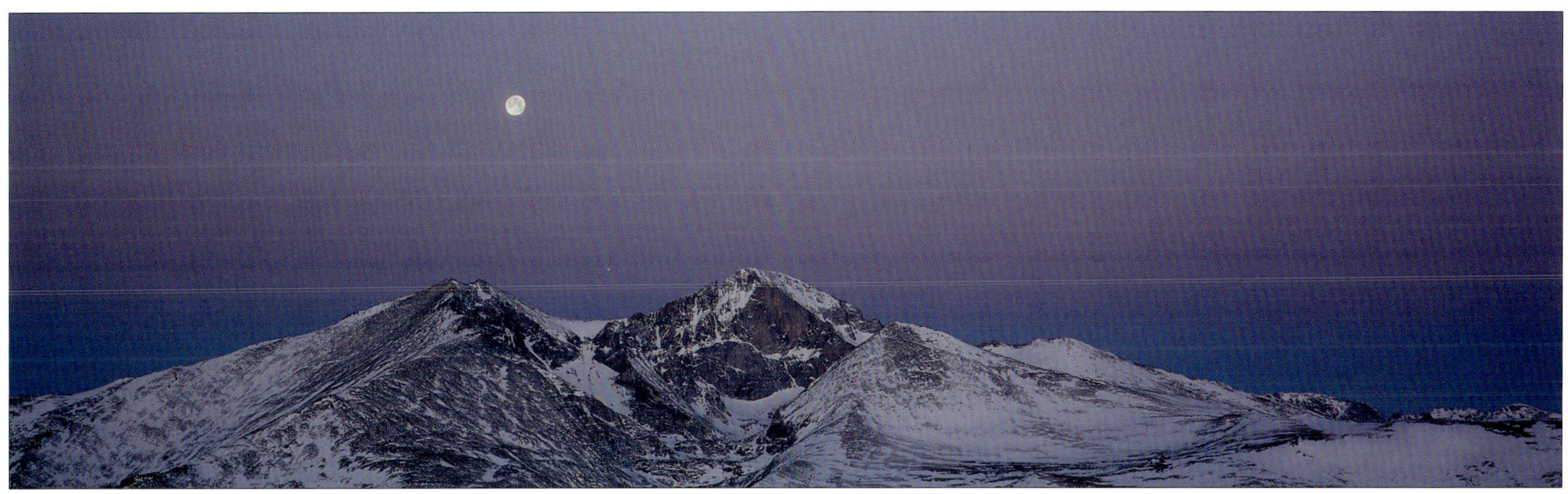

Next Page:

As you approach the Rockies from the east, you travel across a vast expanse—almost desolate—and you wonder if it will ever end. Eventually on the horizon, a slight white brow comes into view and soon rises up in all its grandeur. *Colorado Rocky Mountain Wide* is calling.

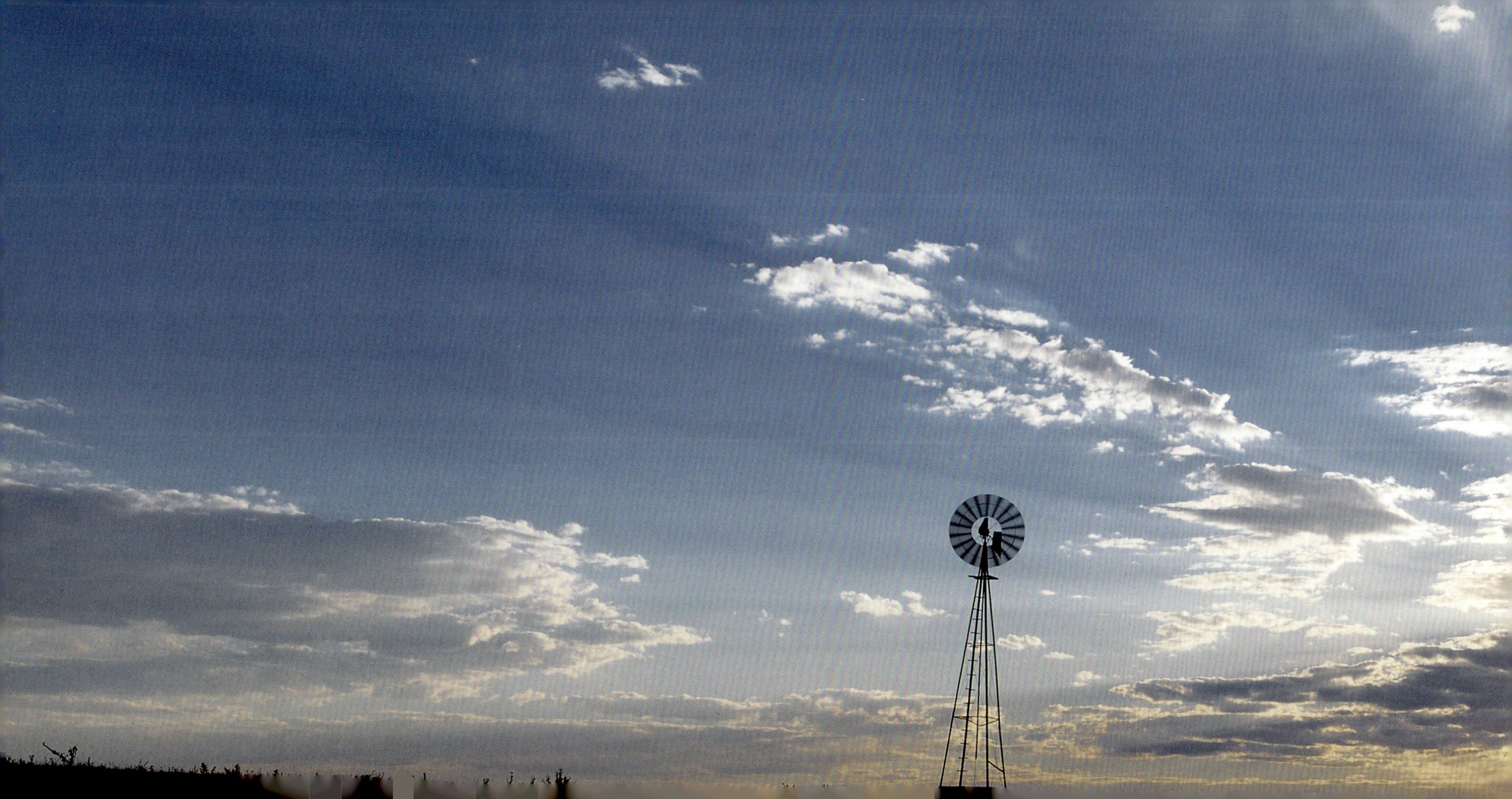

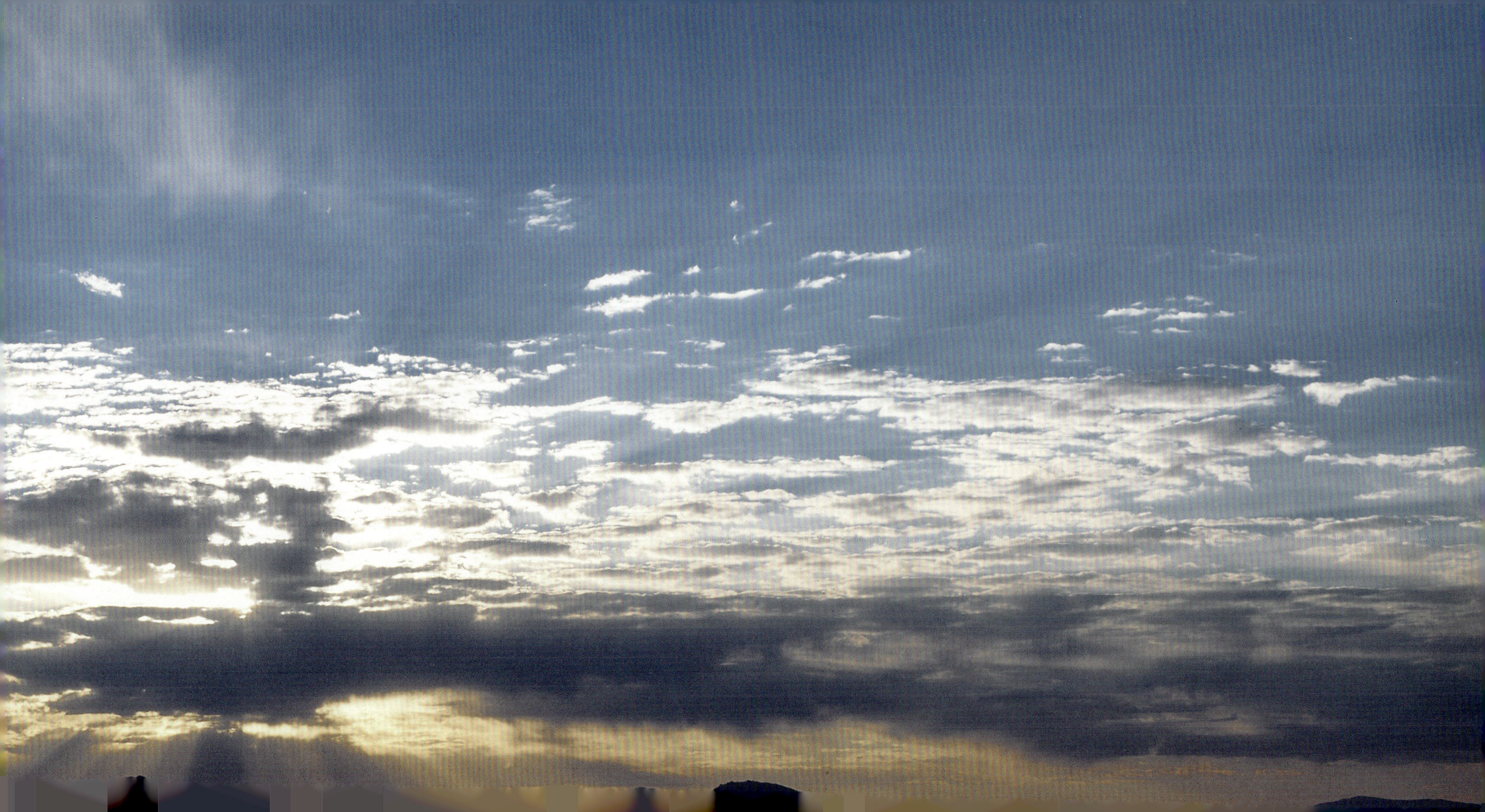

My Story

I have been creating images for a living since graduation from Brooks Institute of Photography in 1969. For many years I owned a photographic gallery on Monterey Bay in California. My wilderness and mountaineering experiences didn't begin until later. When my daughter was a freshman in high school, she and a group of her friends began planning a week-long backpacking trip through the Wenatchee Wilderness in central Washington, using the expert guide services of Reachout Expeditions. I jumped at the opportunity to be chaperone for the

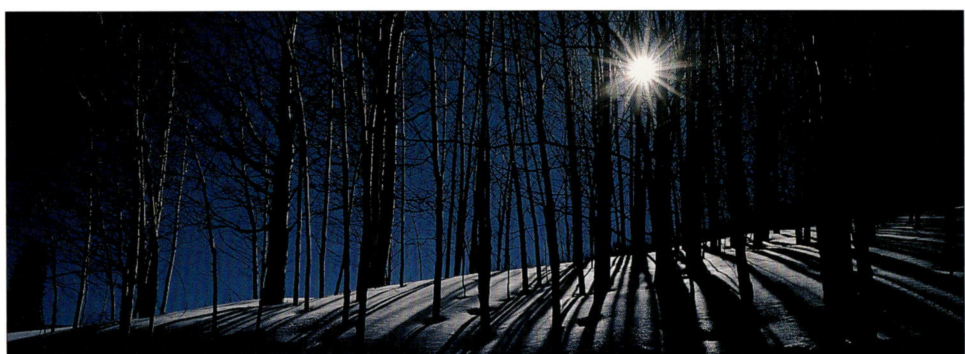

boys and to spend some quality time with my daughter and her friends. Everyone said it was the perfect time to be hiking in this area. Rarely is there rain at that time in July, and we would be able to sleep under the stars without tents. Besides the guides, only one in our group had done any backpacking before. Little did we know that our wilderness initiation would include a summer blizzard. Our third day out, the temperature dropped and by mid-afternoon the rain turned to fluffy white flakes. We stopped early that day, and our guides showed us how to make a low shelter utilizing our ground-cover tarpaulins. By dawn 14 inches of snow had fallen, and the mountains glimmered in the early morning light. For me the adventure was great. I loved it, and I have been going to wild places ever since, making photographs and filming. At every opportunity I bring others with me so they can experience the wonder and beauty of God's creation first-hand. This book is an extension of that sharing. I hope it will inspire you to visit some of these places for yourself. The coordinates

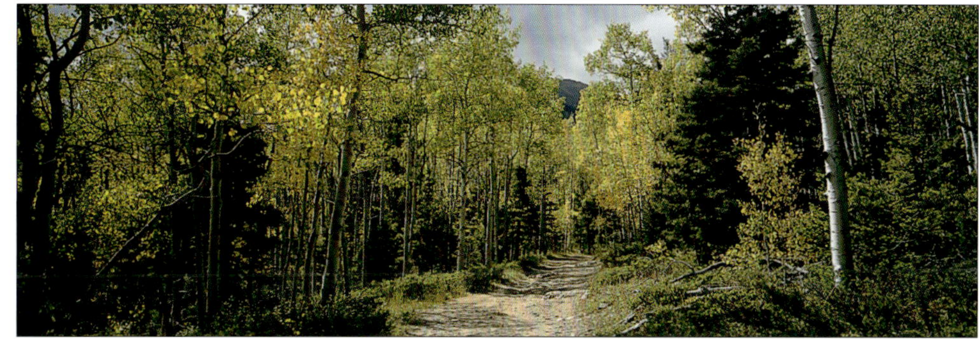

of many of the locations you see in this book are listed on our Web site, www.keenmedia.com. With a map and a GPS unit, you can locate within a couple dozen feet the spots where I created the panographic images™. So proceed to your local outdoor retailer, get the clothes and equipment you need, and head out sometime soon.

Ken

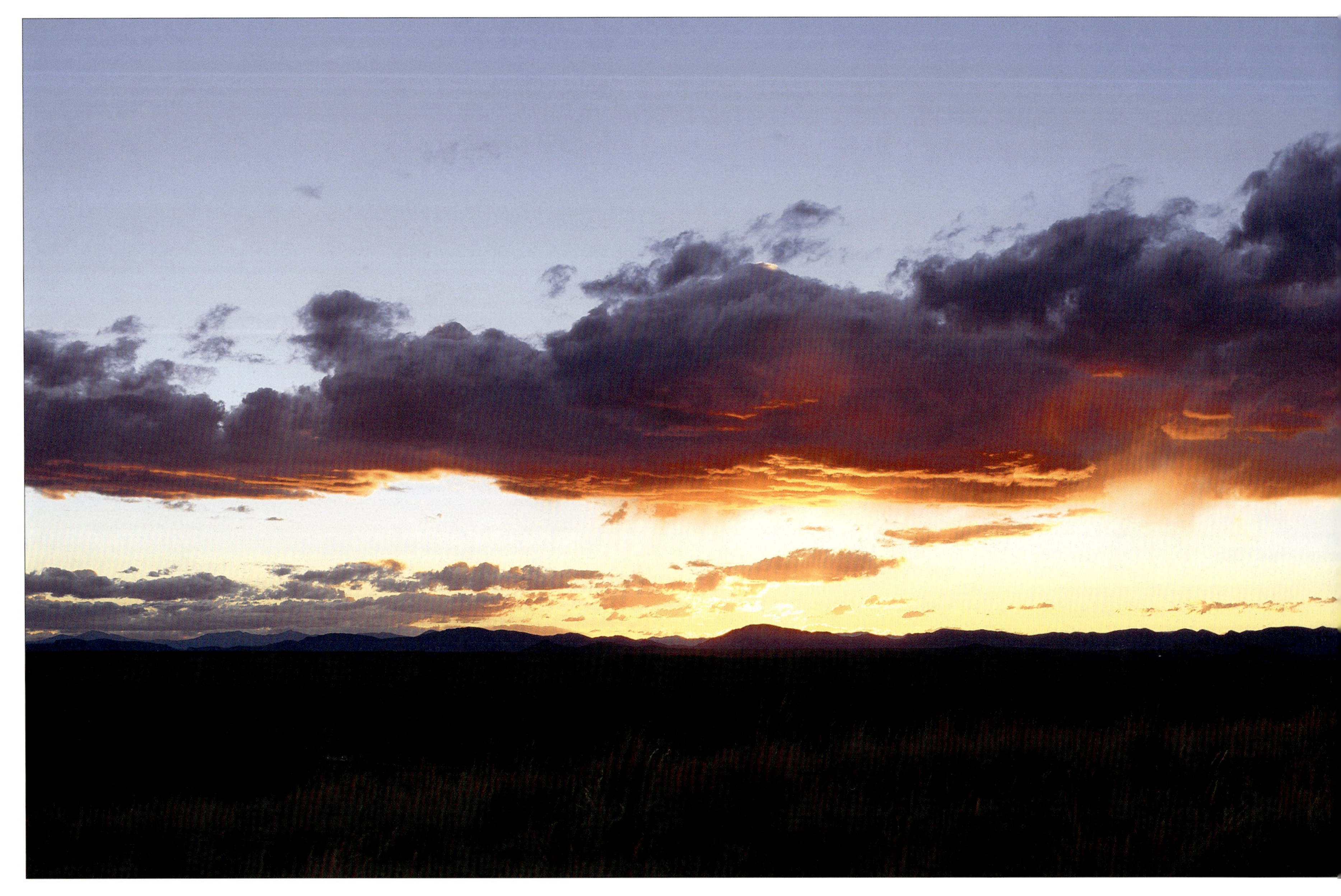

Above the Front Range looking west

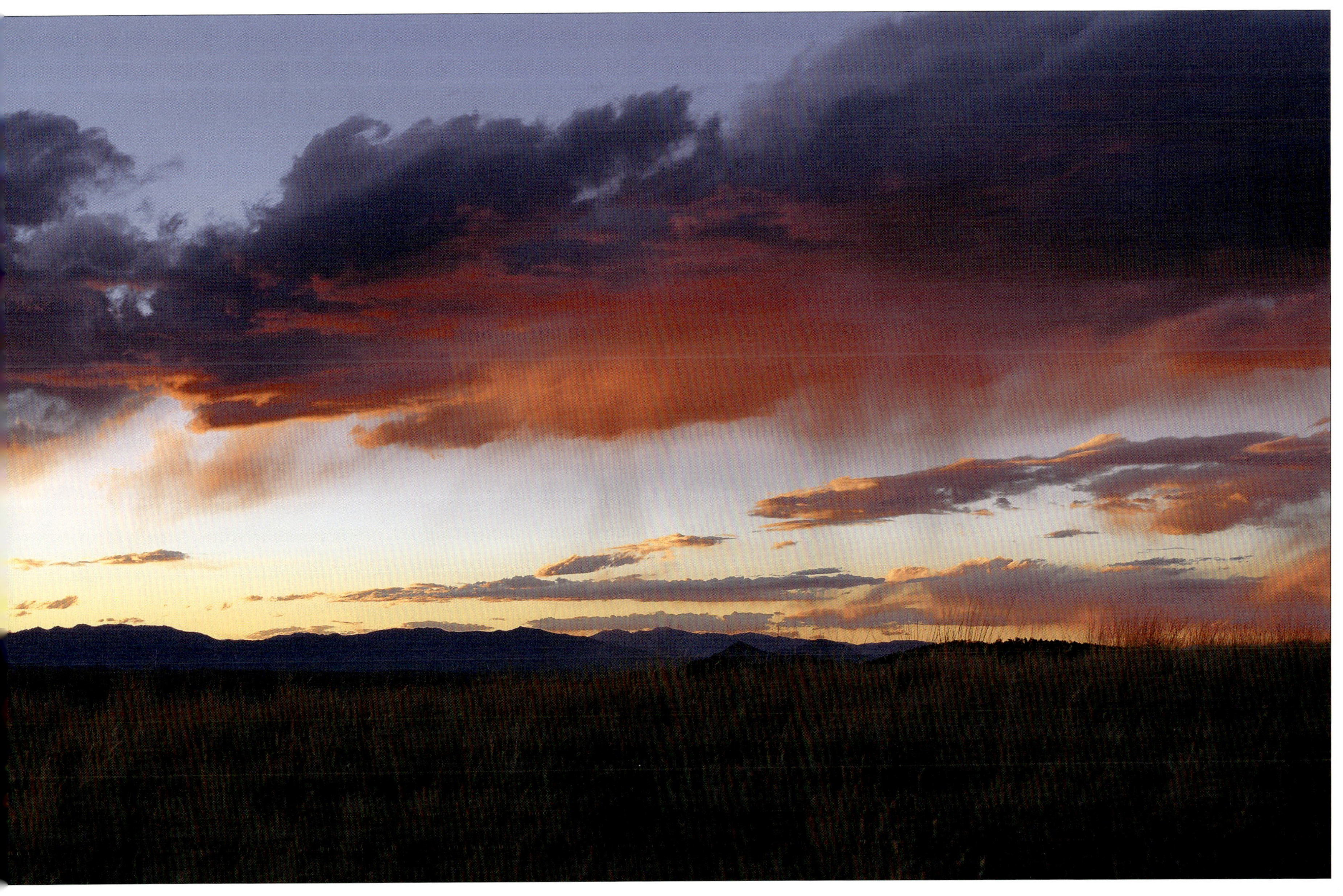

The Mount Sneffels Range rising above Telluride

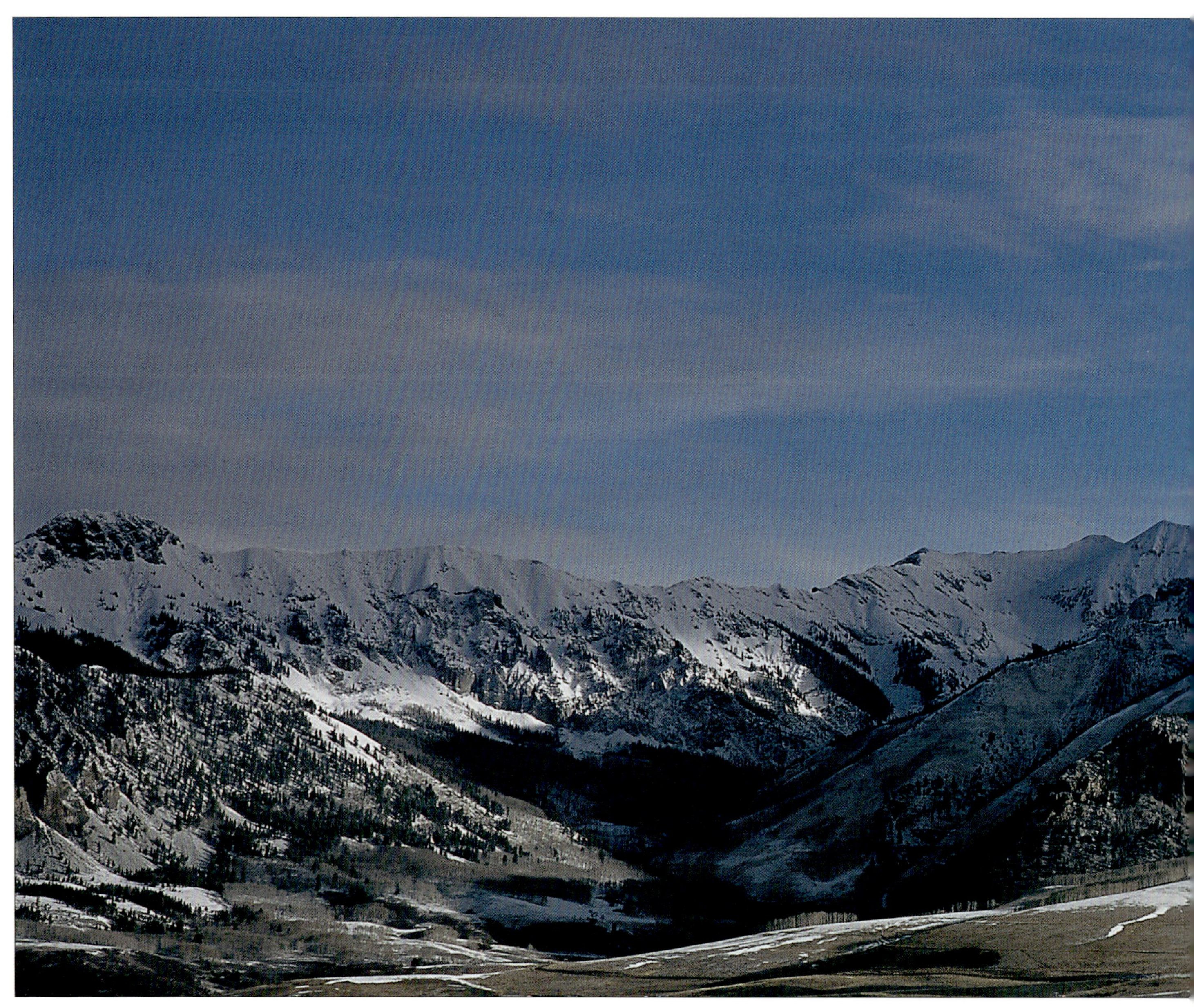

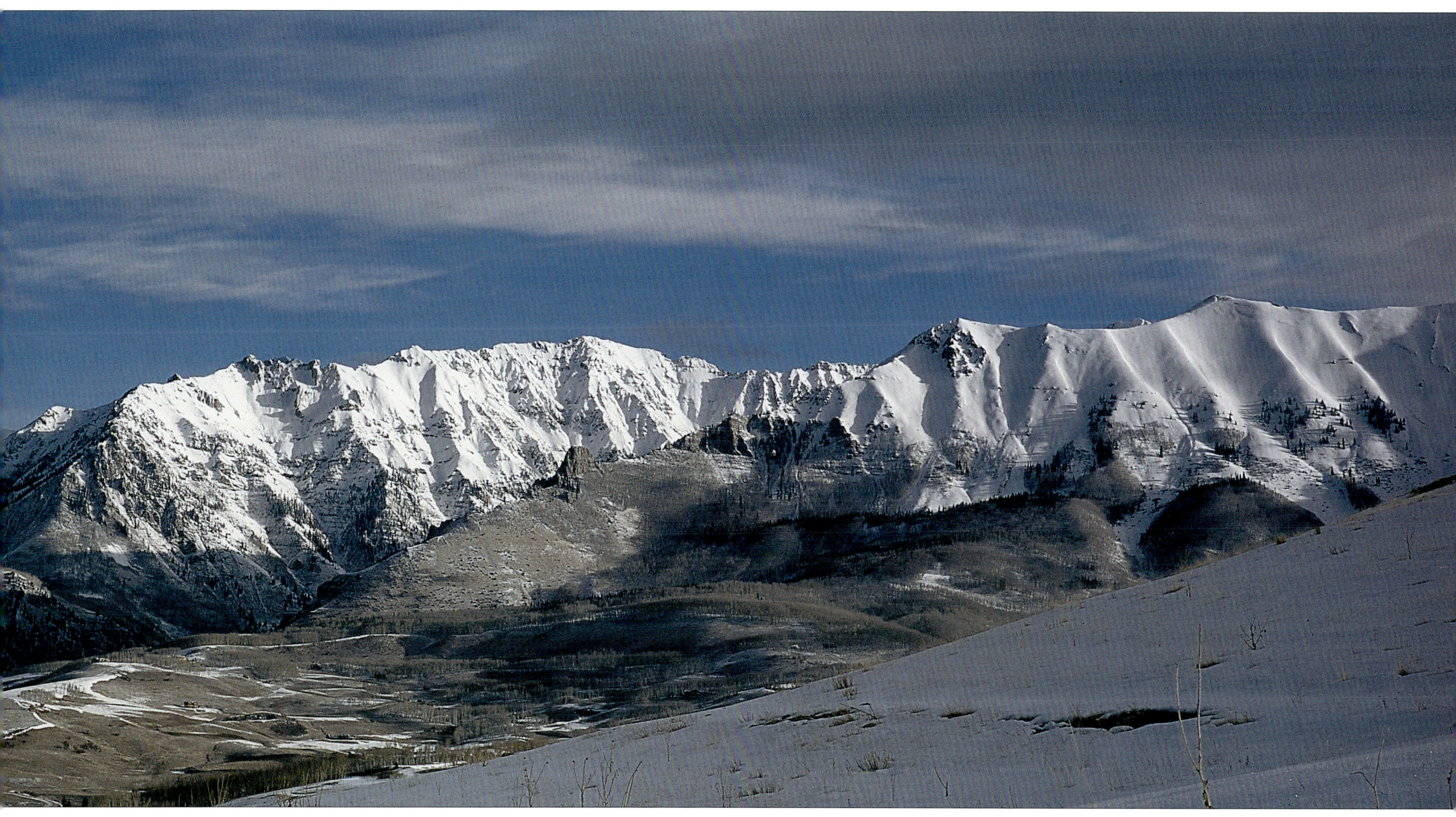

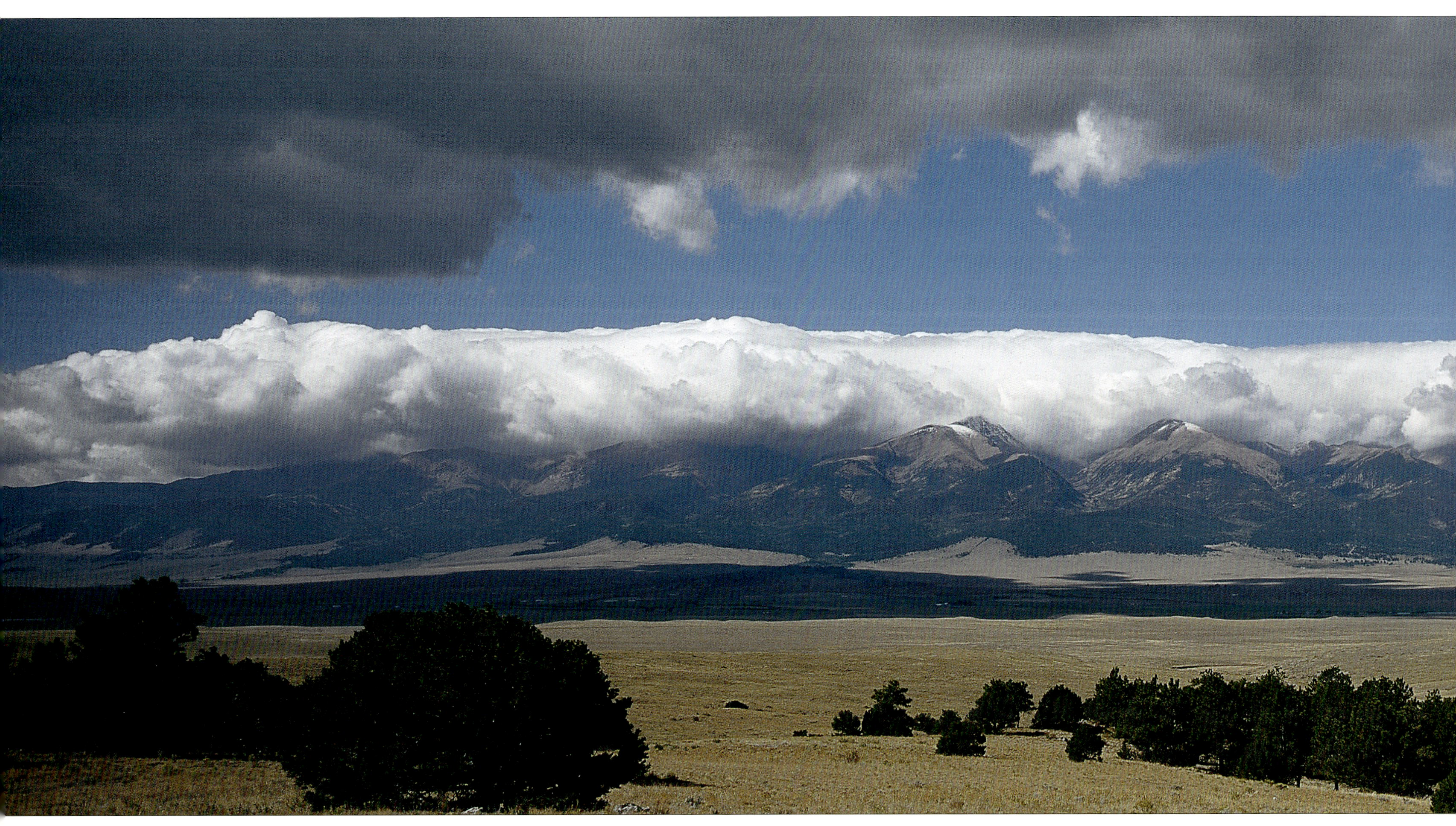

An unusual double storm front passing over the Sangre de Cristo Mountains near Westcliffe

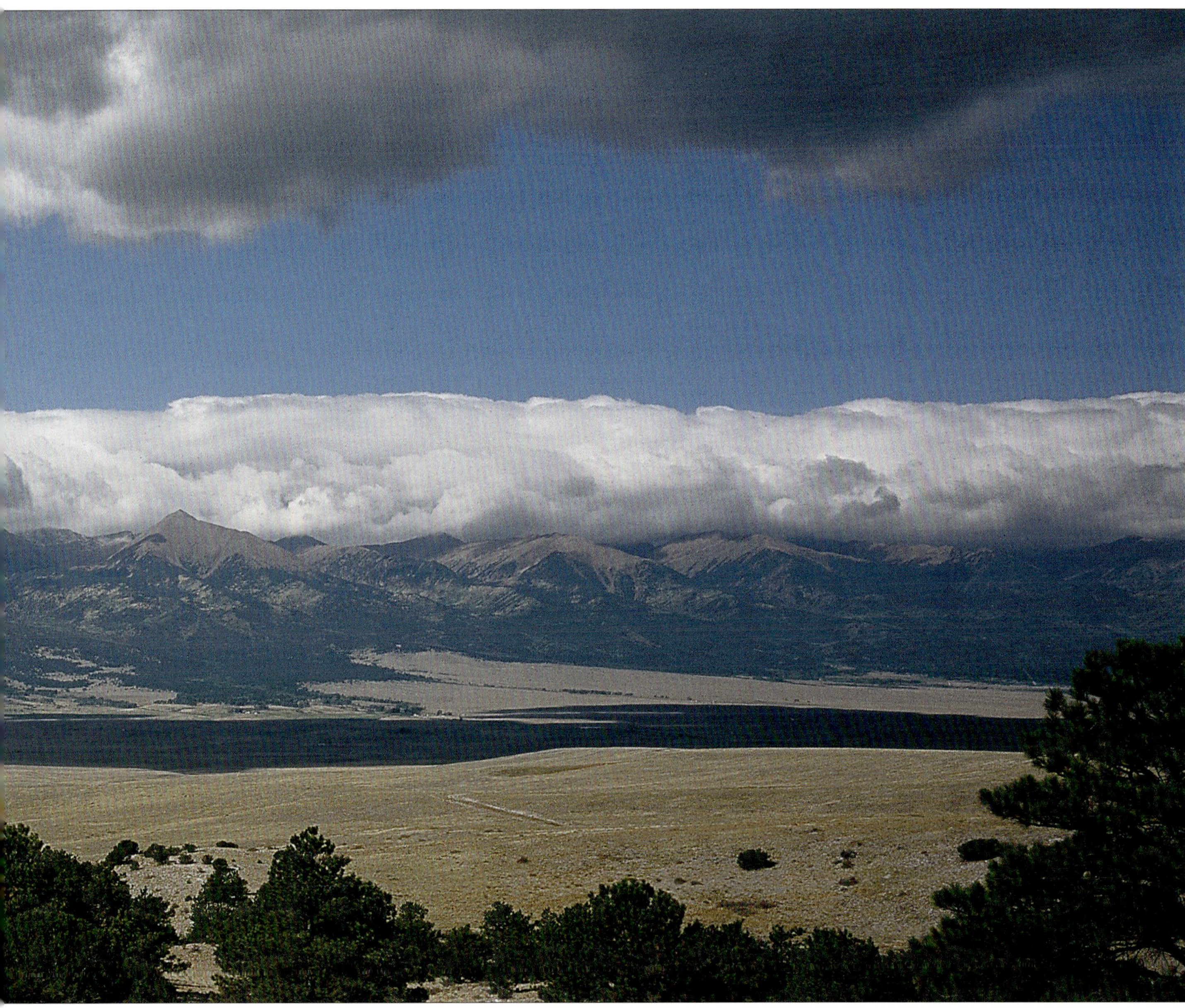

What is a panographic image™?

When I first started my career in photography, my images were all captured on film. I would then enter the lab and make either black-and-white or color photographic prints. Now computers play an increasing role both in my video and still photography. The end result of my work is not always on photographic paper. So a panographic image™ is a panorama I create which may be recorded or reproduced using digital media or video, as well as traditional film and photographic materials.

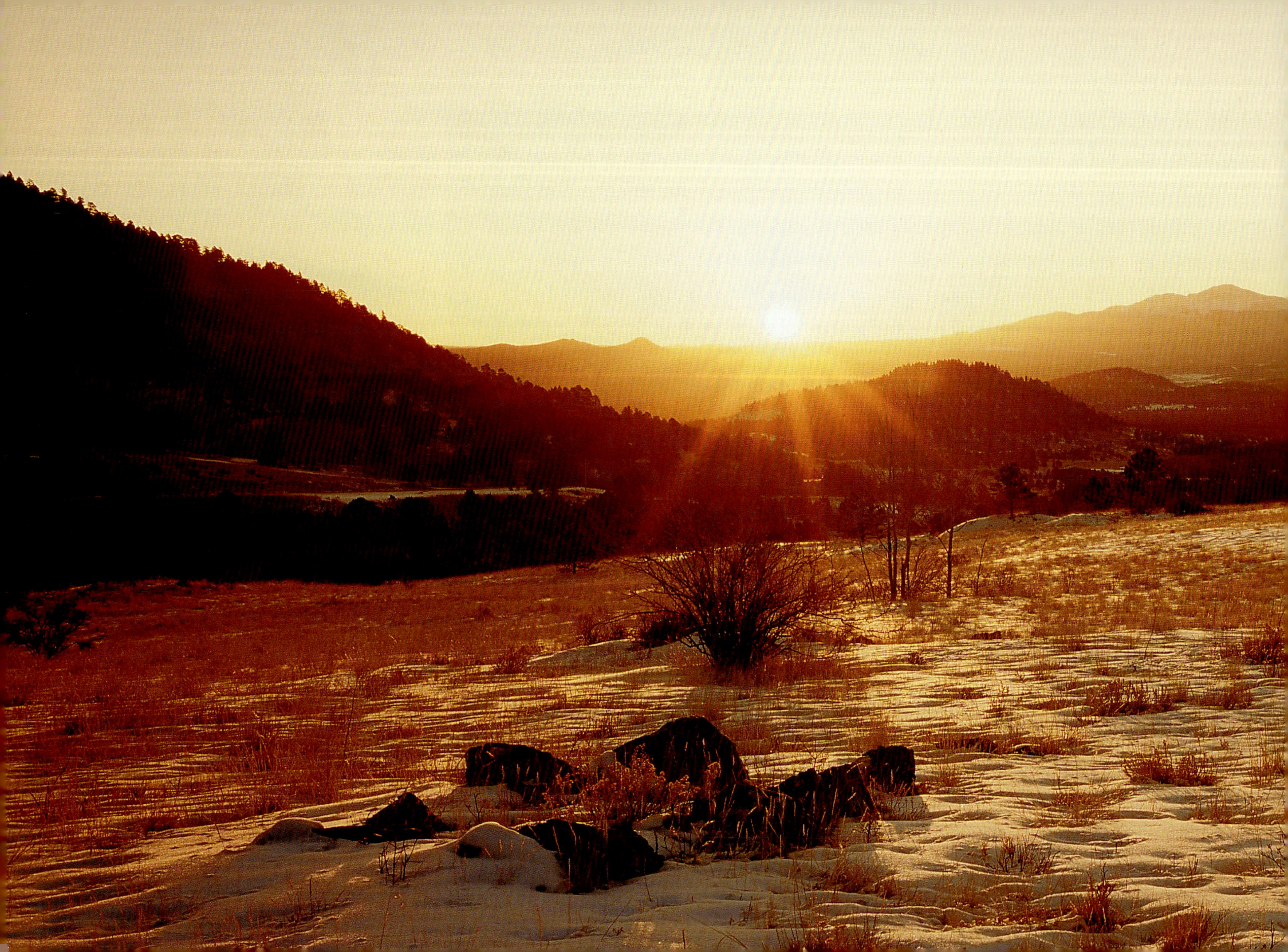

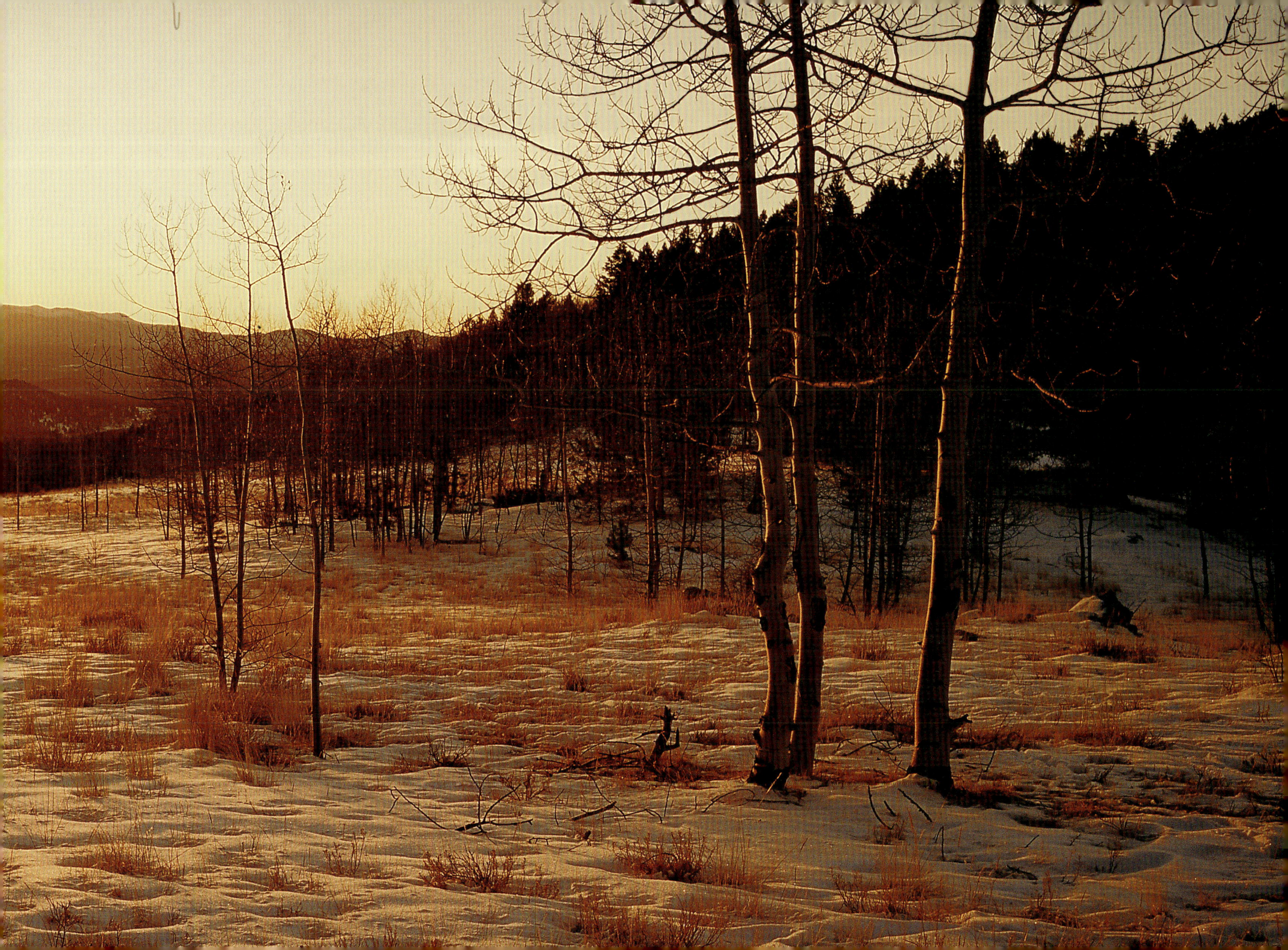

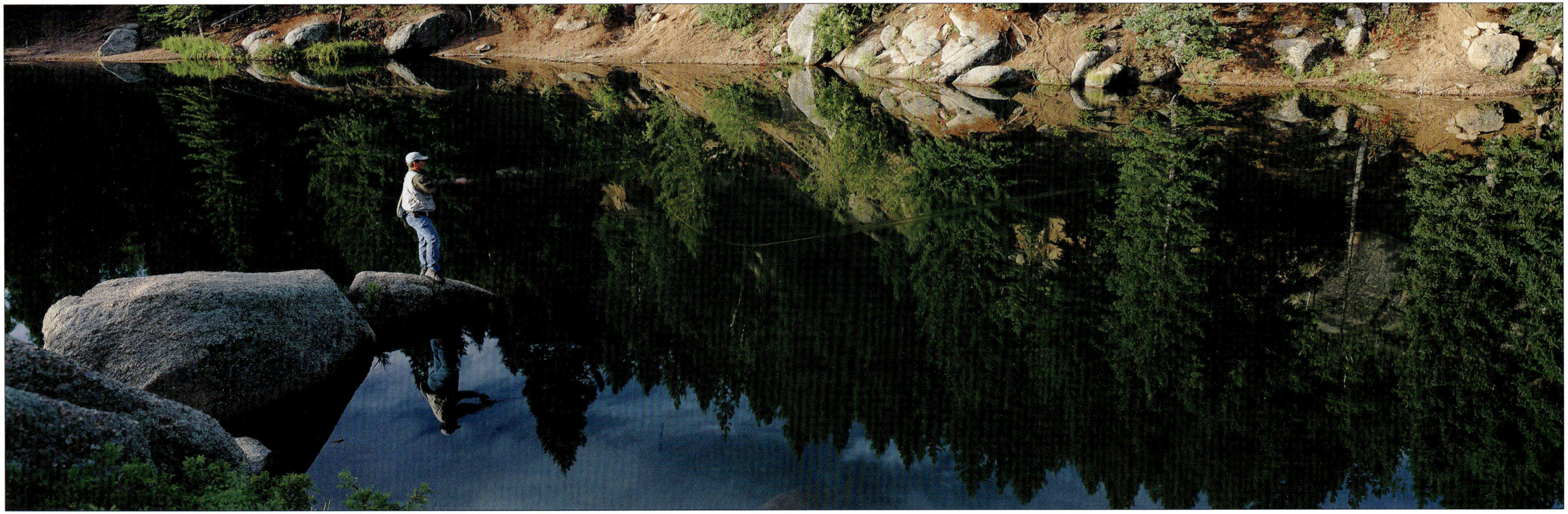

My wife has always wanted me to be a fisherman. I've tried; I just can't catch anything. This is my friend John, a great fly fisherman, at a small hidden lake. You will have to check our Web site to find its precise location. The fishing is great here, unless like me you are catching fleeting images with a camera instead.

Previous Spread: Winter sunrise with Pikes Peak in the distance

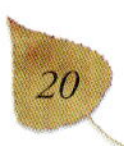

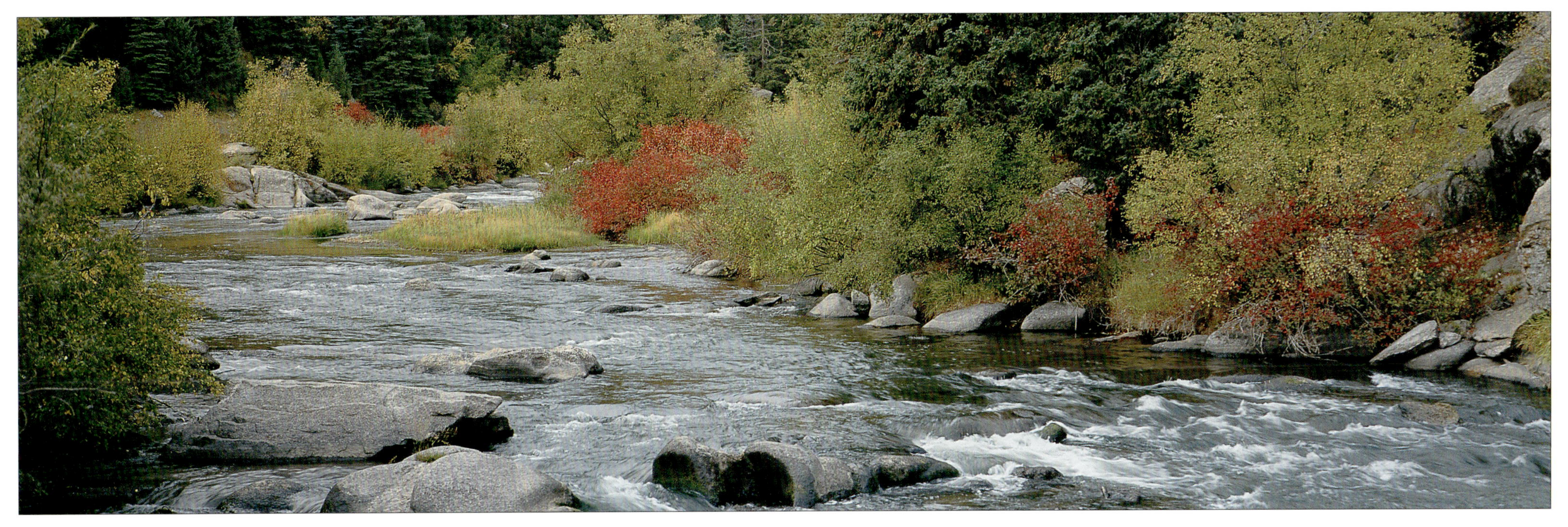

Late summer

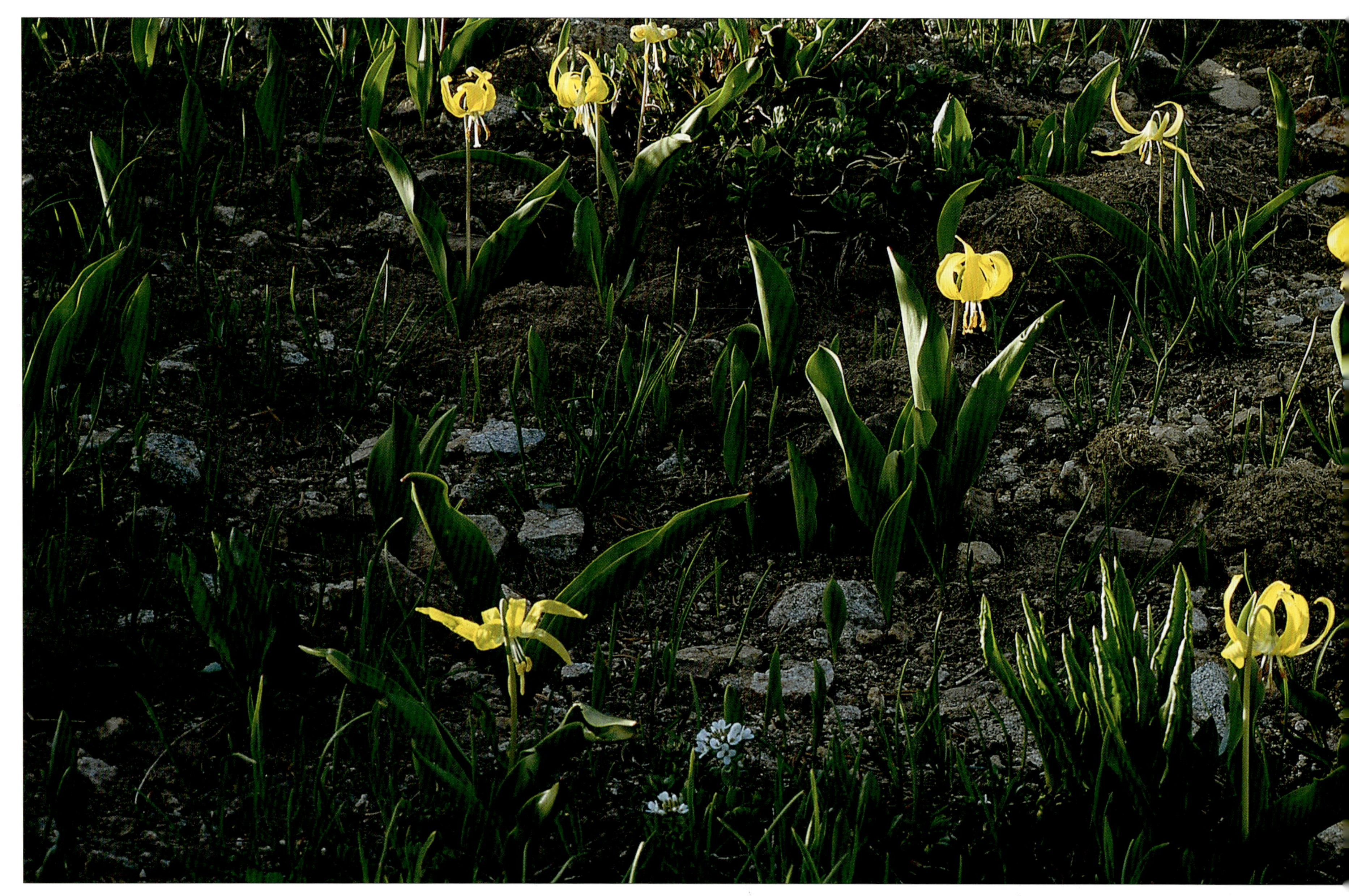

Glacier Lilies (Erythronium grandiflorum)

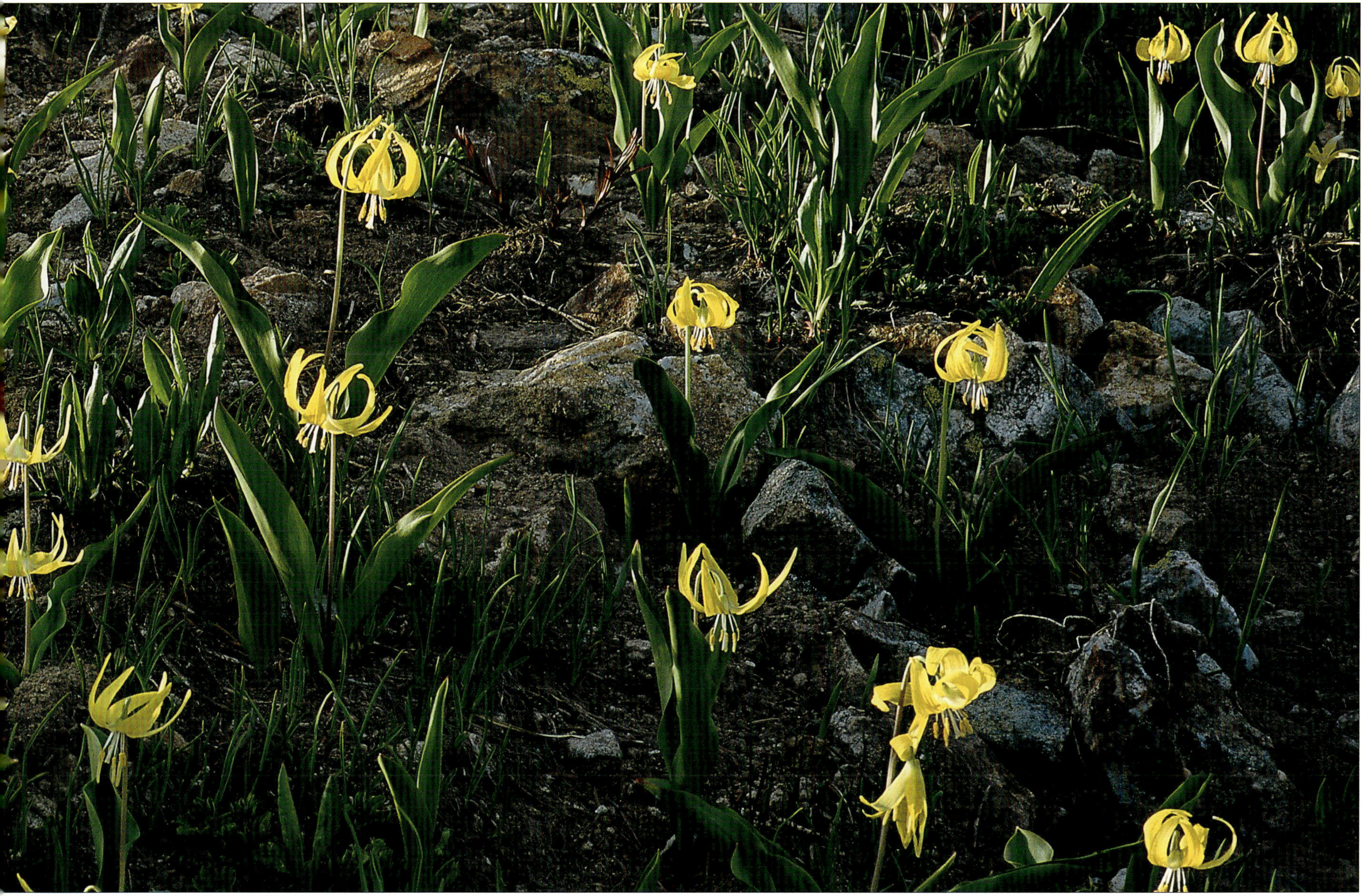

The Ruby Range, Gunnison National Forest

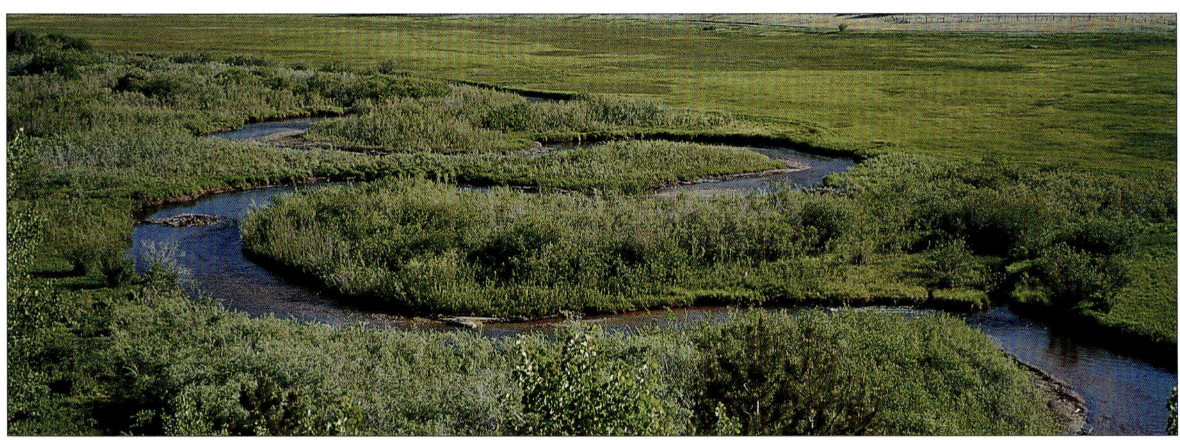

Tarryall Creek, Pike National Forest
Water, the source of life, rushing down from the peaks and meandering through the valleys. Cities and towns on both sides of the continent are nourished from sources in the Rockies.

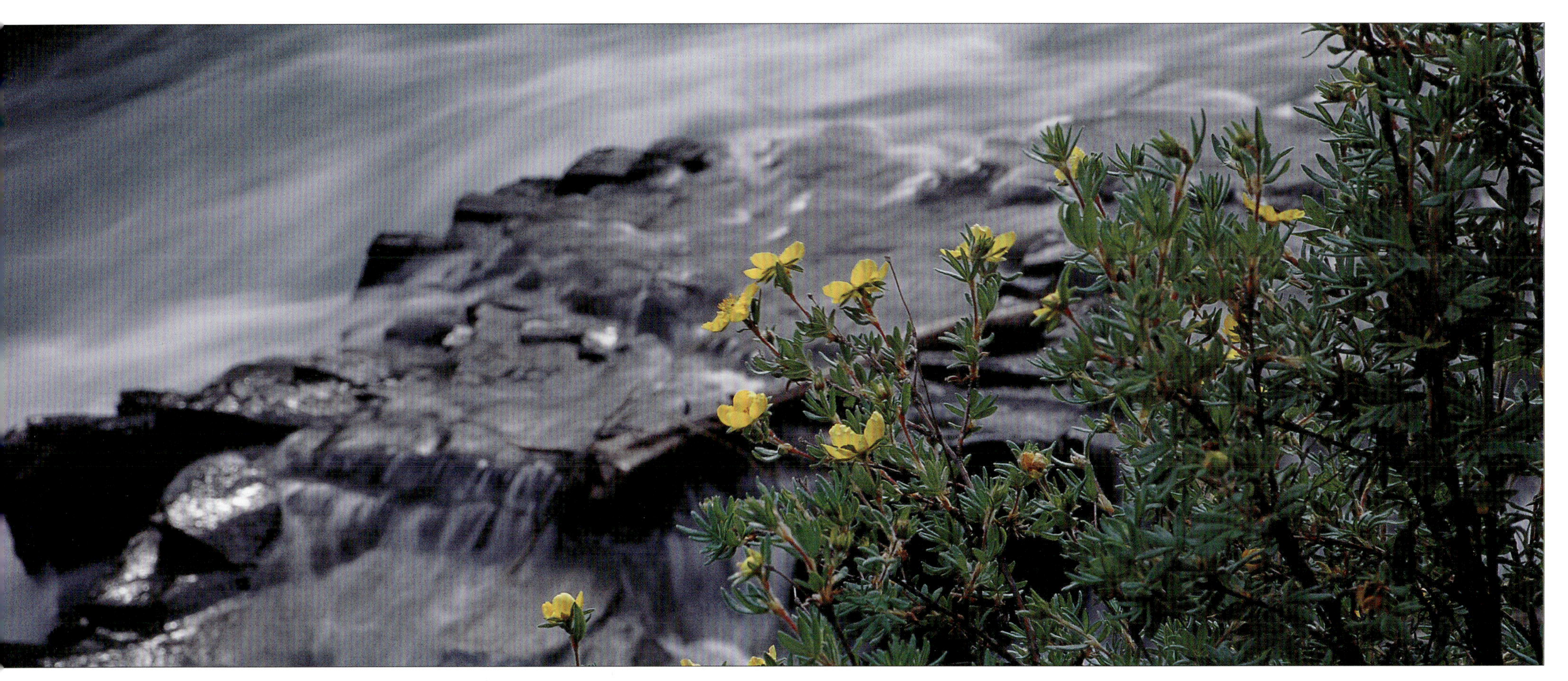

Shrubby Potentilla (Dasiphora fruticosa) contrast with the cool blue-gray water.

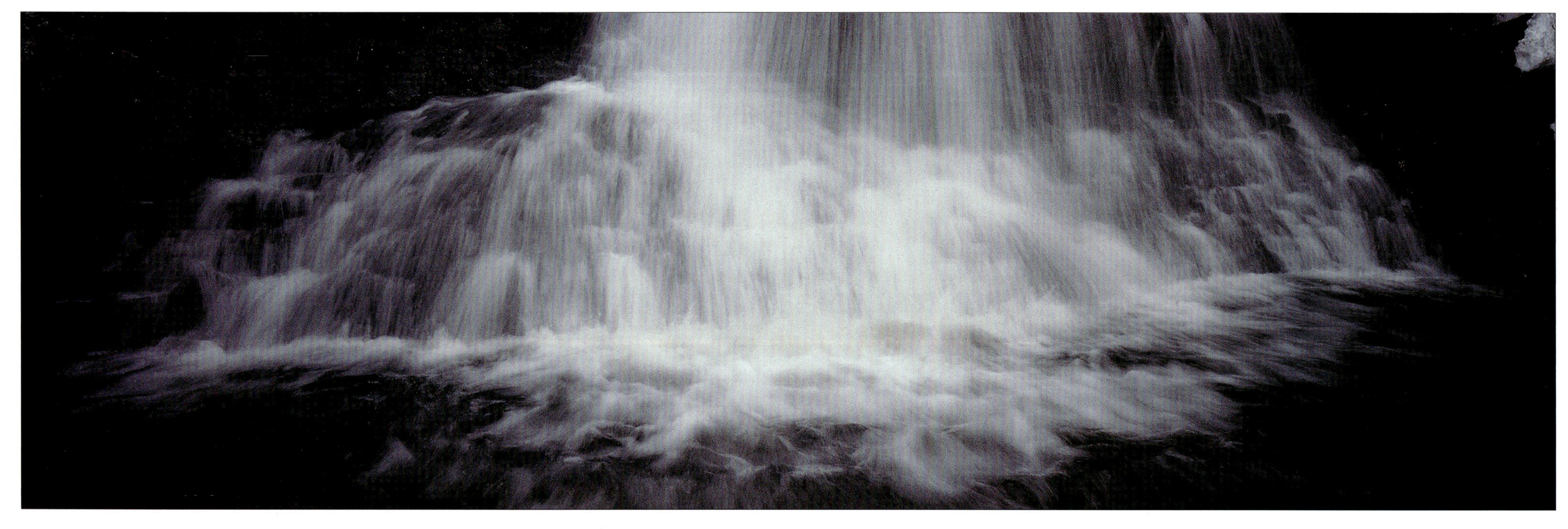

Willow Creek on the eastern side of the Sangre de Cristo Mountains, Rio Grande National Forest

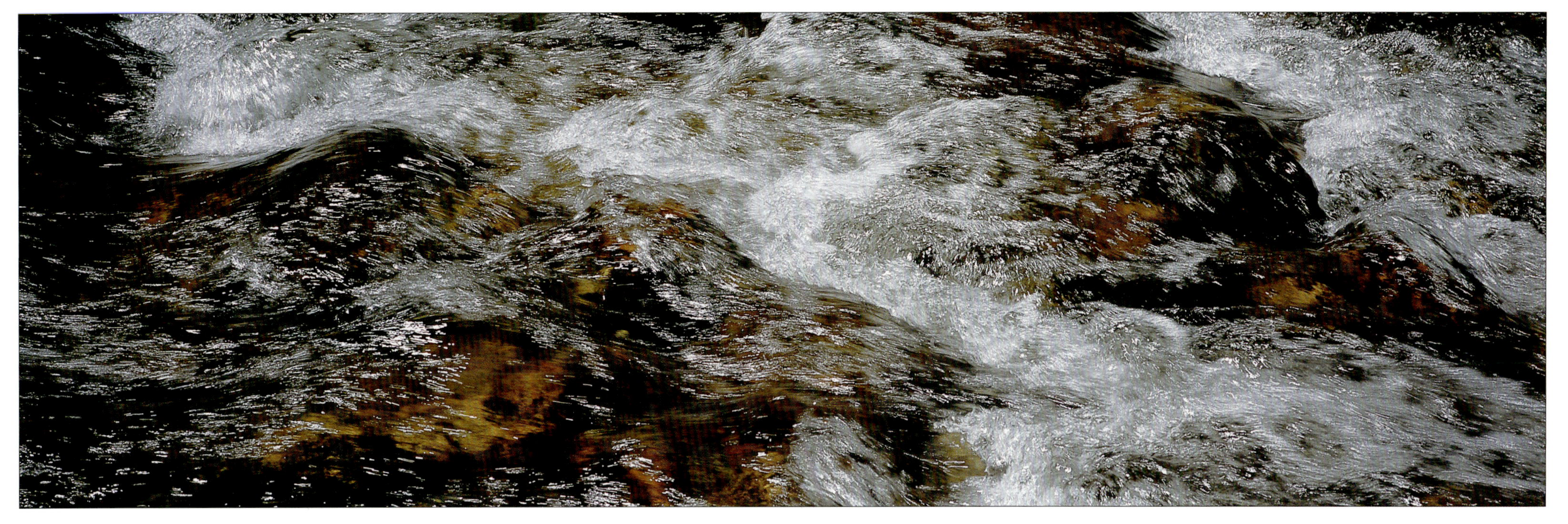

Sunlight dancing on the water of Tomichi Creek

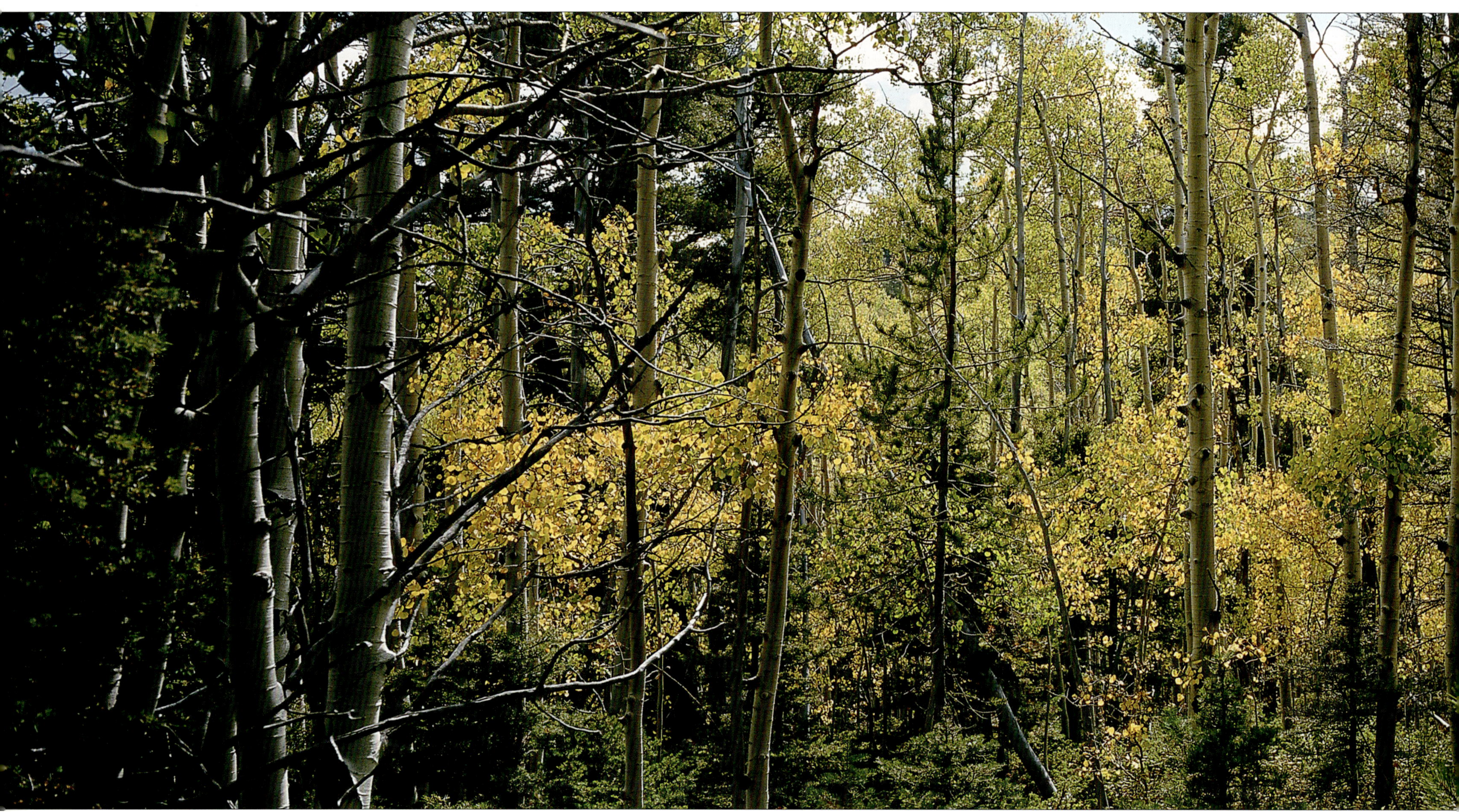

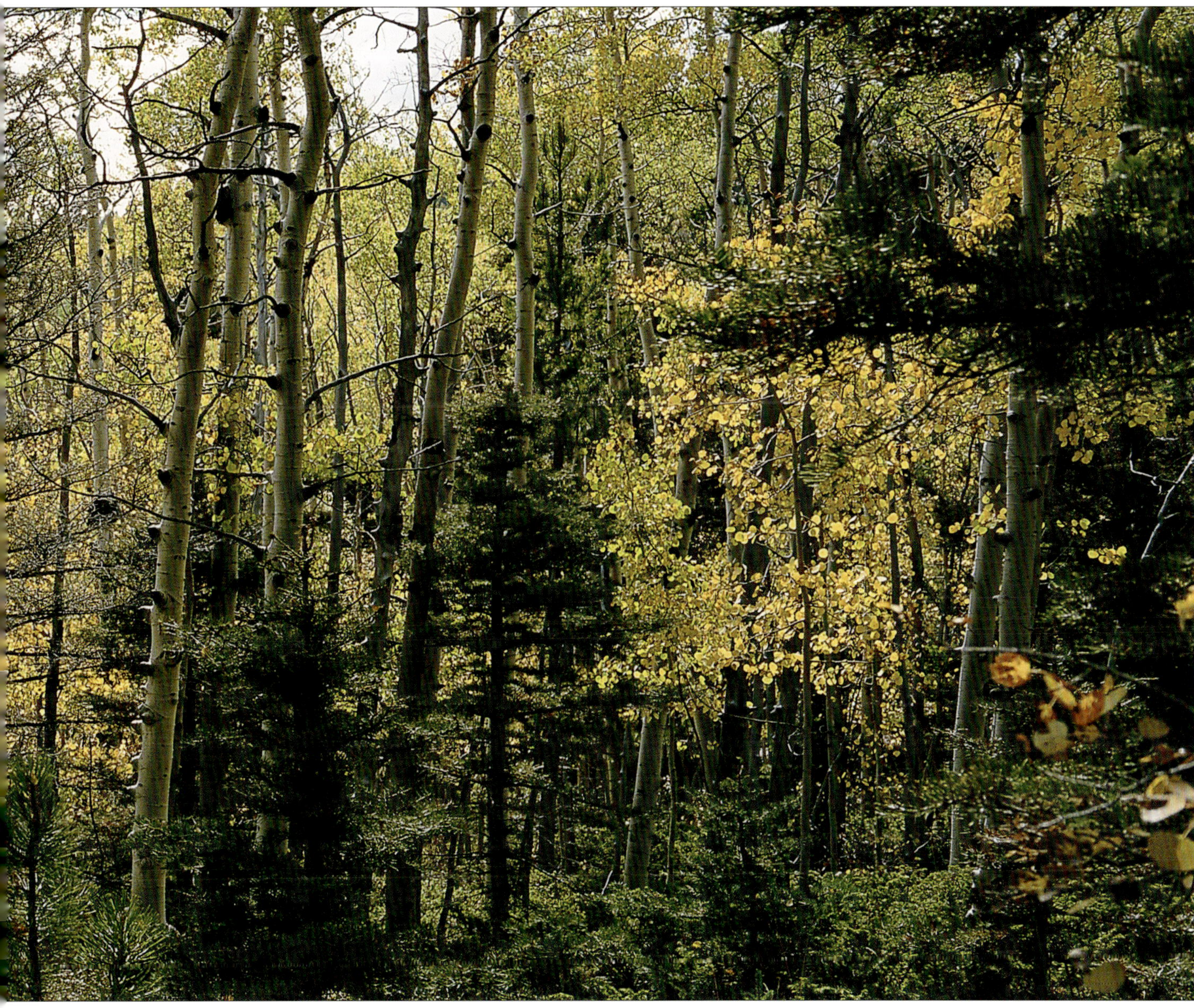

Sangre de Cristo Mountains near Westcliffe

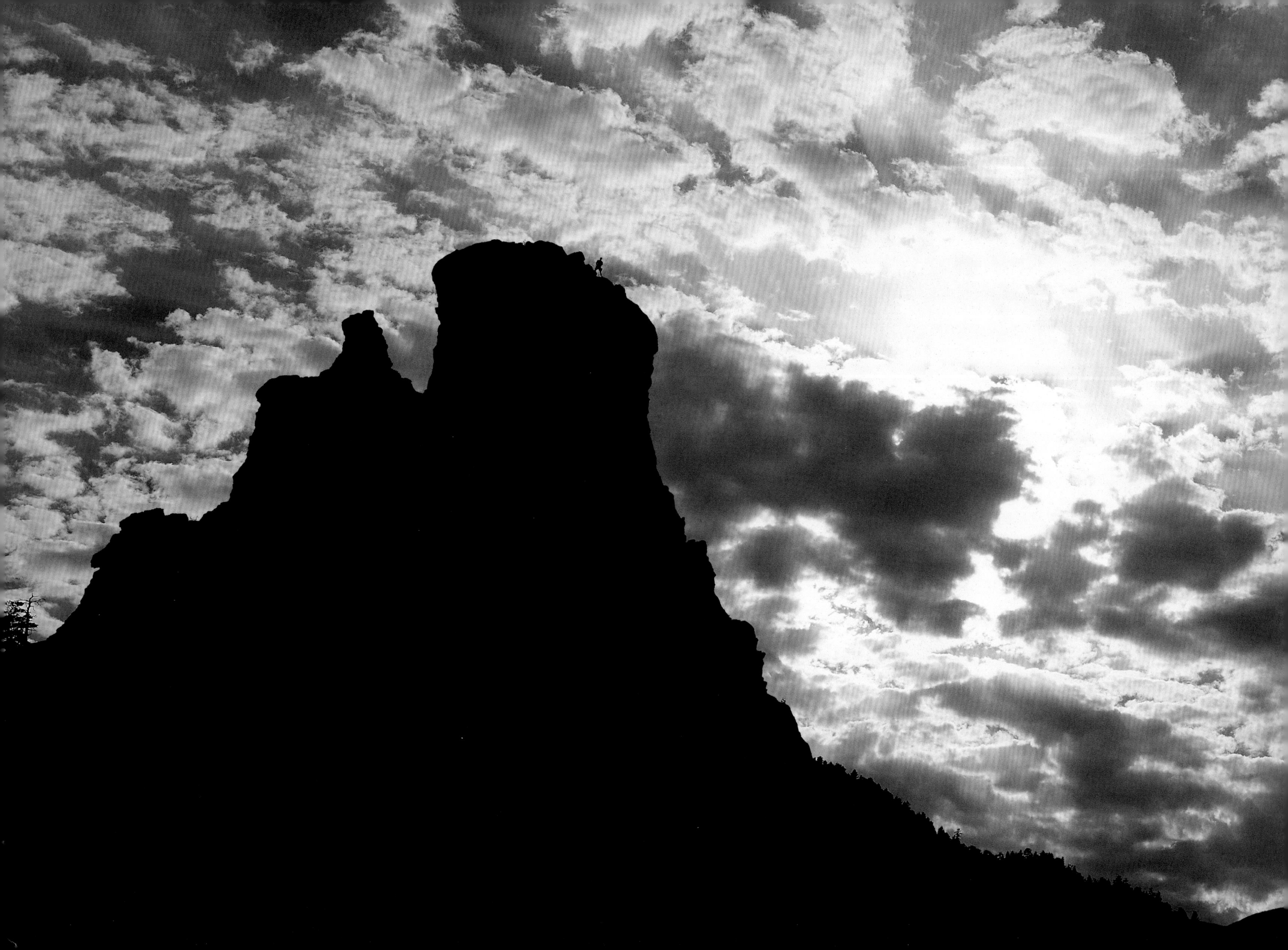

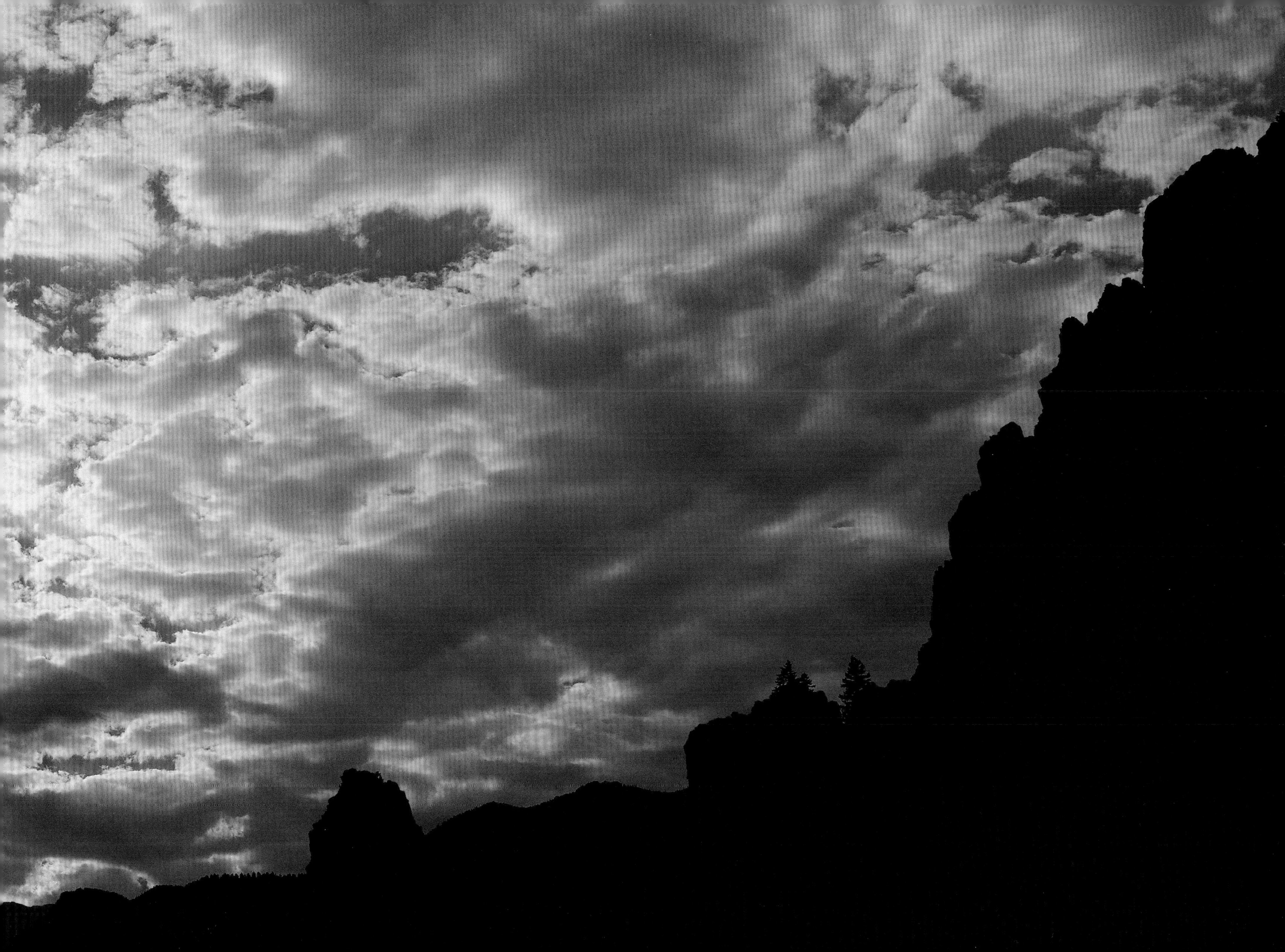

From Pulpit Rock looking towards Pikes Peak

Previous Spread: A climber in North Cheyenne Canyon

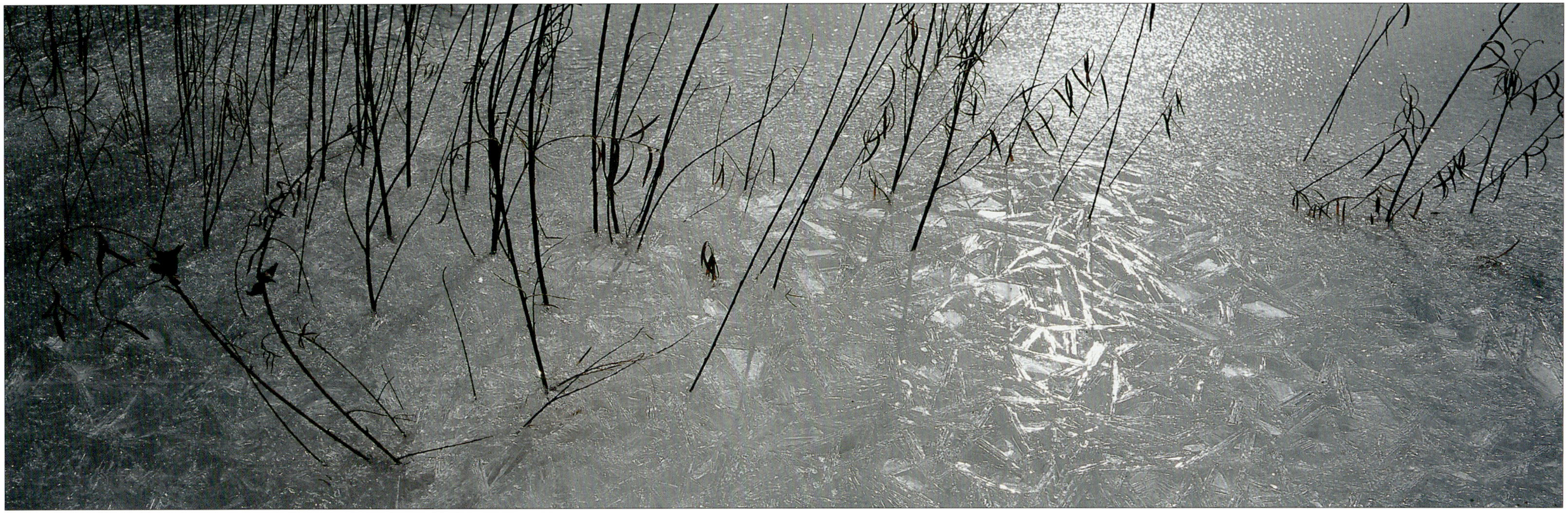

Unusual patterns in the ice on an unnamed small stream

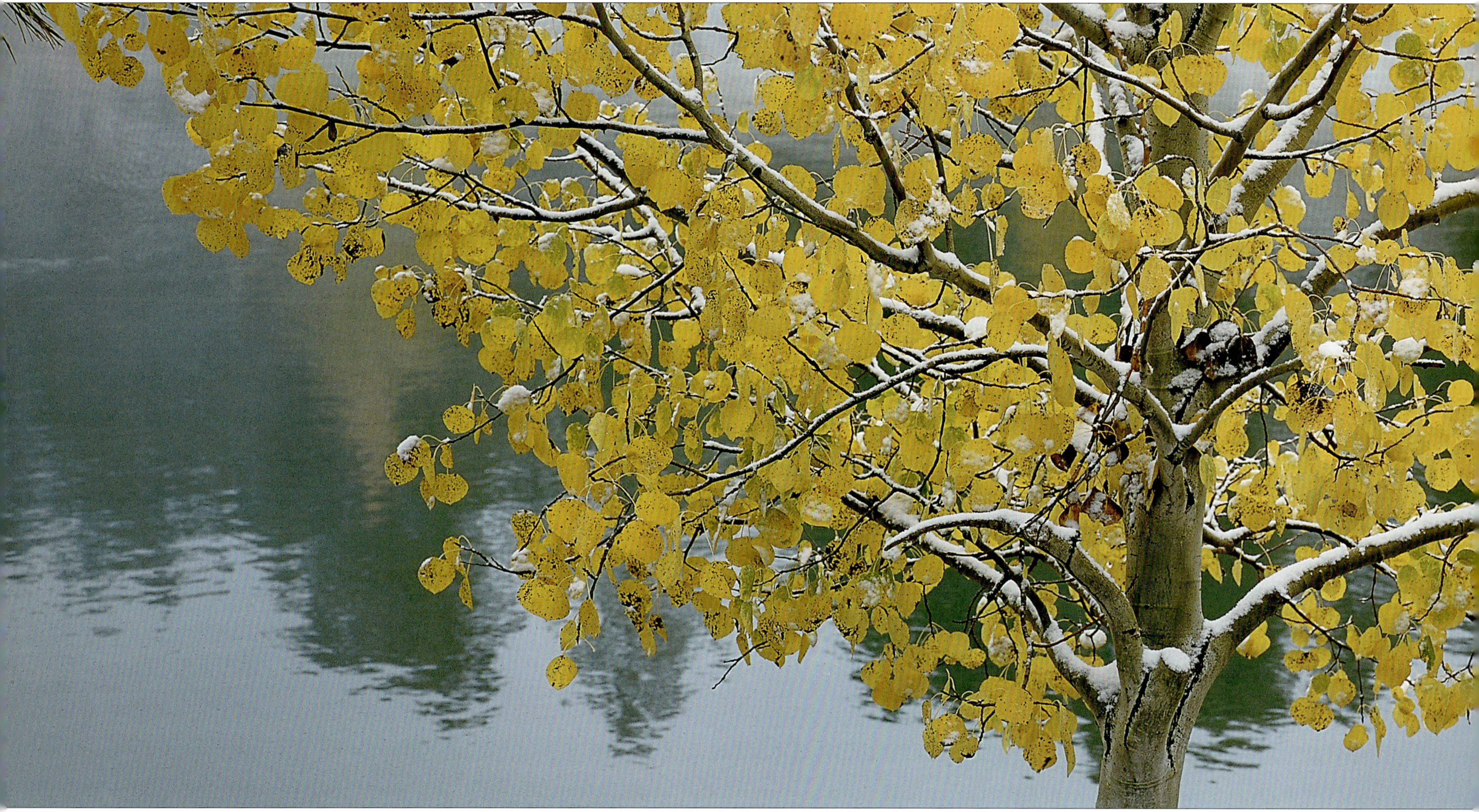

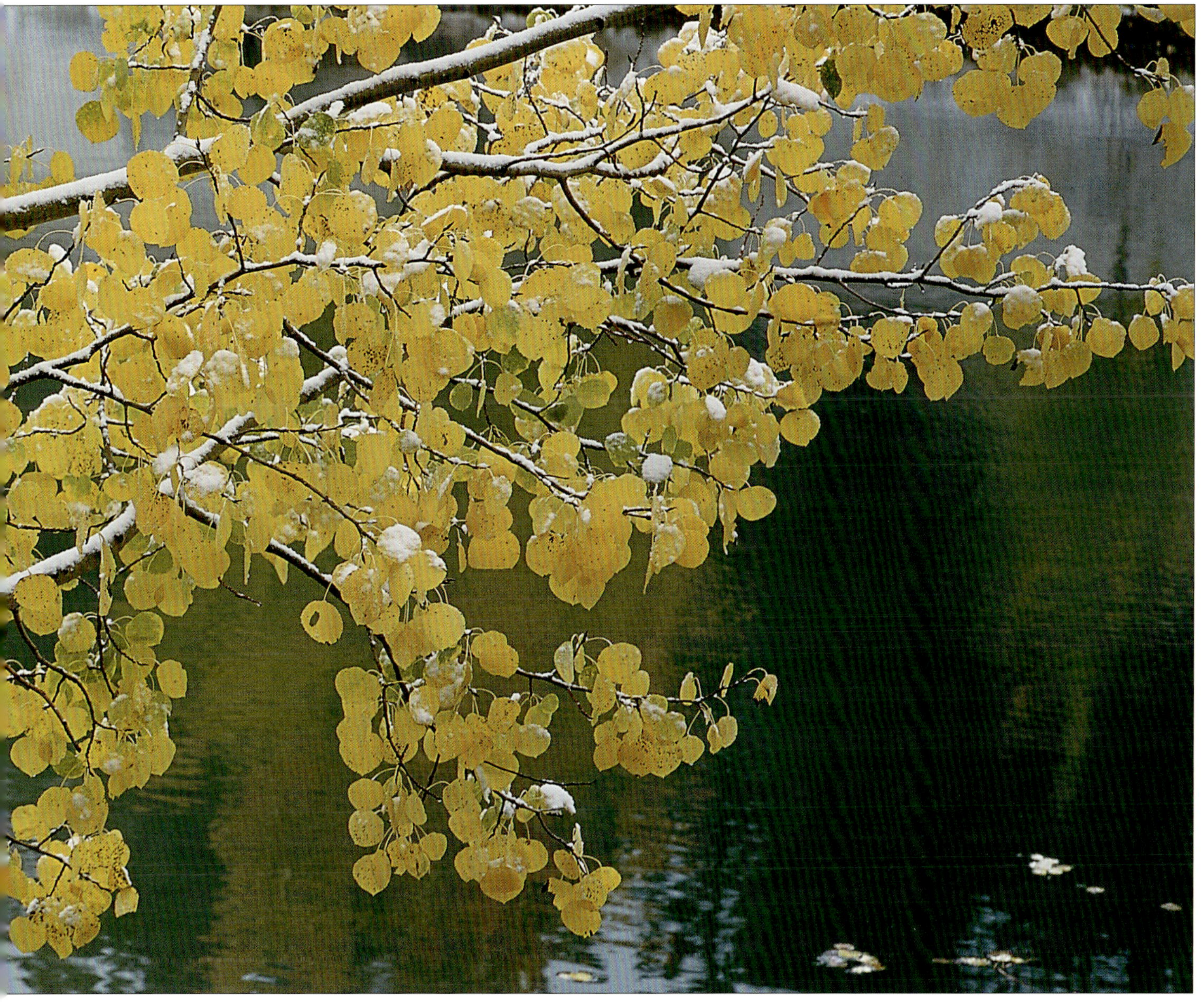

Early fall in the Black Forest

Twin Lakes, looking towards the northern boundary of the Collegiate Peaks Wilderness. The Colorado Trail descends from these peaks and passes around this lake on its way through the San Isabel National Forest.

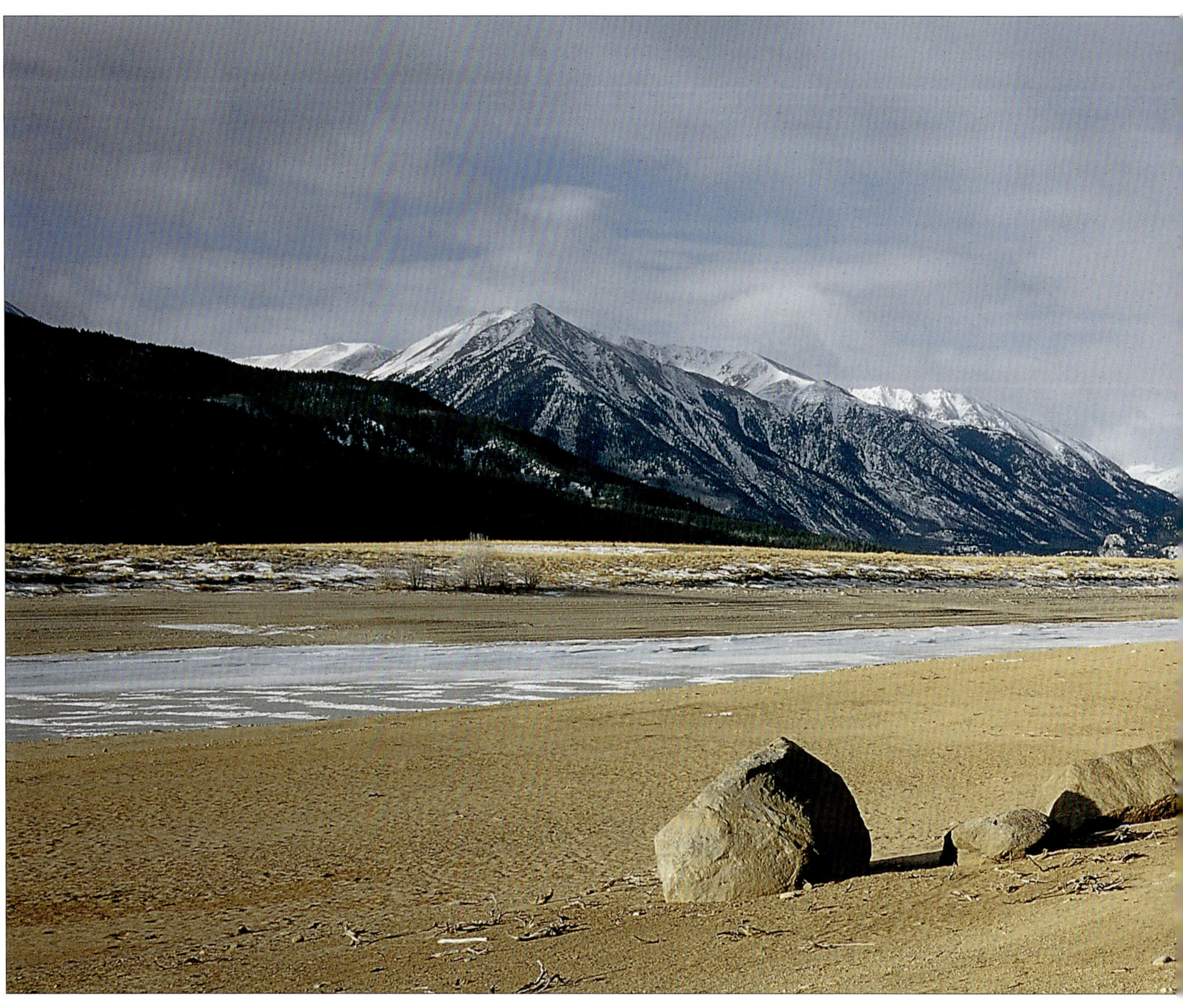

The Collegiate Peaks Wilderness

This area encompasses nearly 168,000 acres, and within its boundaries are eight of Colorado's highest peaks. Numerous other peaks in this area, although less than 14,000 feet high, are much more challenging to climb. But climbing isn't the only reason to come here: Quiet solitude can be found just a few miles into the wilderness.

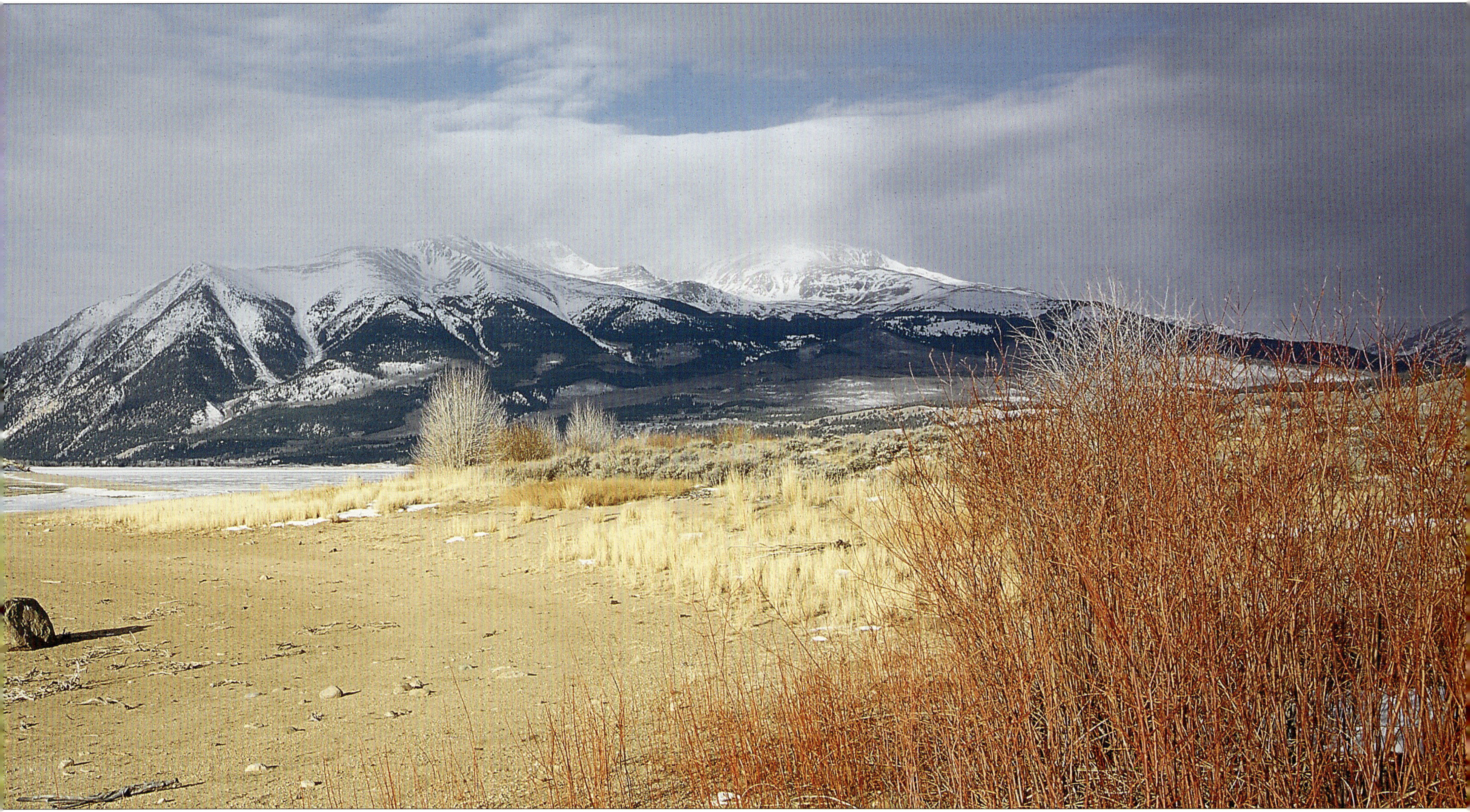

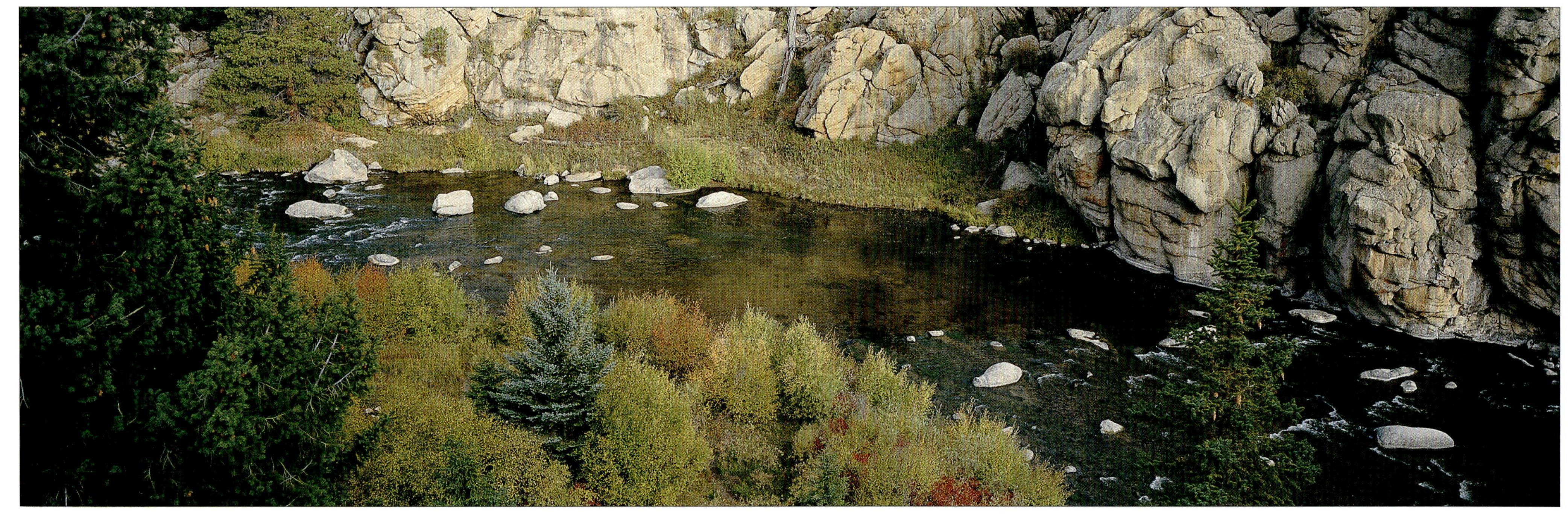

The South Platte River in Elevenmile Canyon

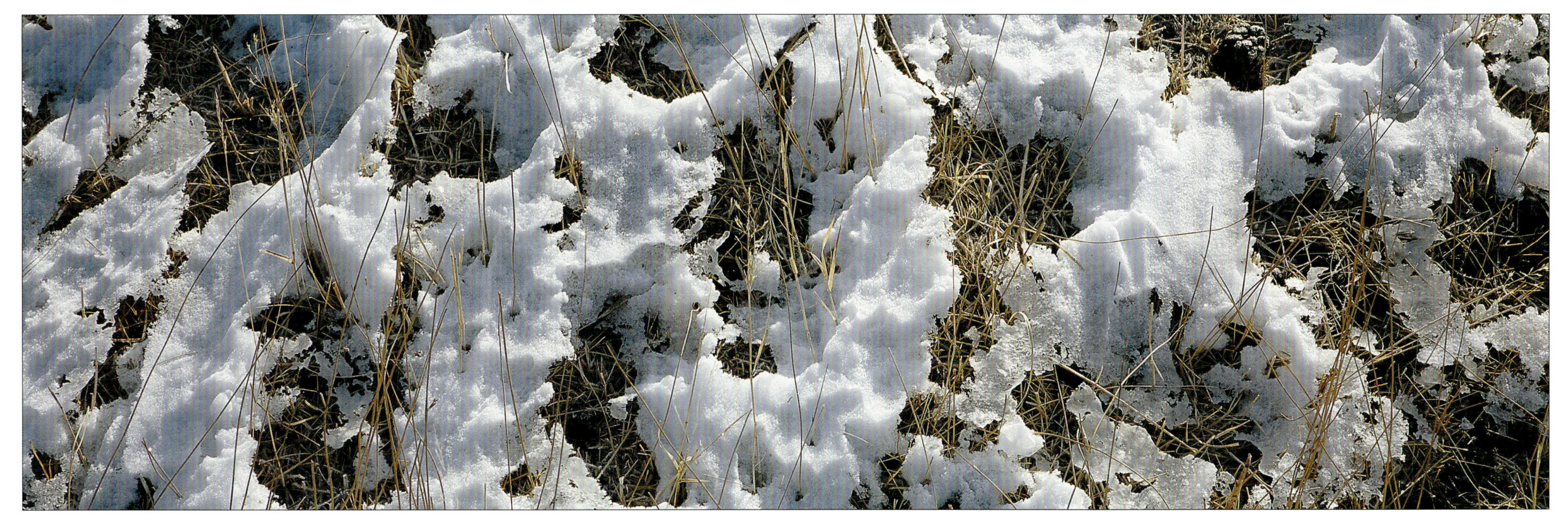

The patterns in the snow were created by a herd of elk wintering in this meadow.

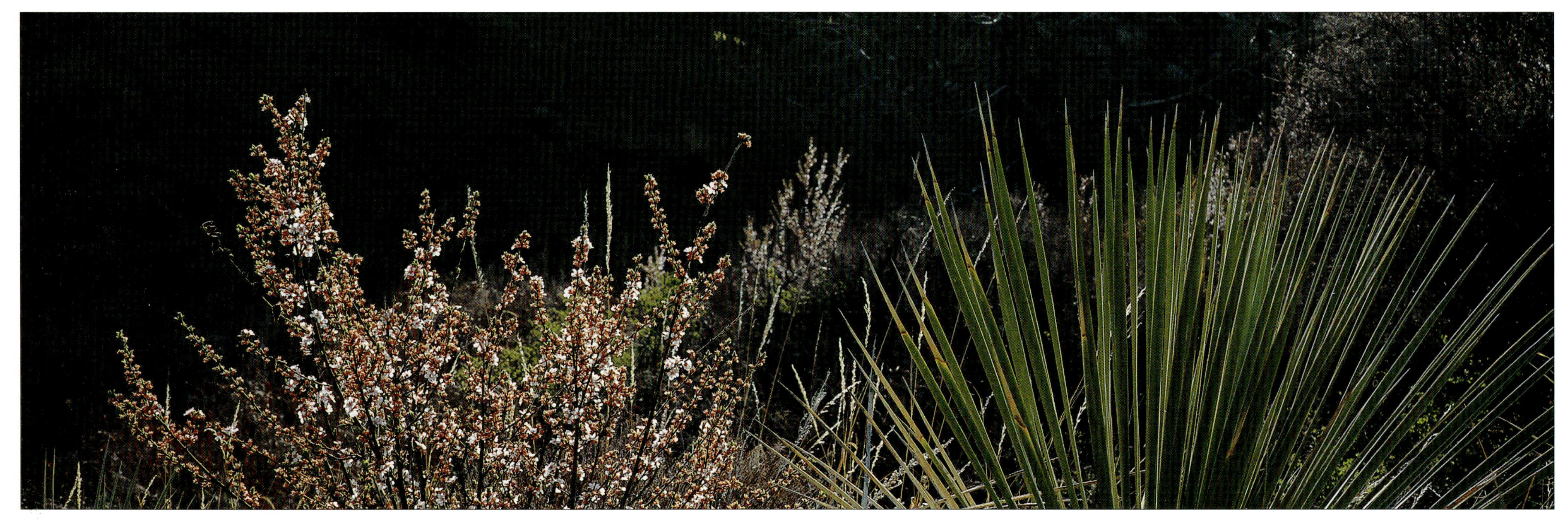

In the Rockies there are places where wildflowers and blooms will be right next to yucca plants—an interesting contrast.

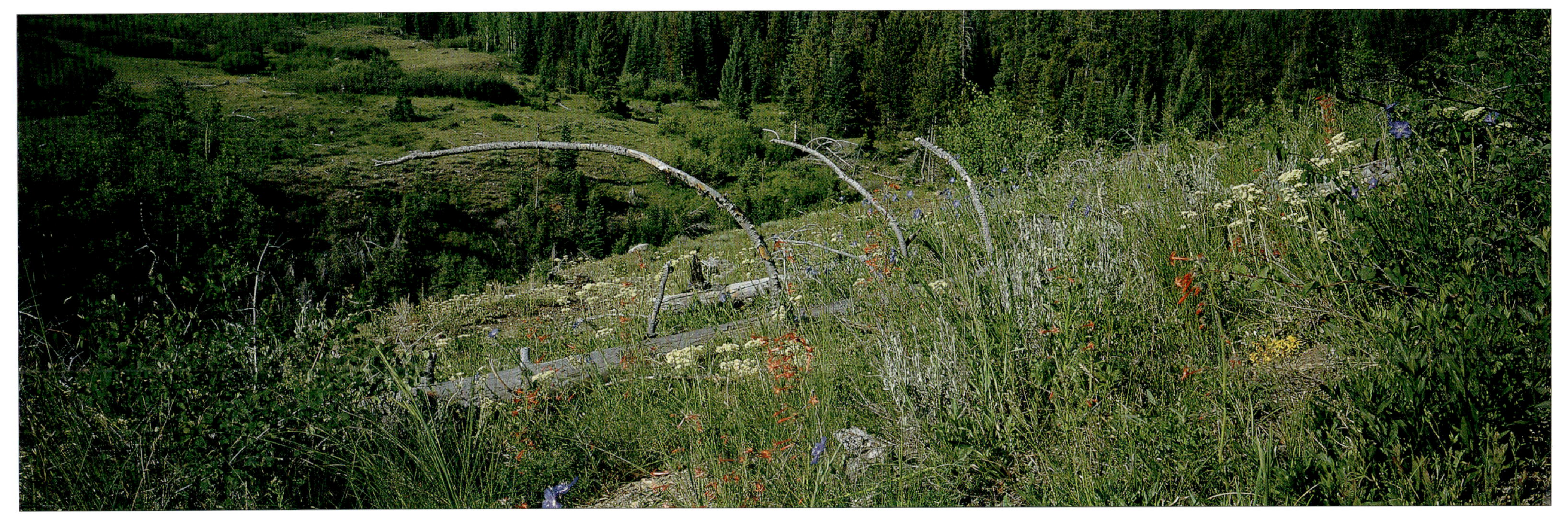

Just off the Oh-be-joyful Trail near Crested Butte

How many of these flowers can you name?

Log on to our Web site at www.keenmedia.com and let us know what you see here.

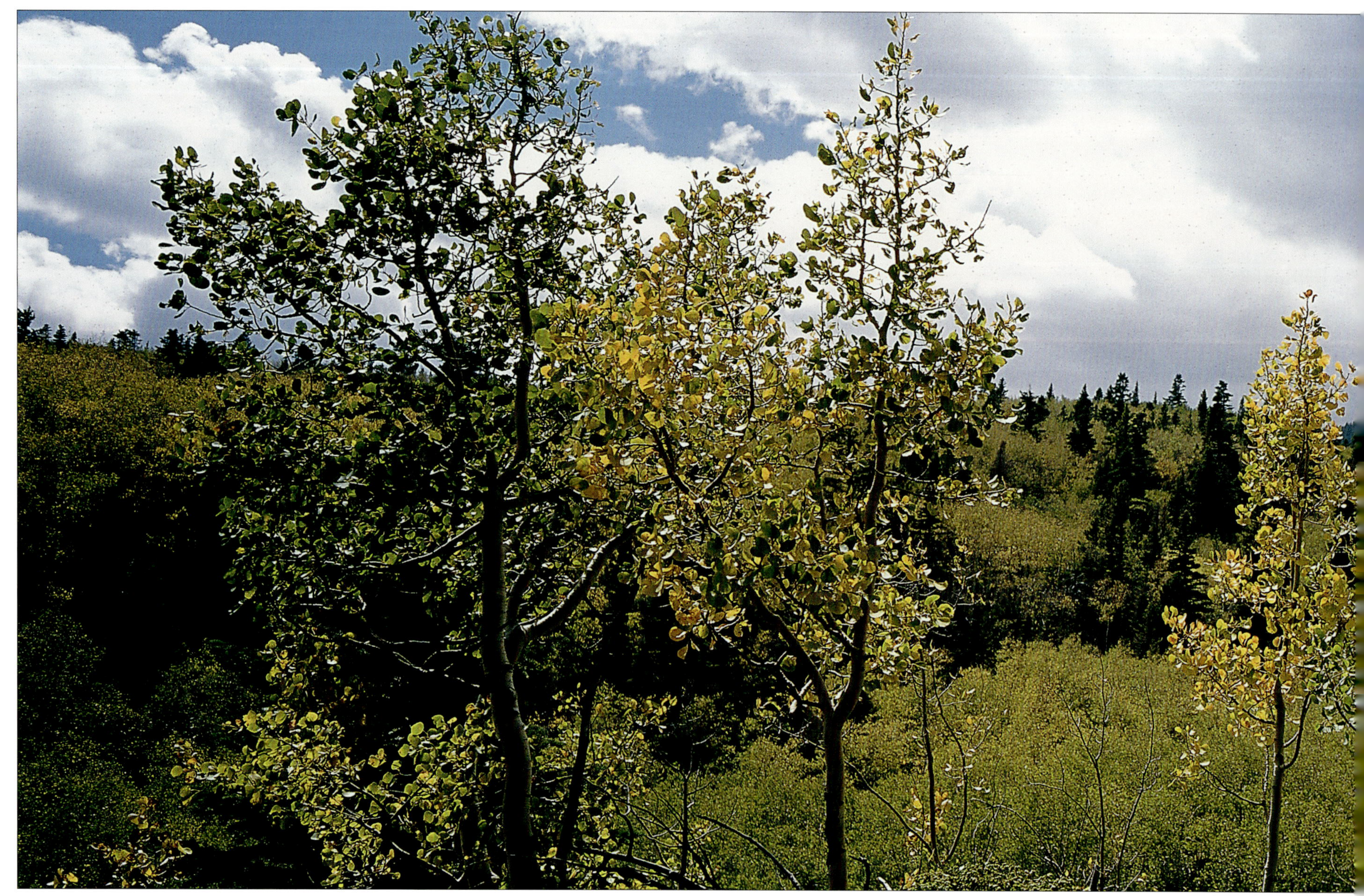

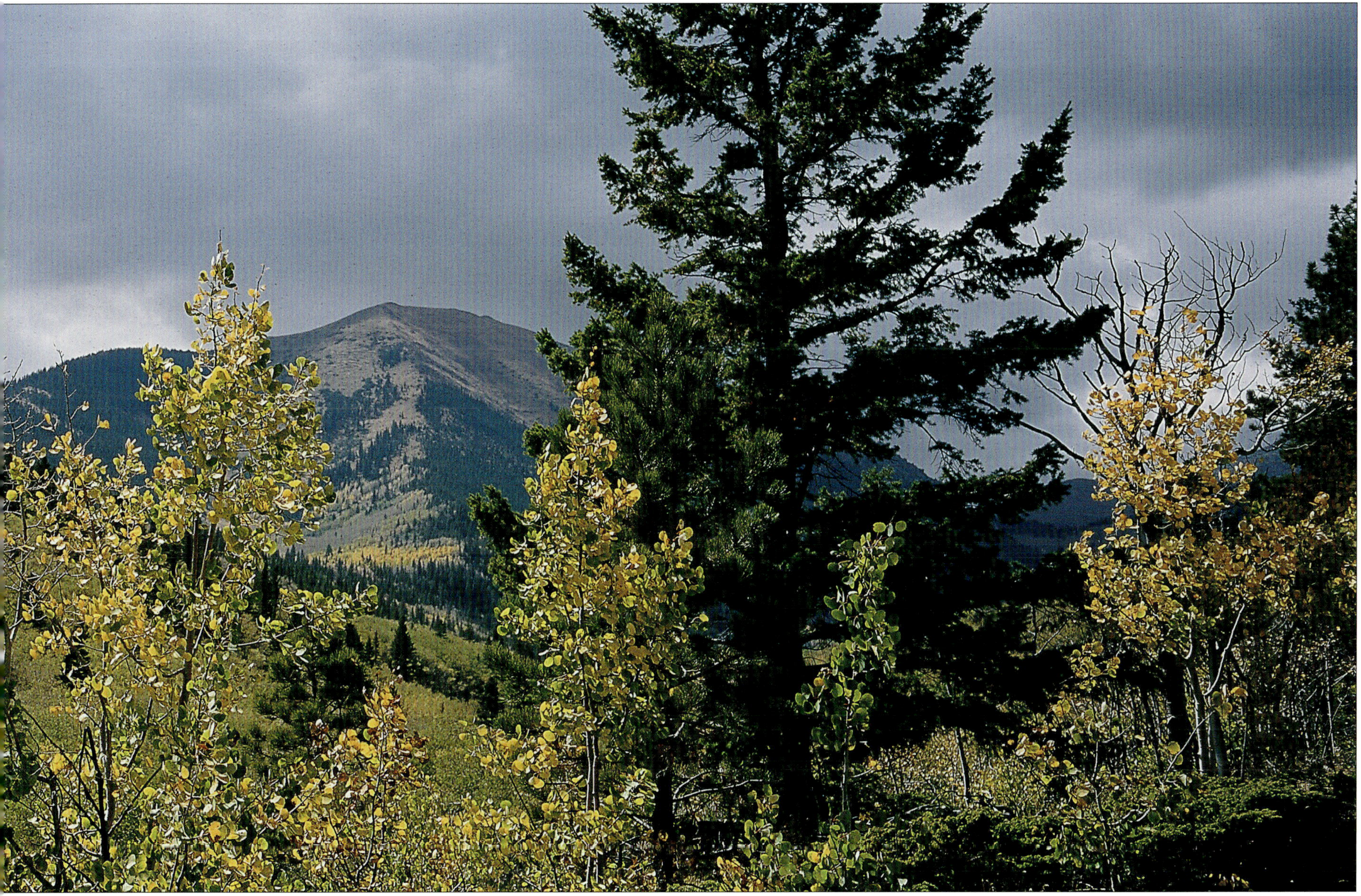

View from the Rainbow Trail in the Sangre de Cristo Mountains

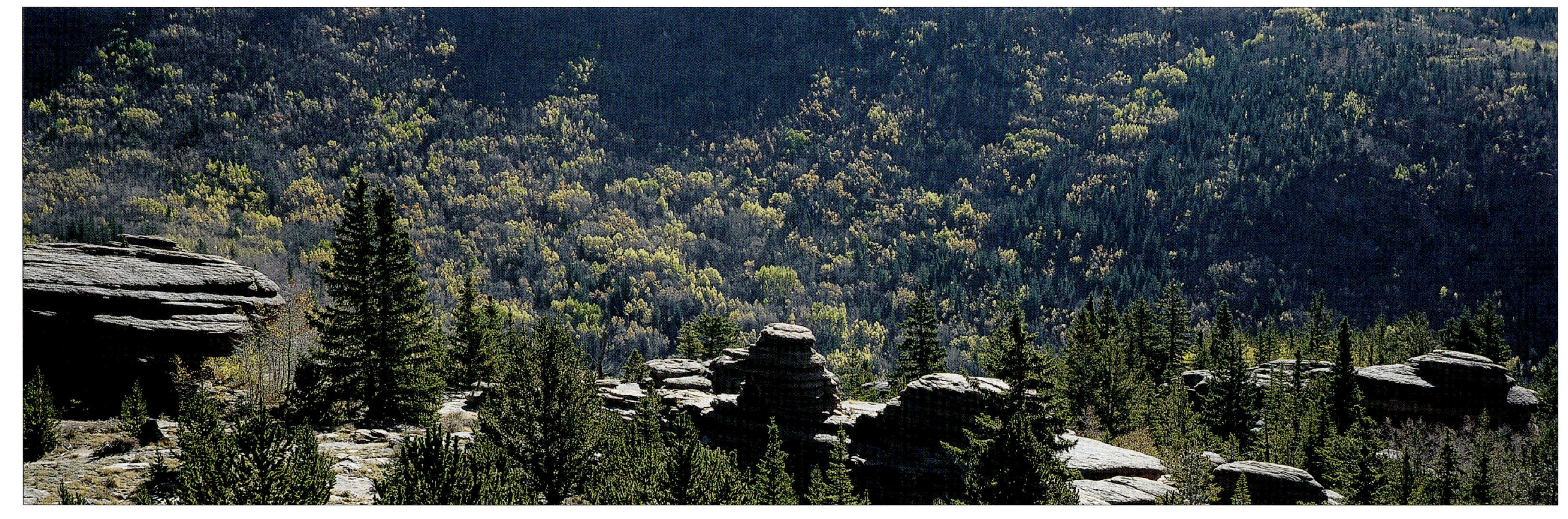

Pancake Rocks, Pike National Forest

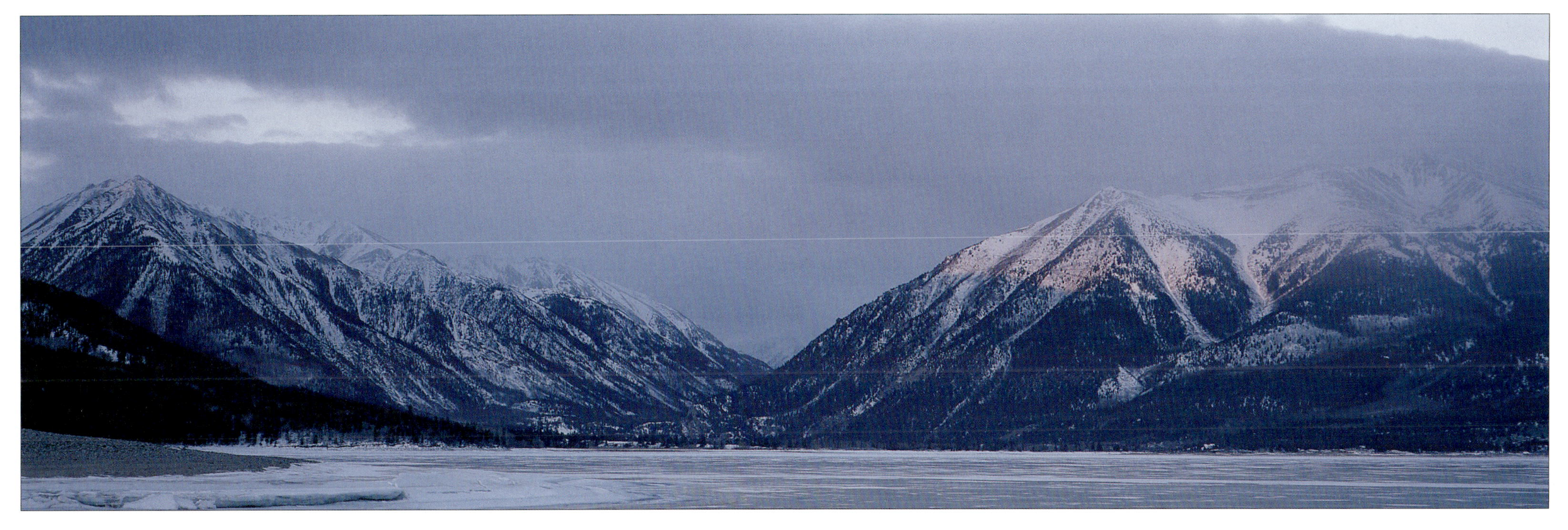

Dawn on Perry Peak, the Sawatch Range

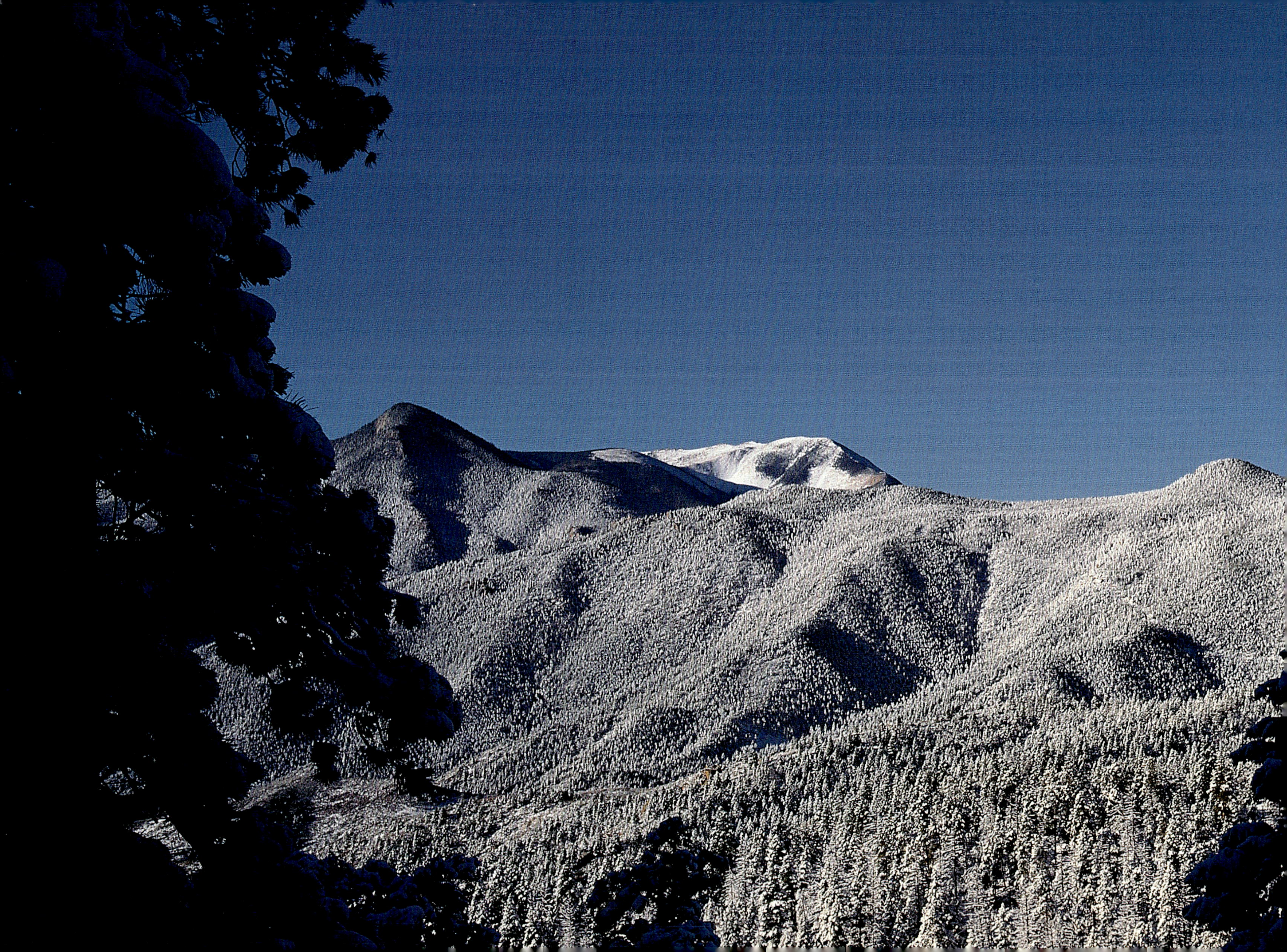

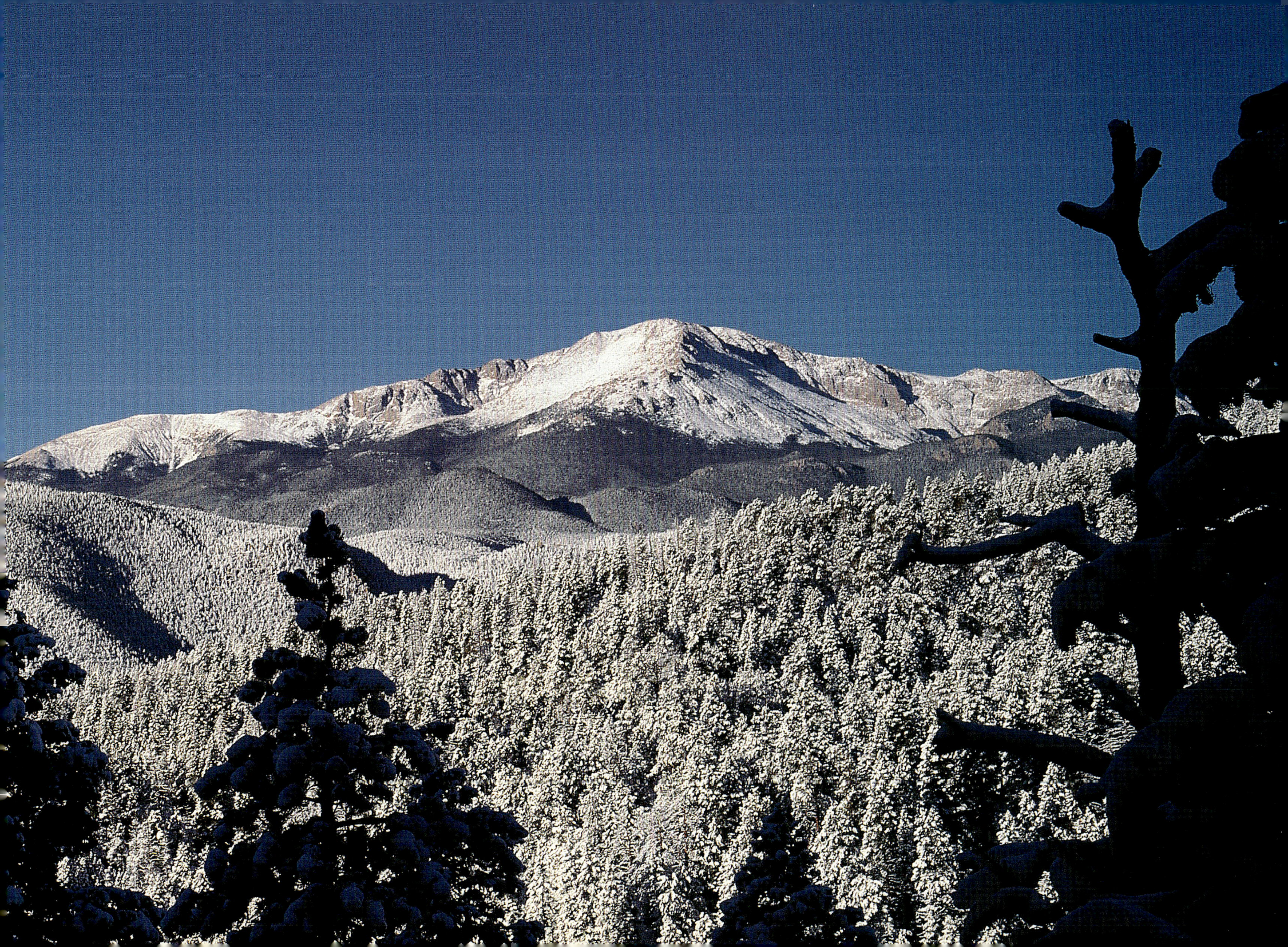

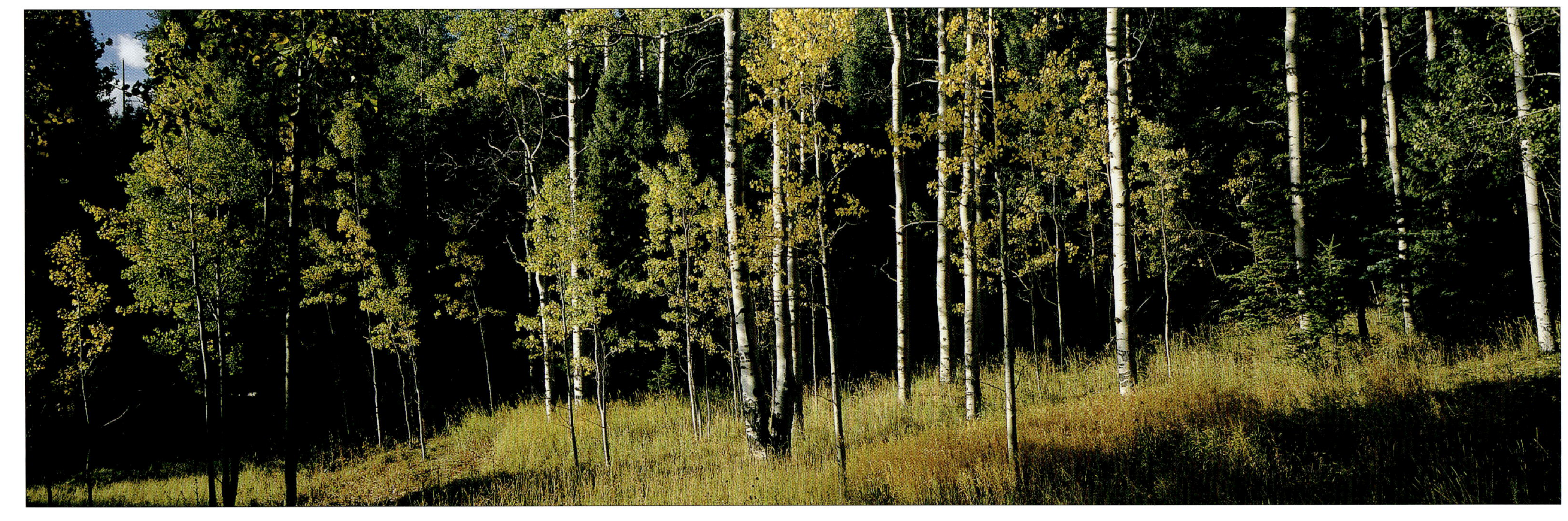

The Wet Mountains

Previous Spread: The first snow of the season on Pikes Peak as seen from Waldo Canyon

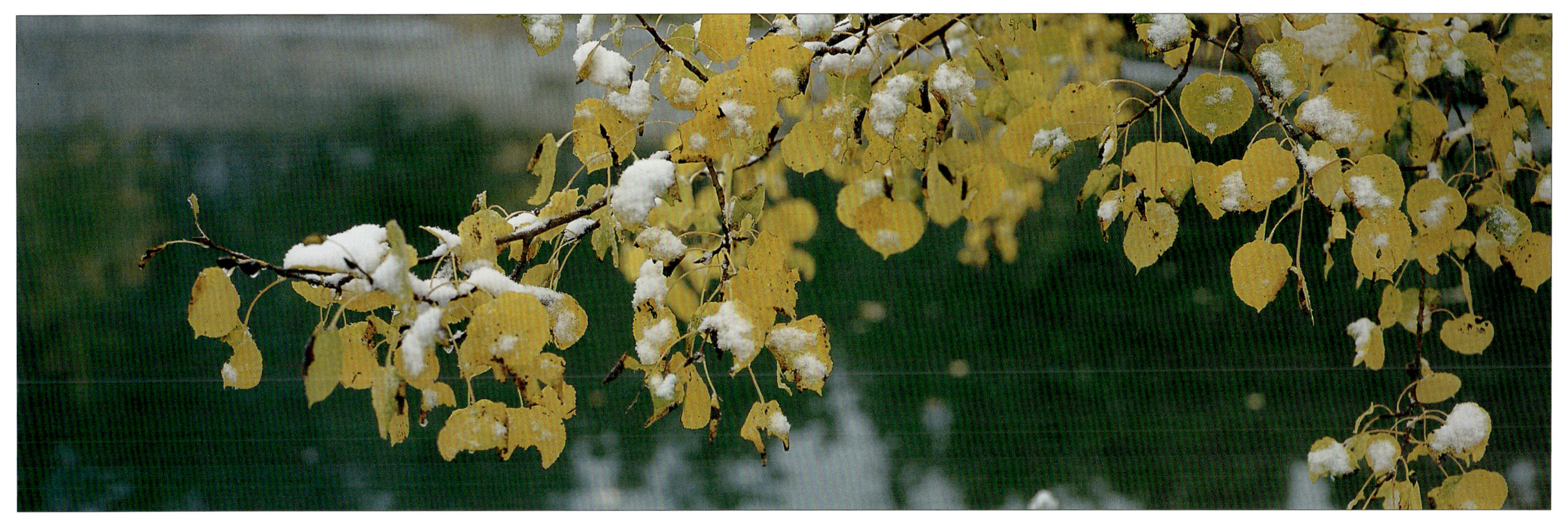

Fox Run Park

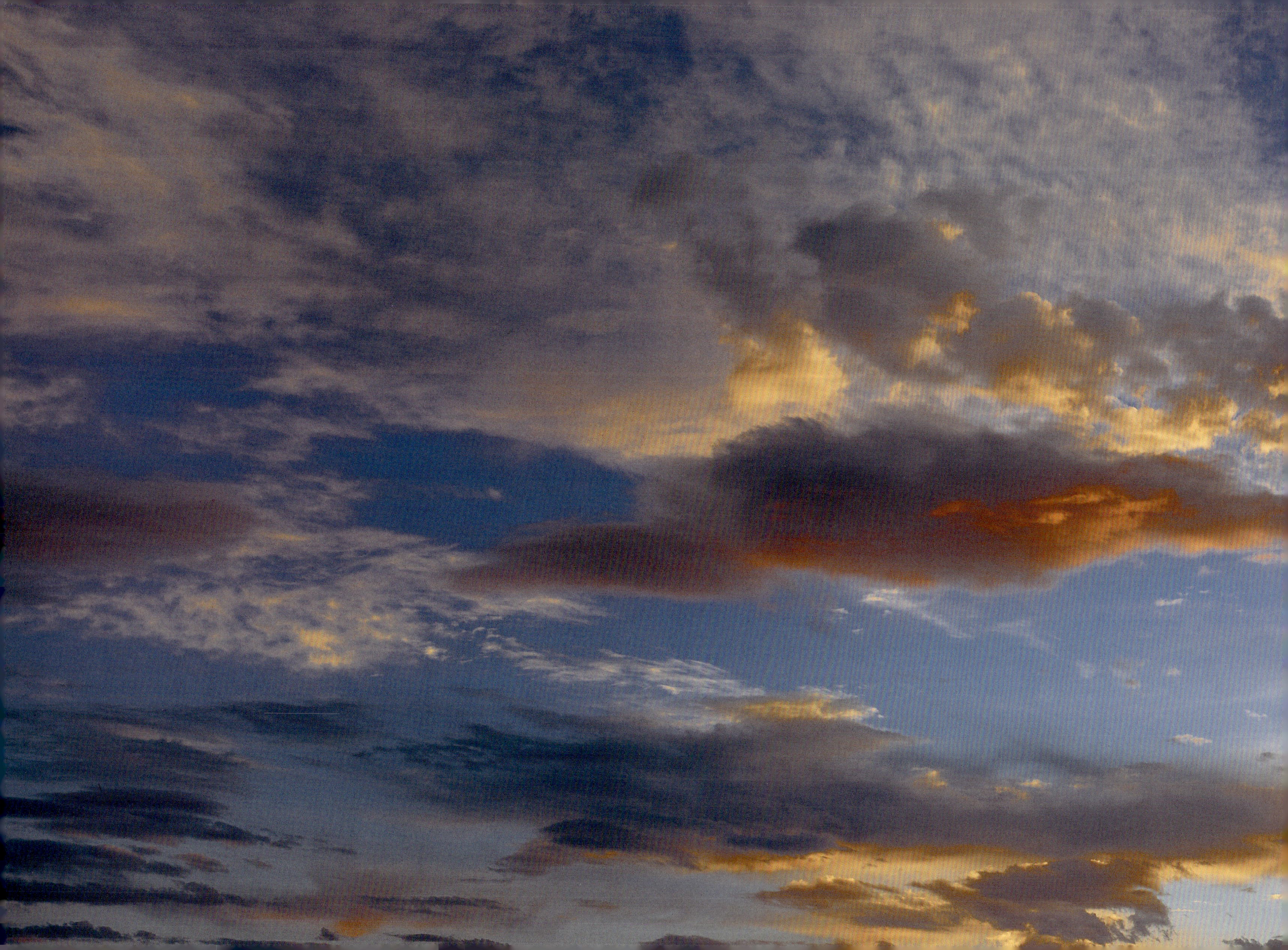

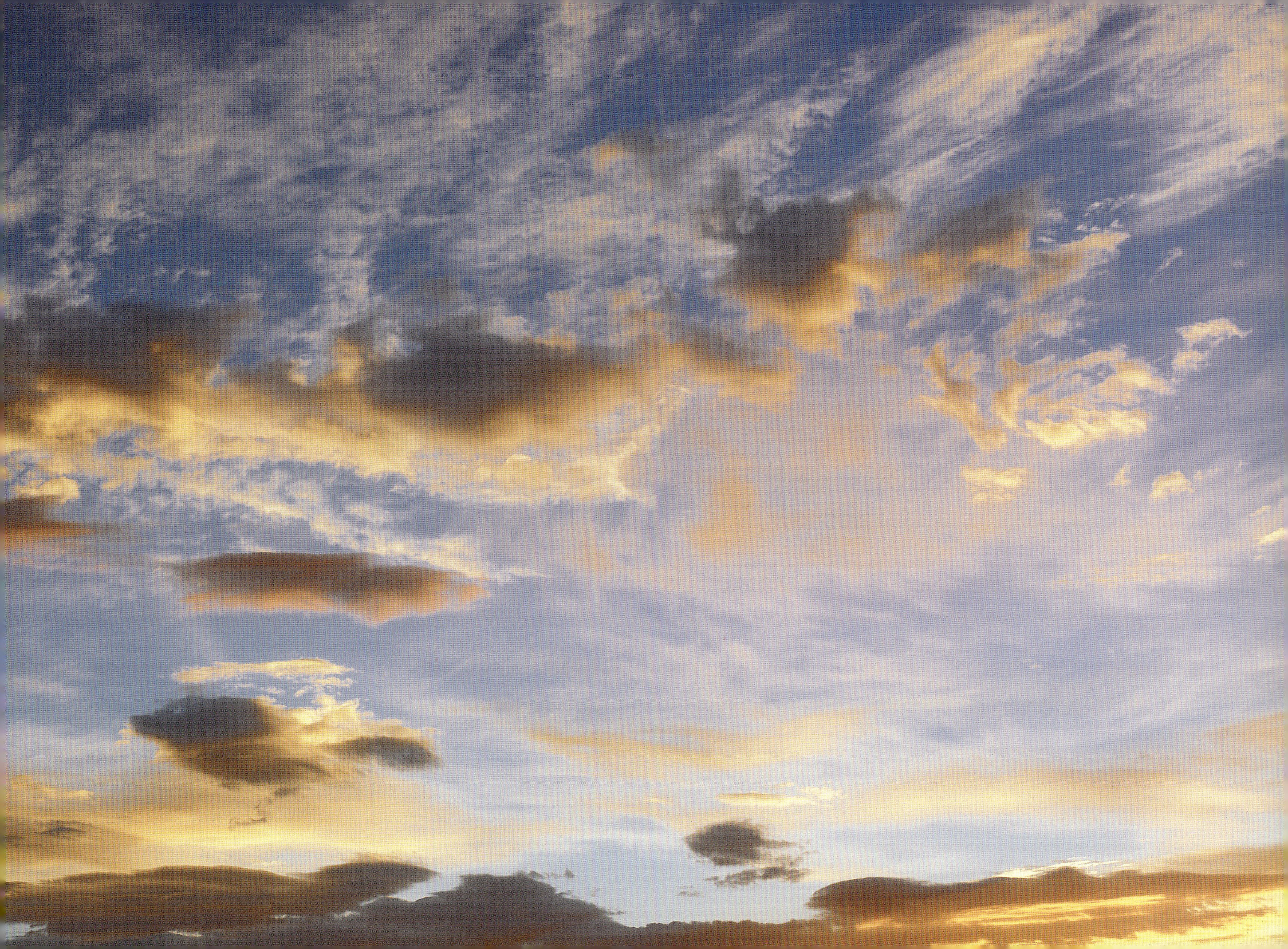

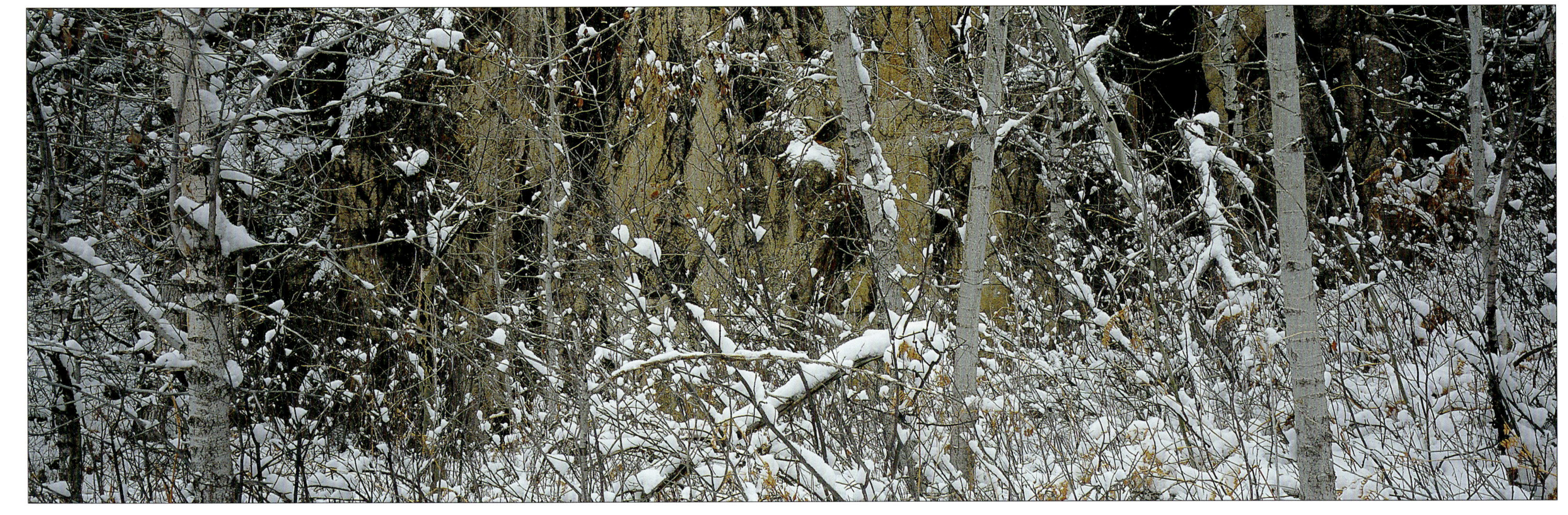

Rocky Mountain National Park

Previous Spread: A Colorado dawn

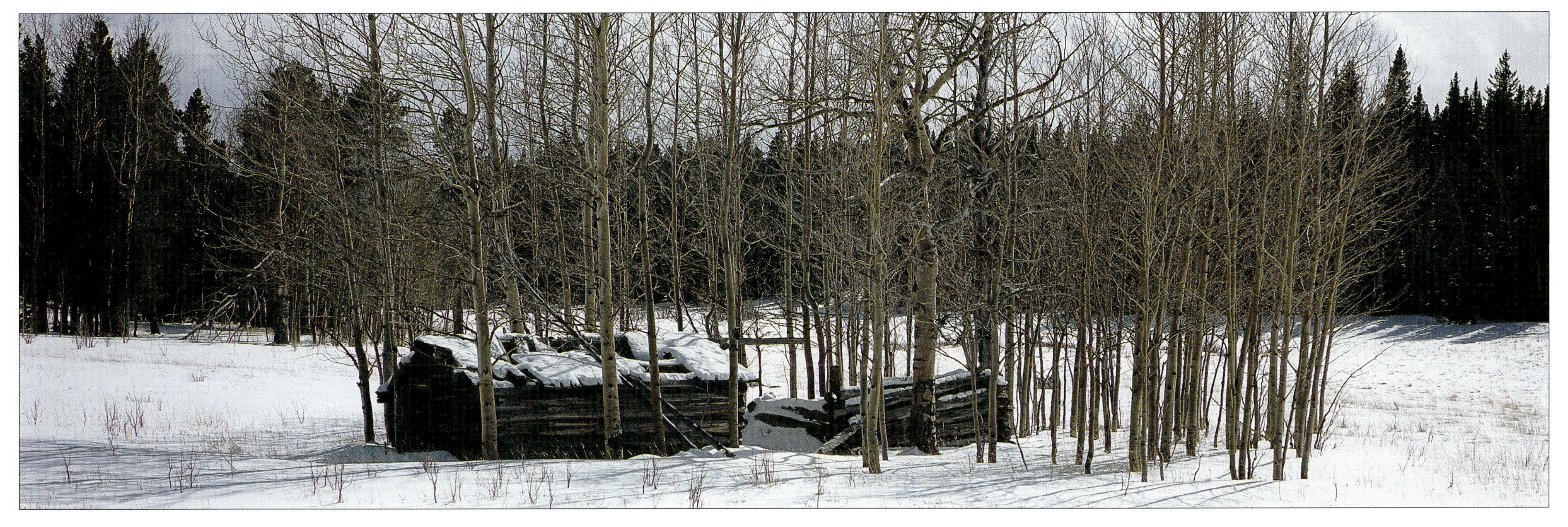

An old ranch near Ward, Colorado

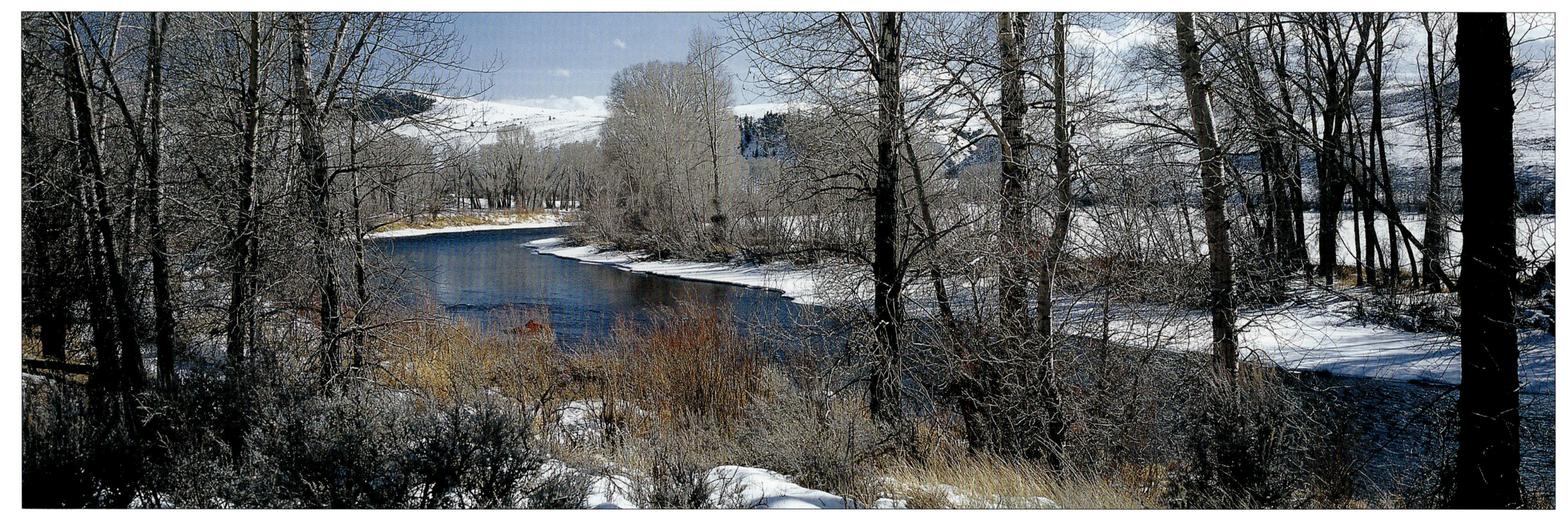

The Colorado River near its source

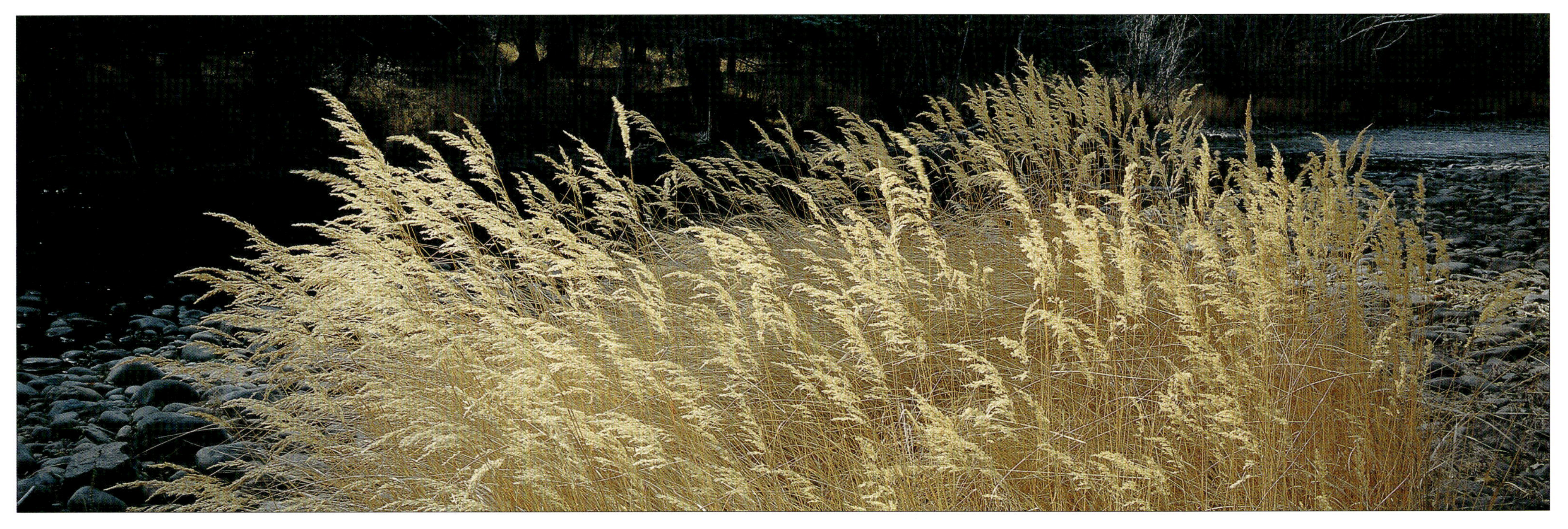

South Fork Rio Grande River

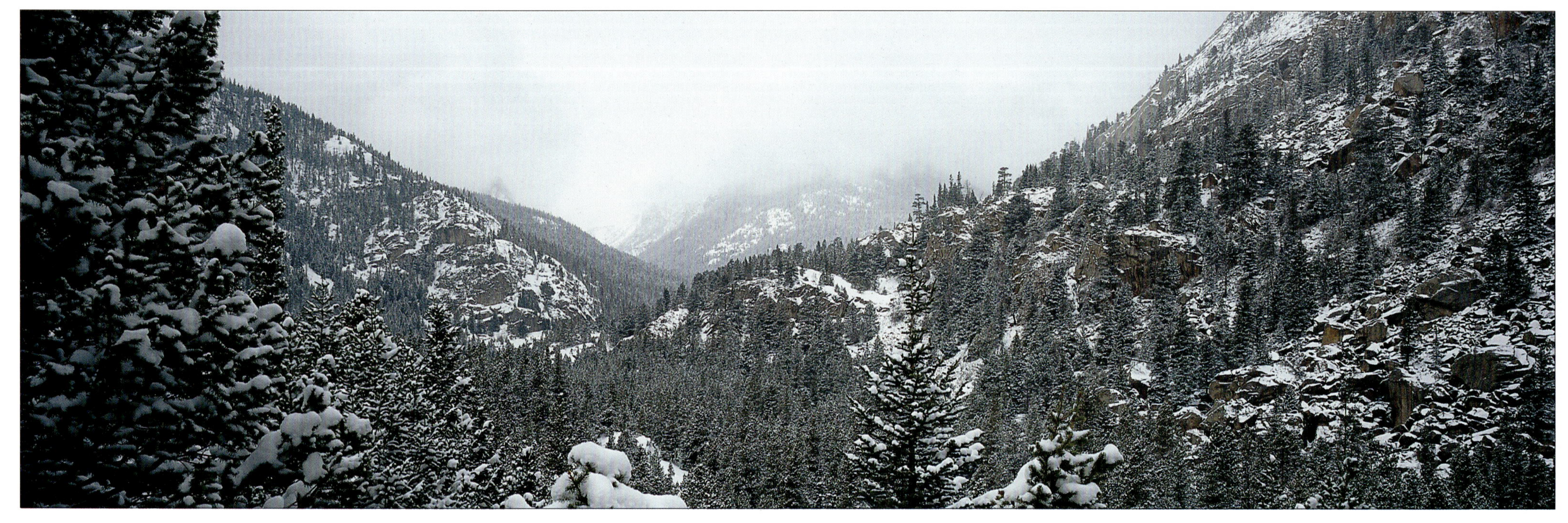

South Lateral Moraine in Rocky Mountain National Park

On the 17th of March 2001, my wife Roann joined me on her very first winter camping trip. We hiked a couple miles up Fern Lake Trail in Rocky Mountain National Park. It was snowing lightly—just her kind of snow, with no wind. I made a number of panographic images™ of the freshly fallen snow on the trees while she was busy identifying birds and animal footprints. We hiked back down through four or five inches of new snow in plenty of time to make camp close to the car. Early the next morning, well before sunrise, we drove up Trailridge Road to the point where the road was closed for the winter. I climbed up the rock that you see on the left to photograph the first light of dawn hitting Longs Peak. Near the top I stamped out a small ledge in the snow and balanced my tripod on a few rocks. I waited there about an hour and a half for the right lighting, but there was very little color in the sky that morning, and I only made a few images. With cold fingers and toes, I climbed back down to join Roann in the car to warm up a little. As I sat there I could see that the sun was about to pass right up behind a crack in the rock—an opportunity to make a good silhouette. Quickly getting the camera out of the trunk, I made a few exposures and realized I would need to move the car to get in the right position to make any more images. I drove the car backwards 20 or 30 feet and returned to move my camera to the right position. Just as I set the tripod down, a gust of wind blew the snow off the tree. The sun backlit the blowing flakes and created the beautiful panographic image™ on the next page. A moment later it was gone.

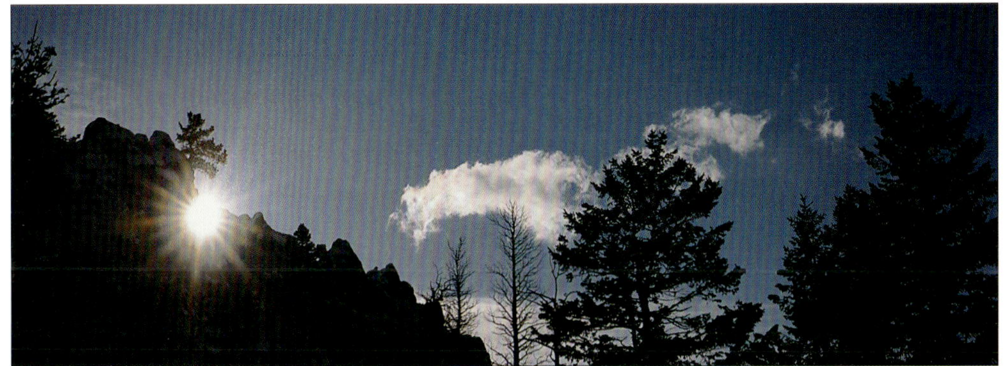

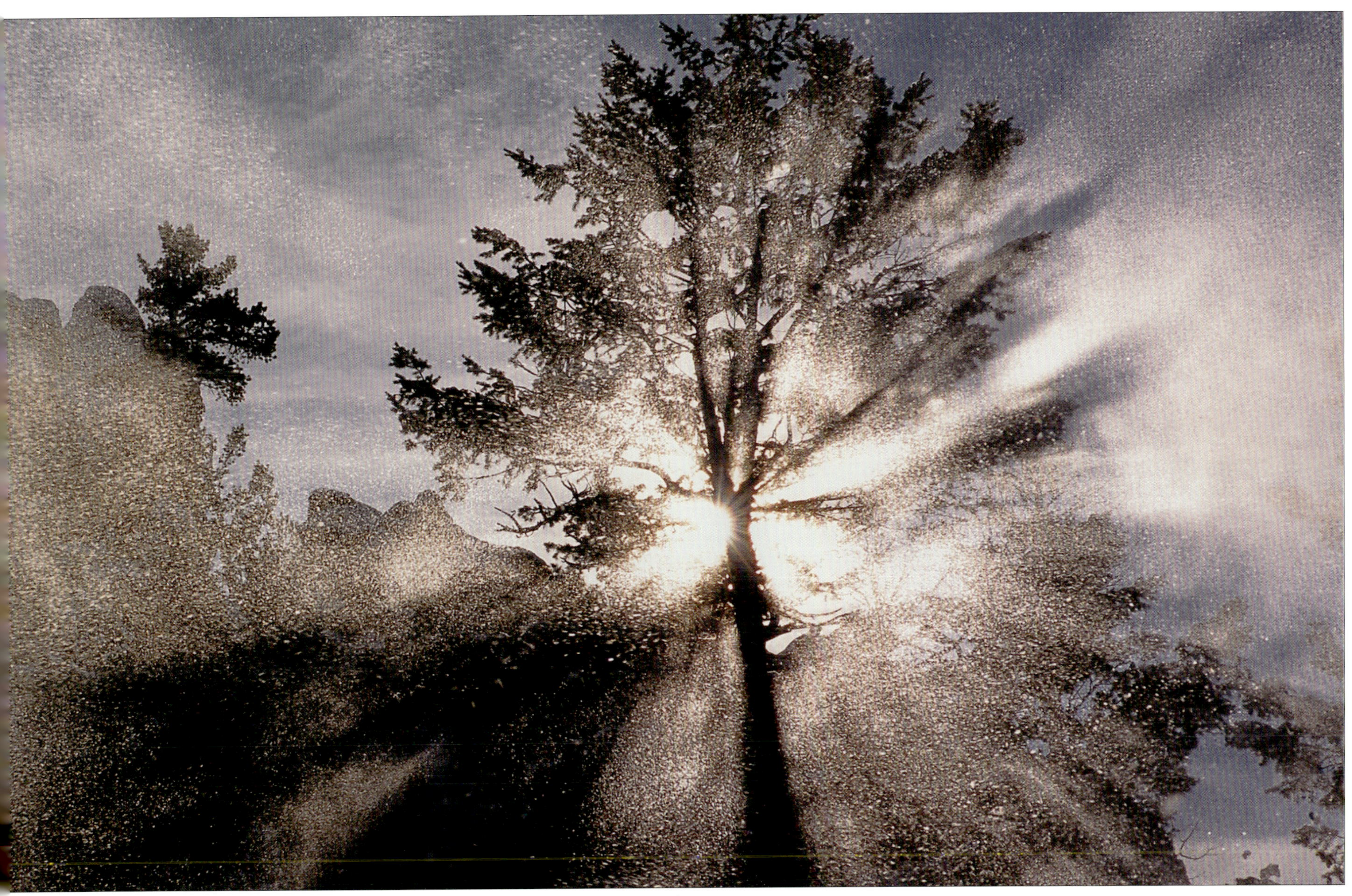

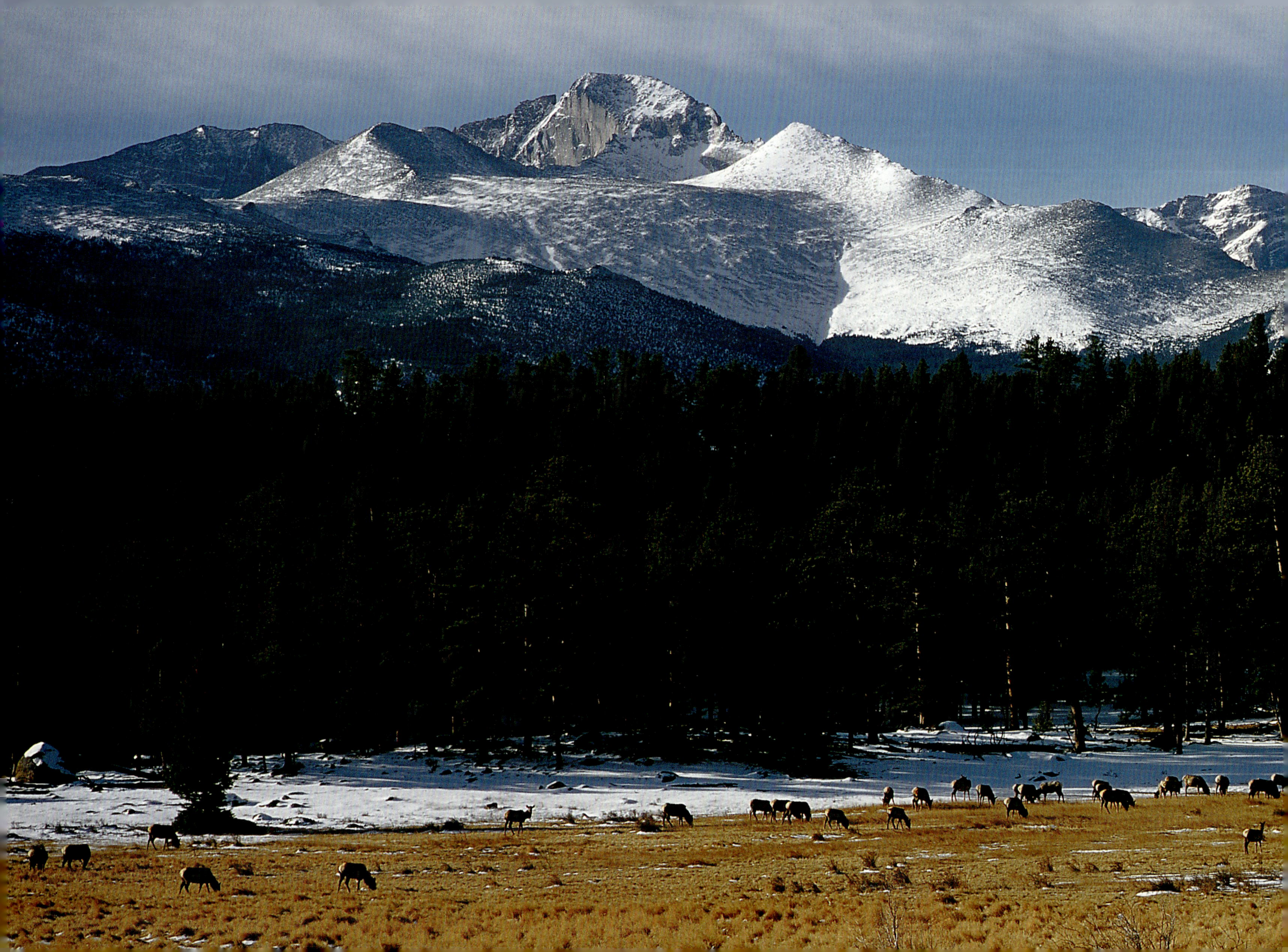

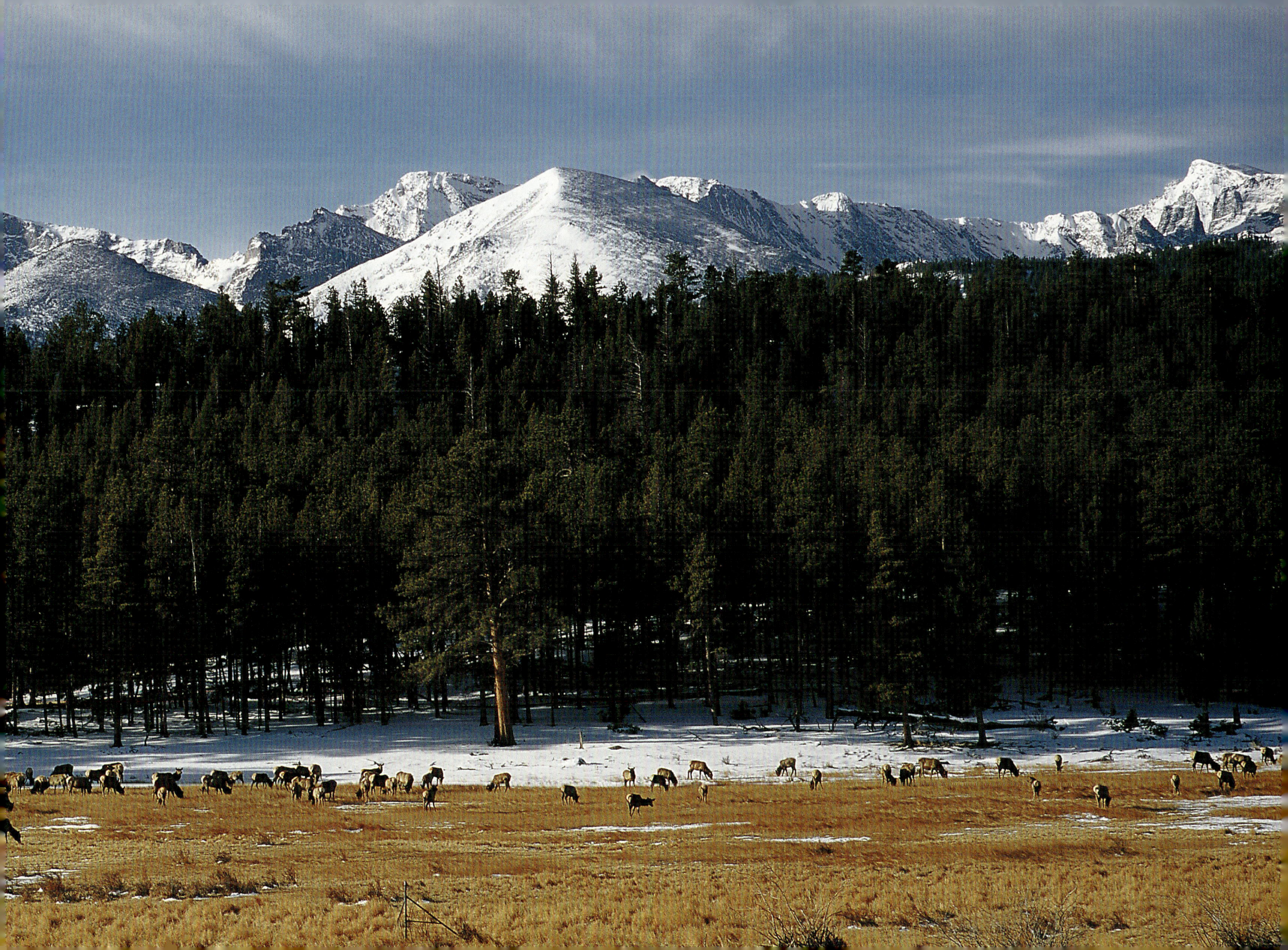

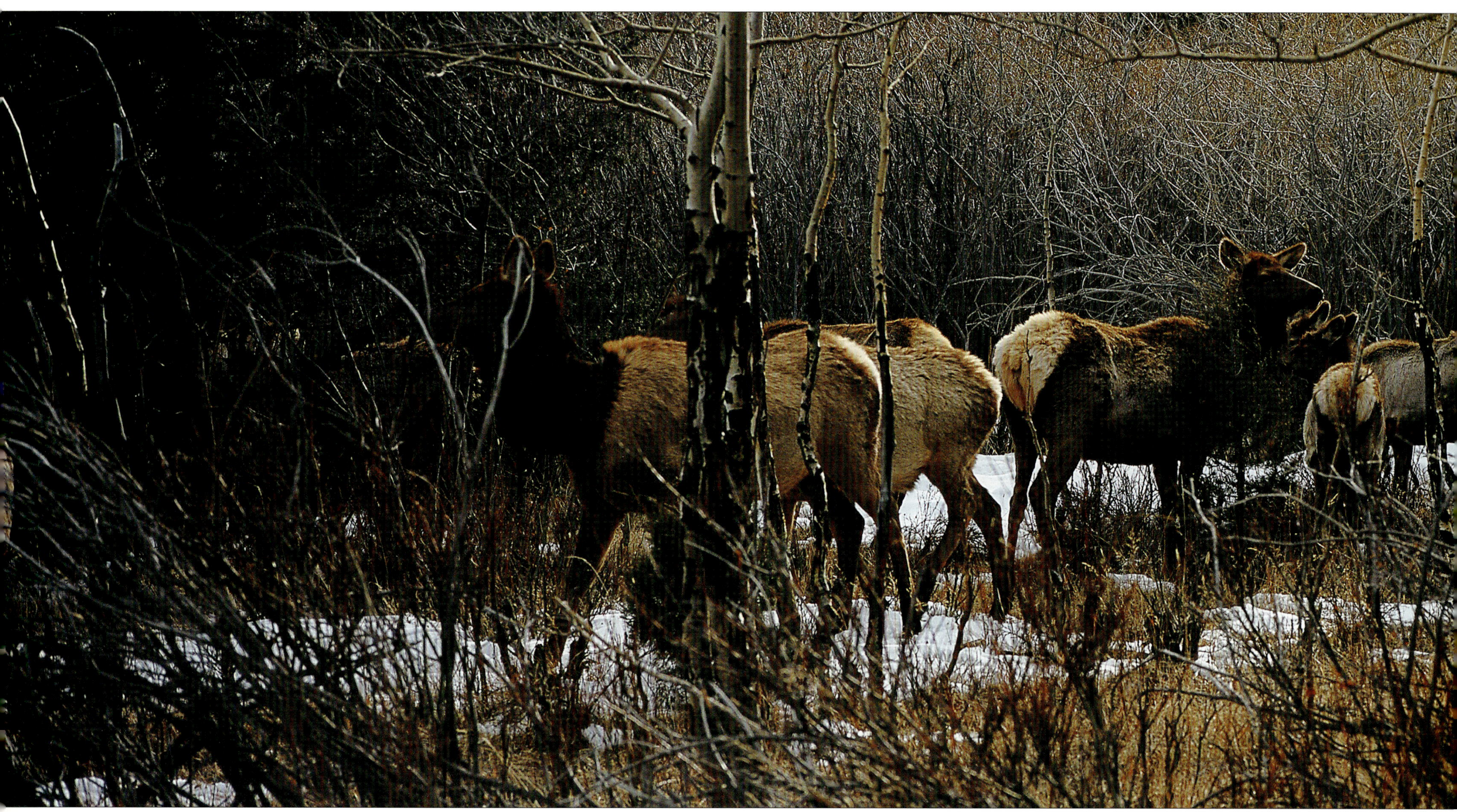

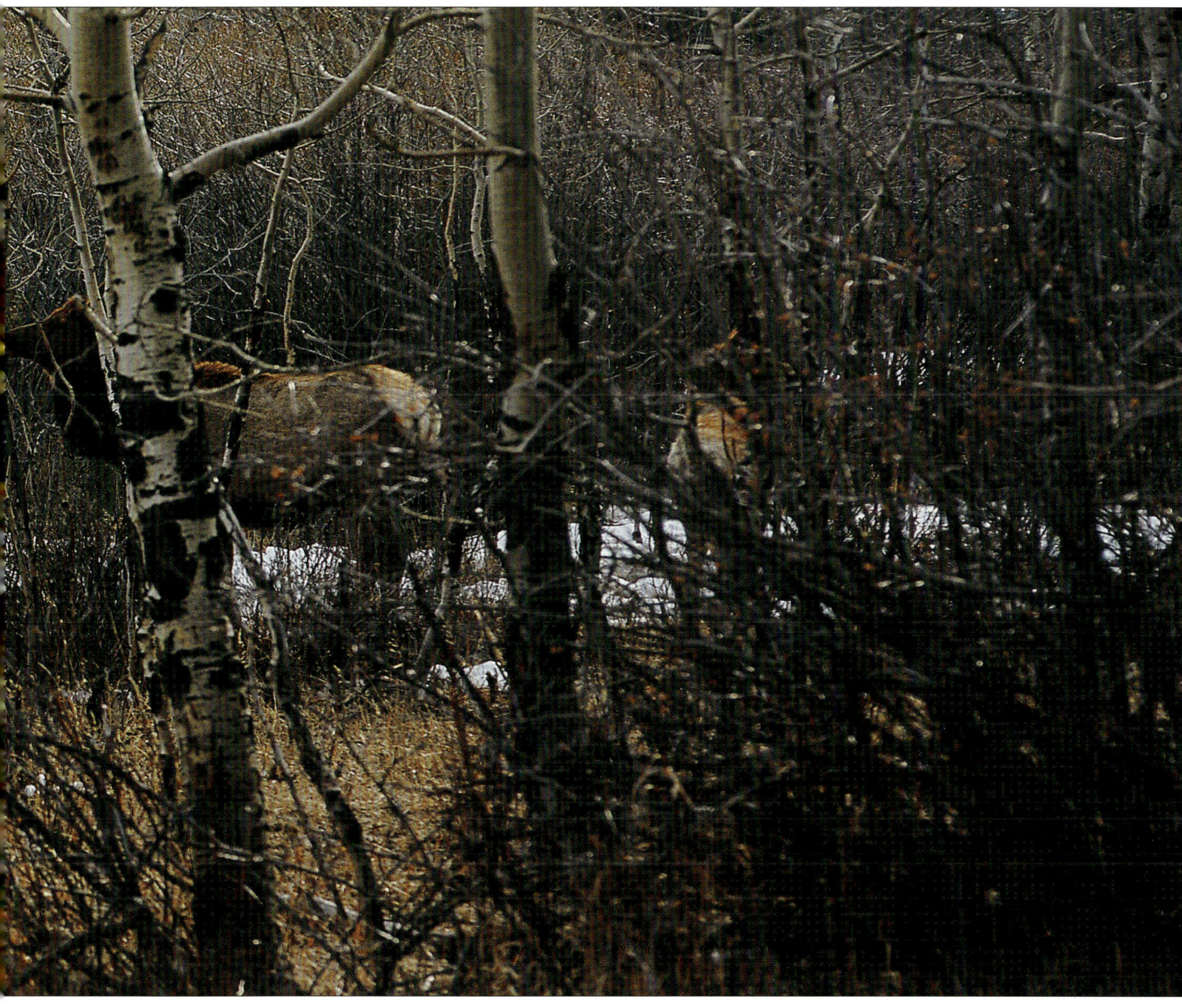

Rocky Mountain National Park

One winter day I spent about three hours hiking along with a herd of several hundred elk. I'm sure I began to smell like one of them, because after a while they let me get to within twenty feet of them.

Previous Spread: Elk in Rocky Mountain National Park

Winter grazing land for deer and elk

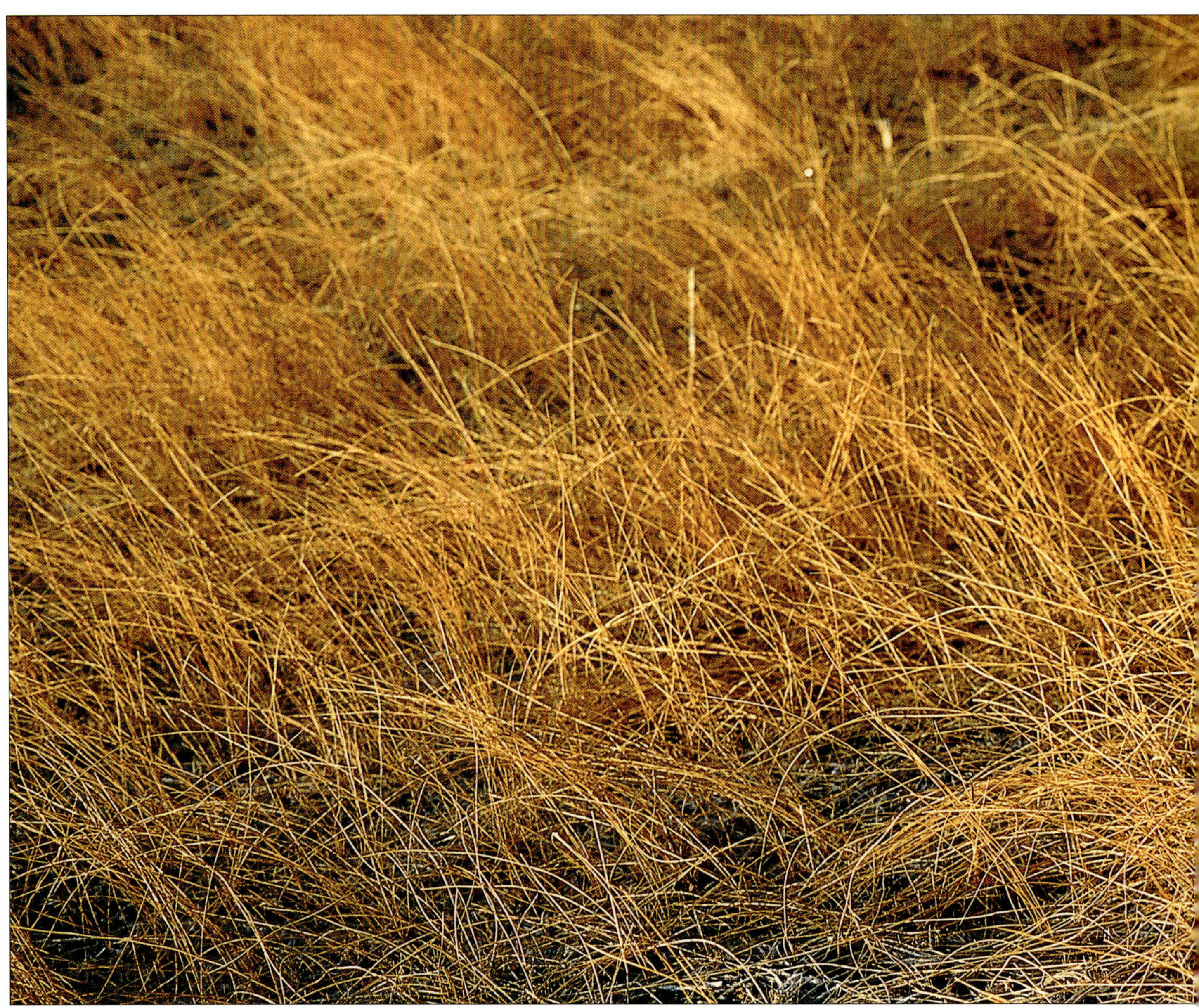

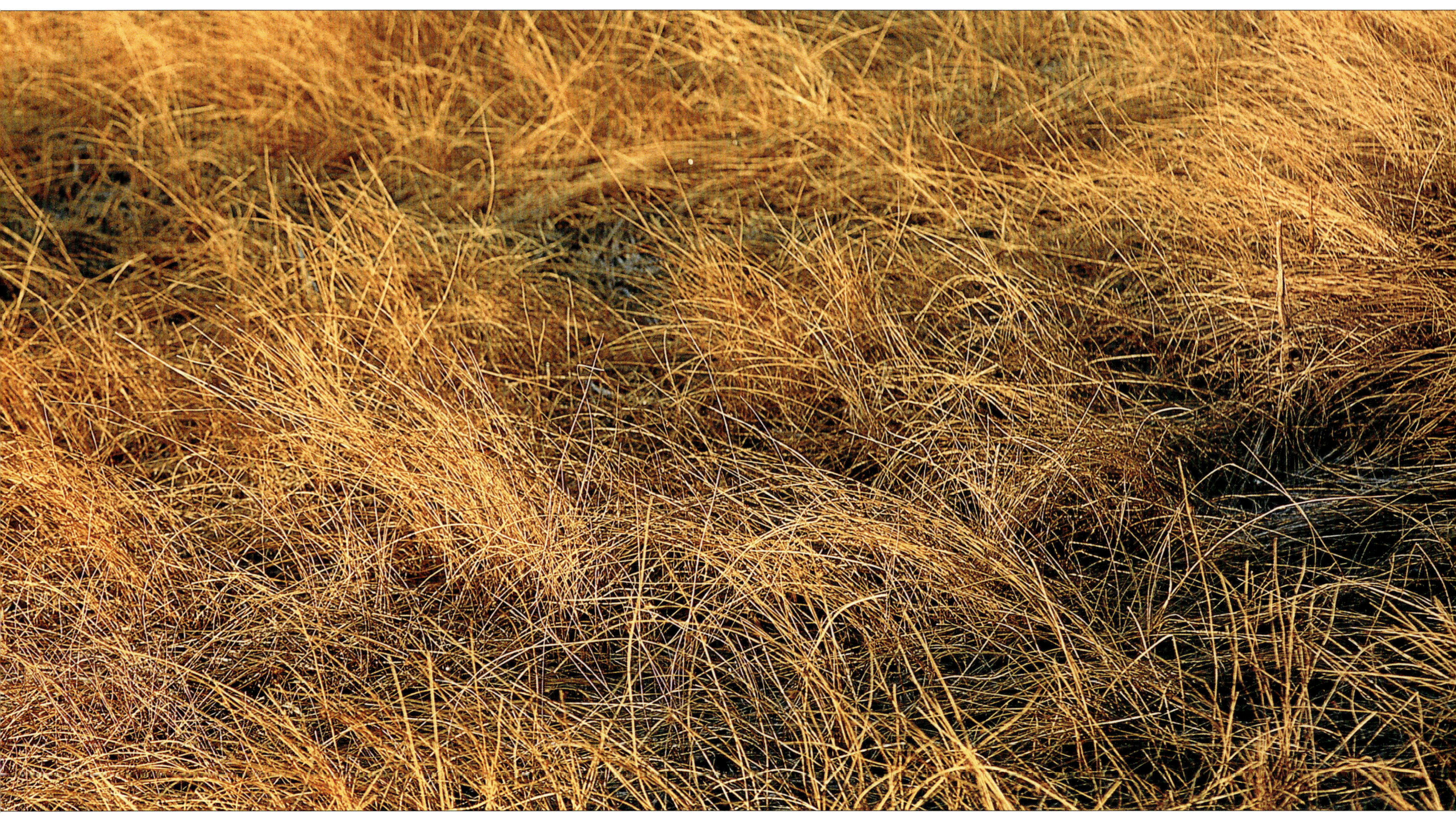

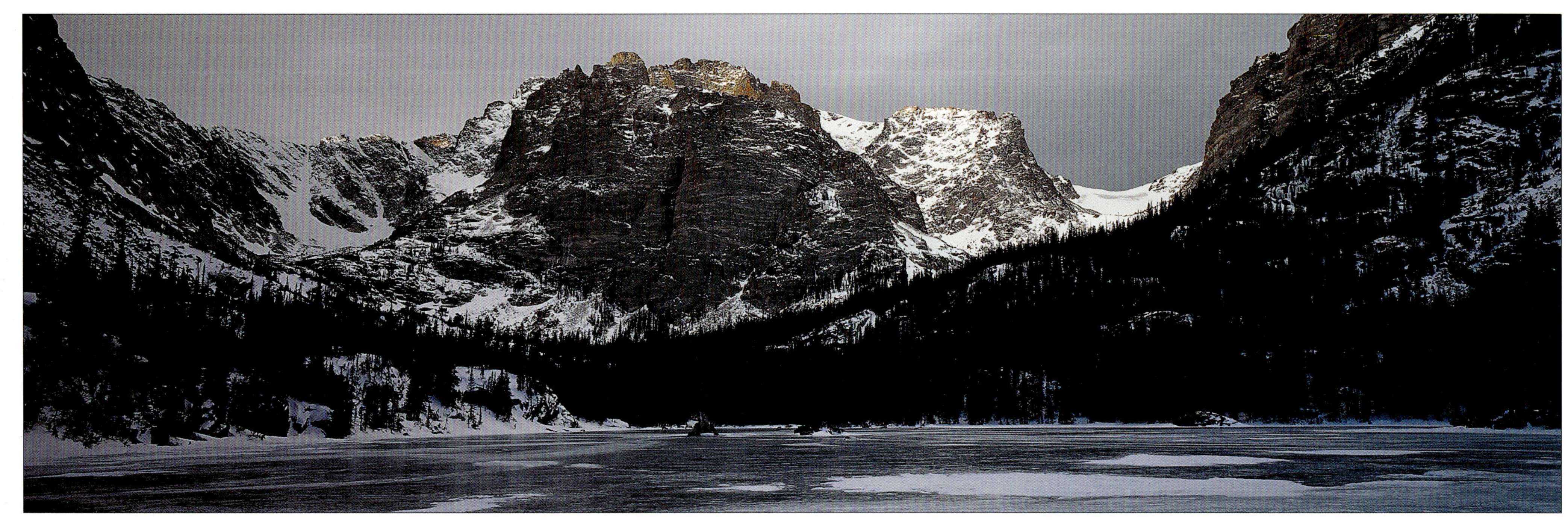

The Lock, Rocky Mountain National Park

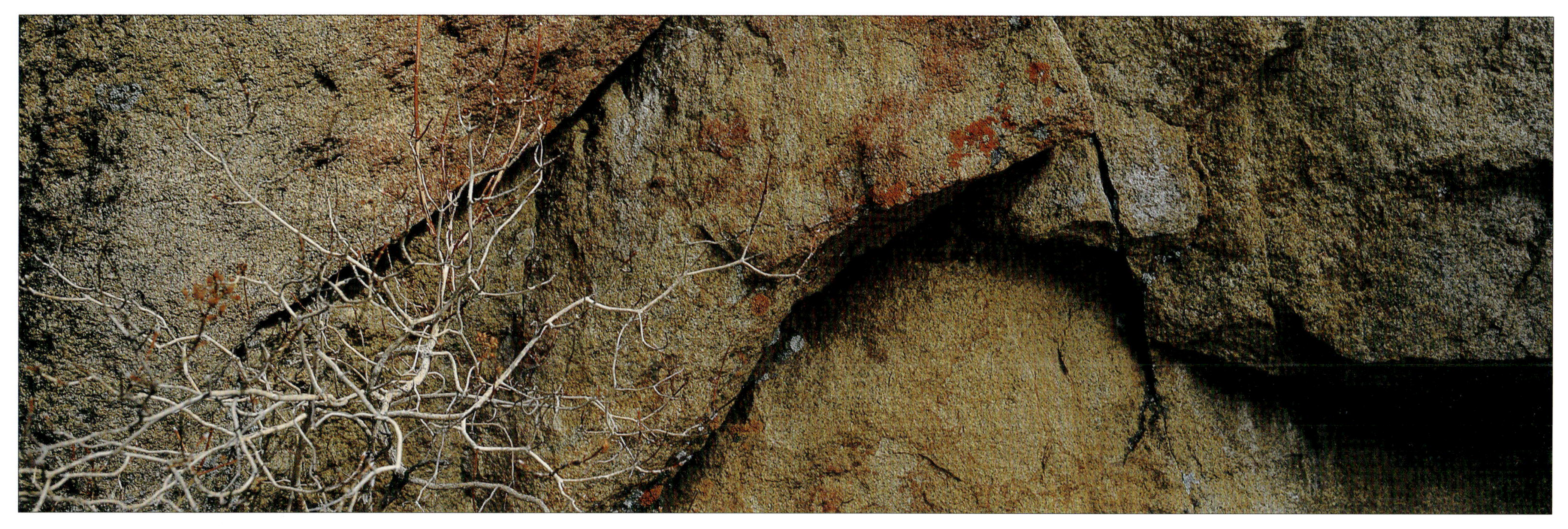

Rocky Mountain National Park

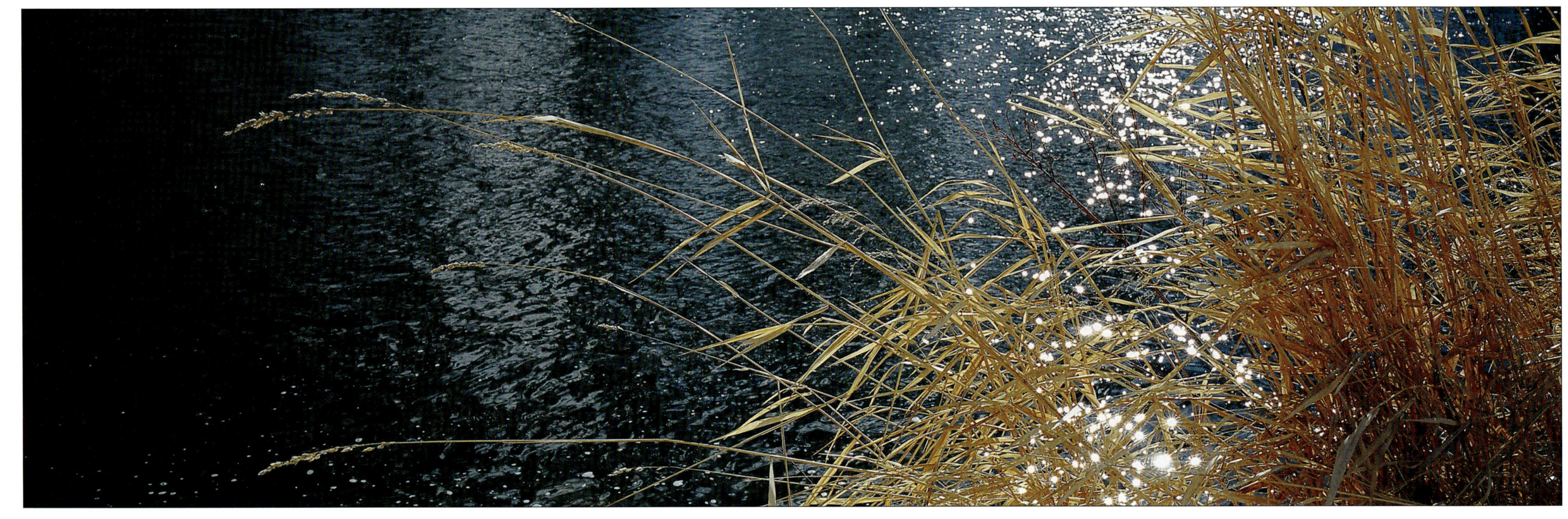

Along the Colorado River

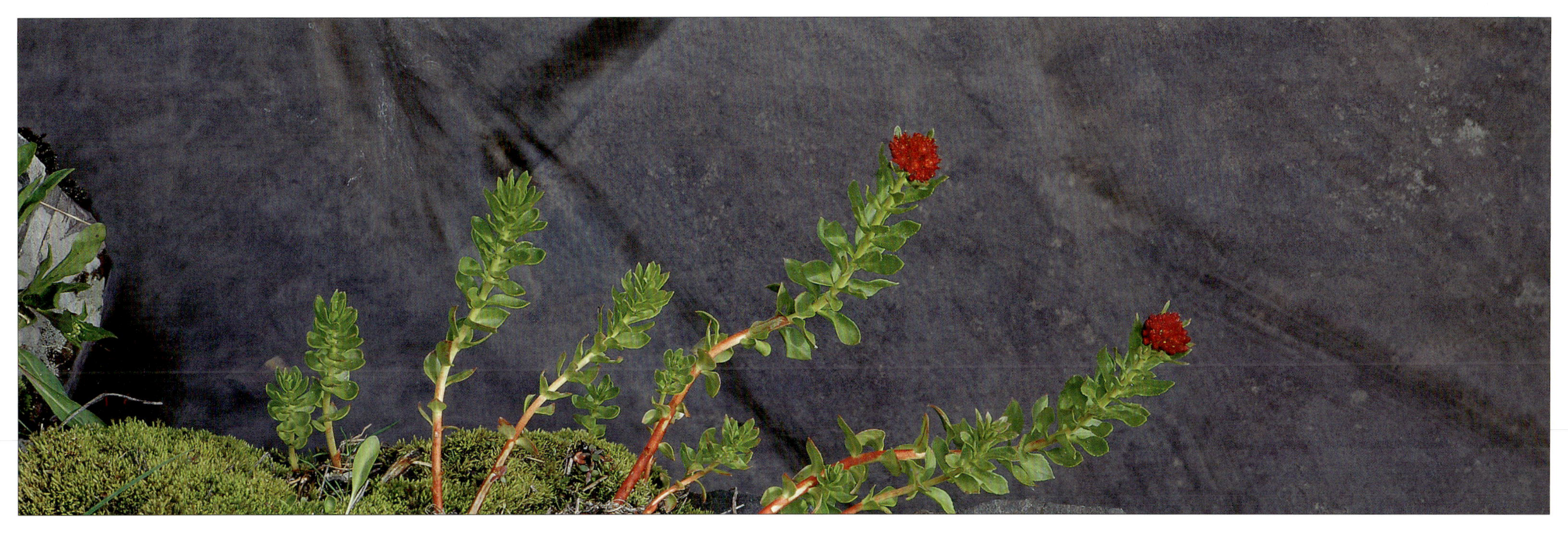

Kings Crown (Rhodiola integrifolia) growing just above a clear stream flowing over slate

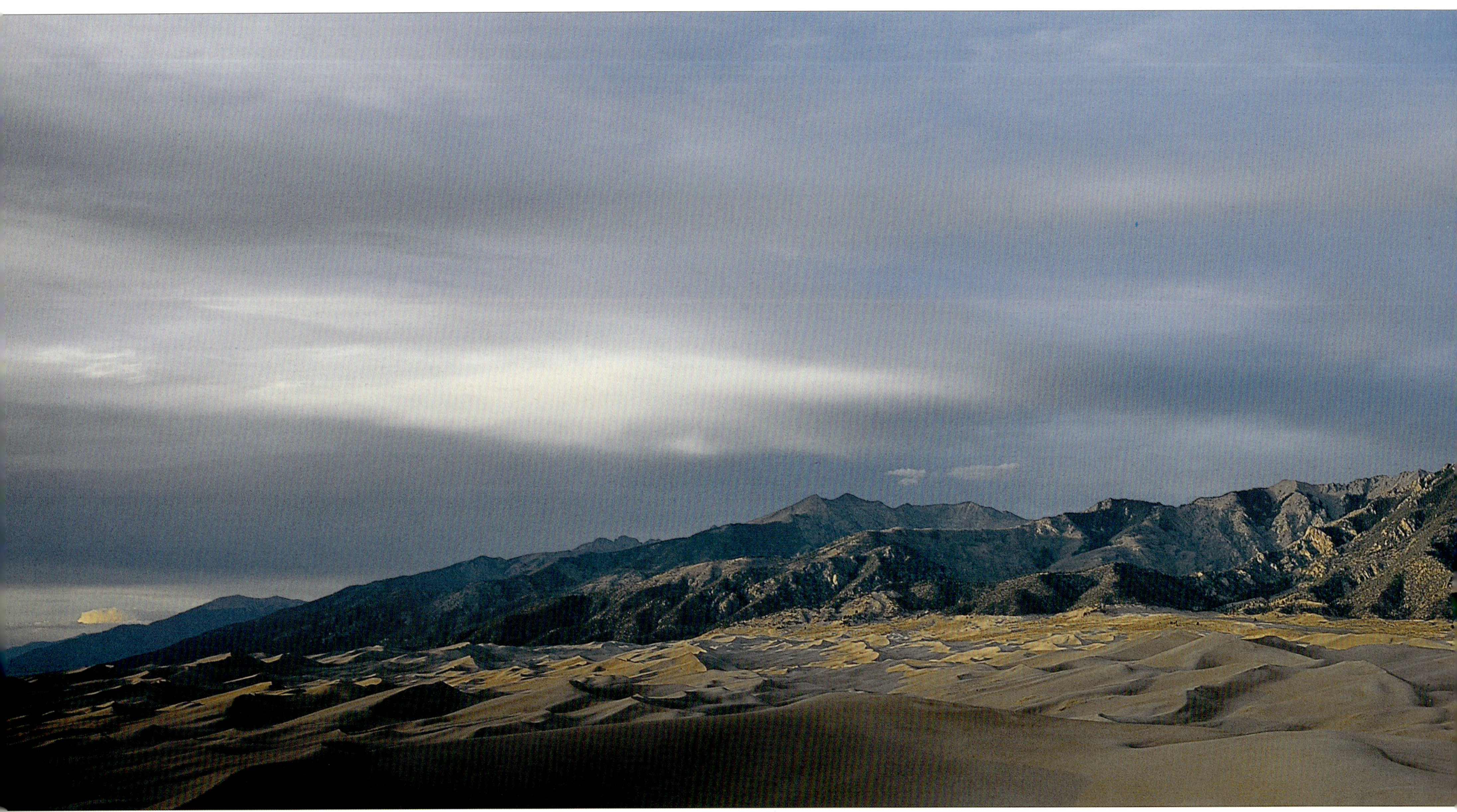

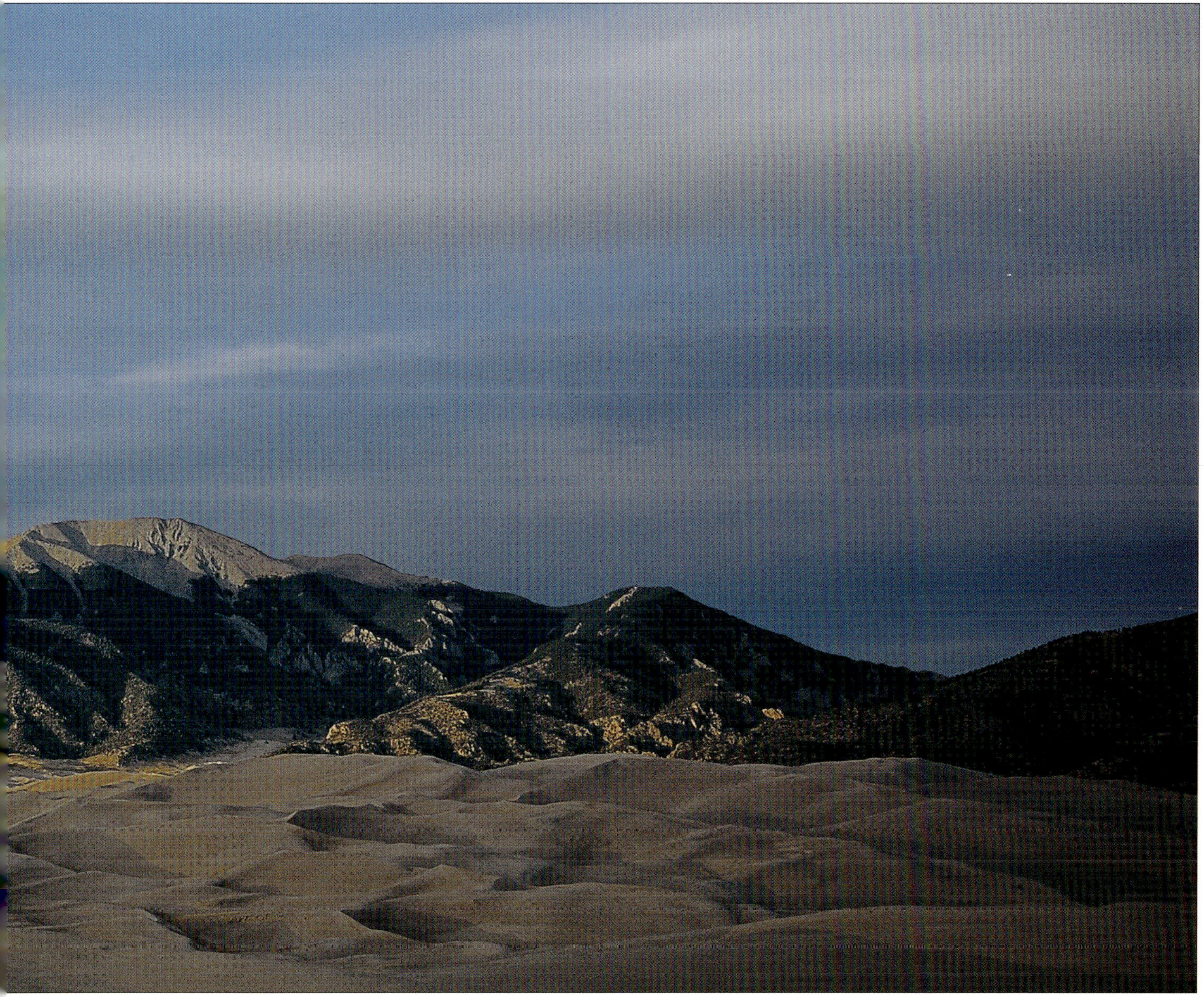

The Great Sand Dunes National Monument

Next Spread: Wind and grass patterns in the sand

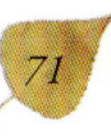

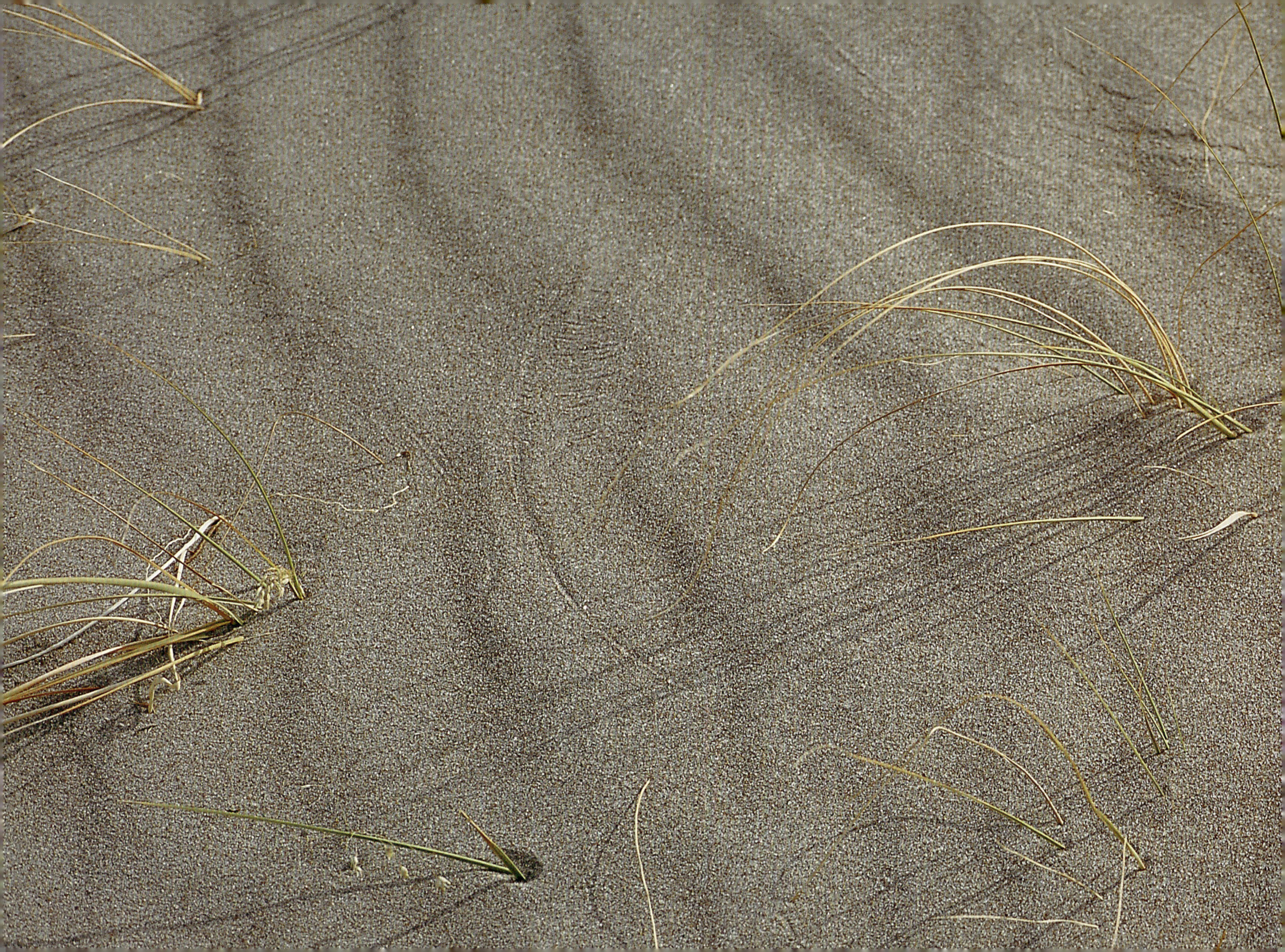

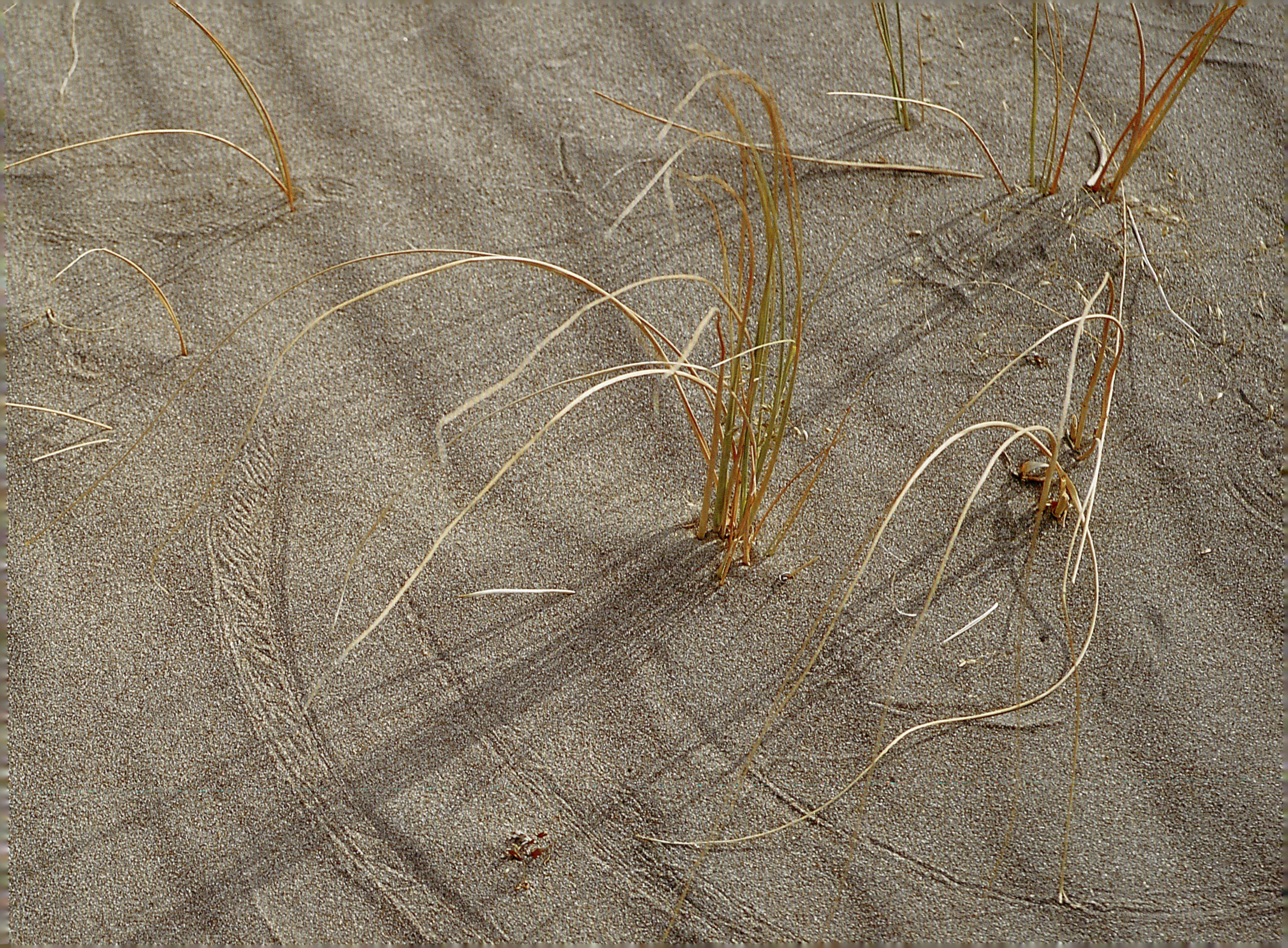

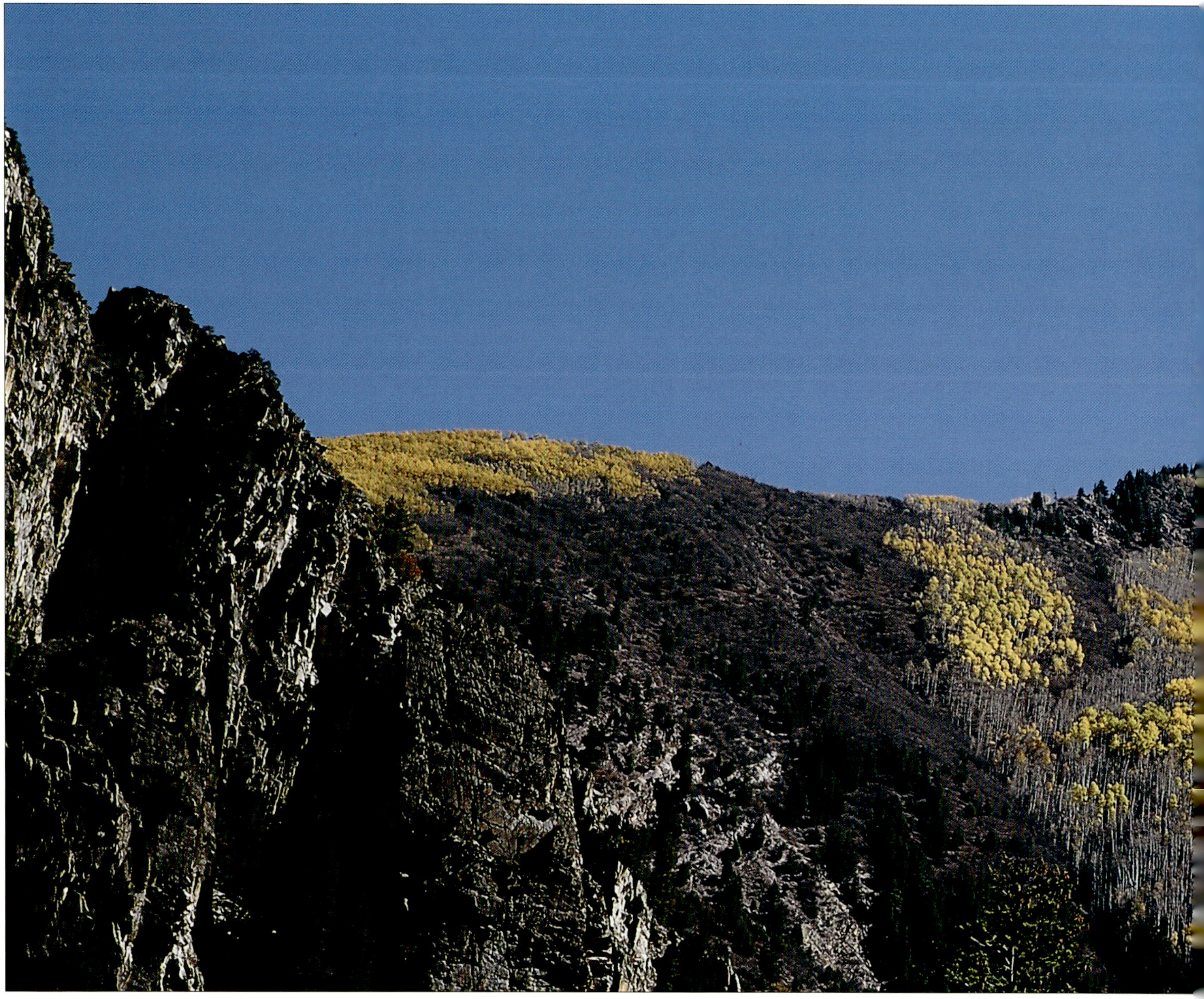

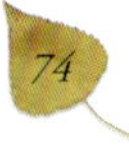

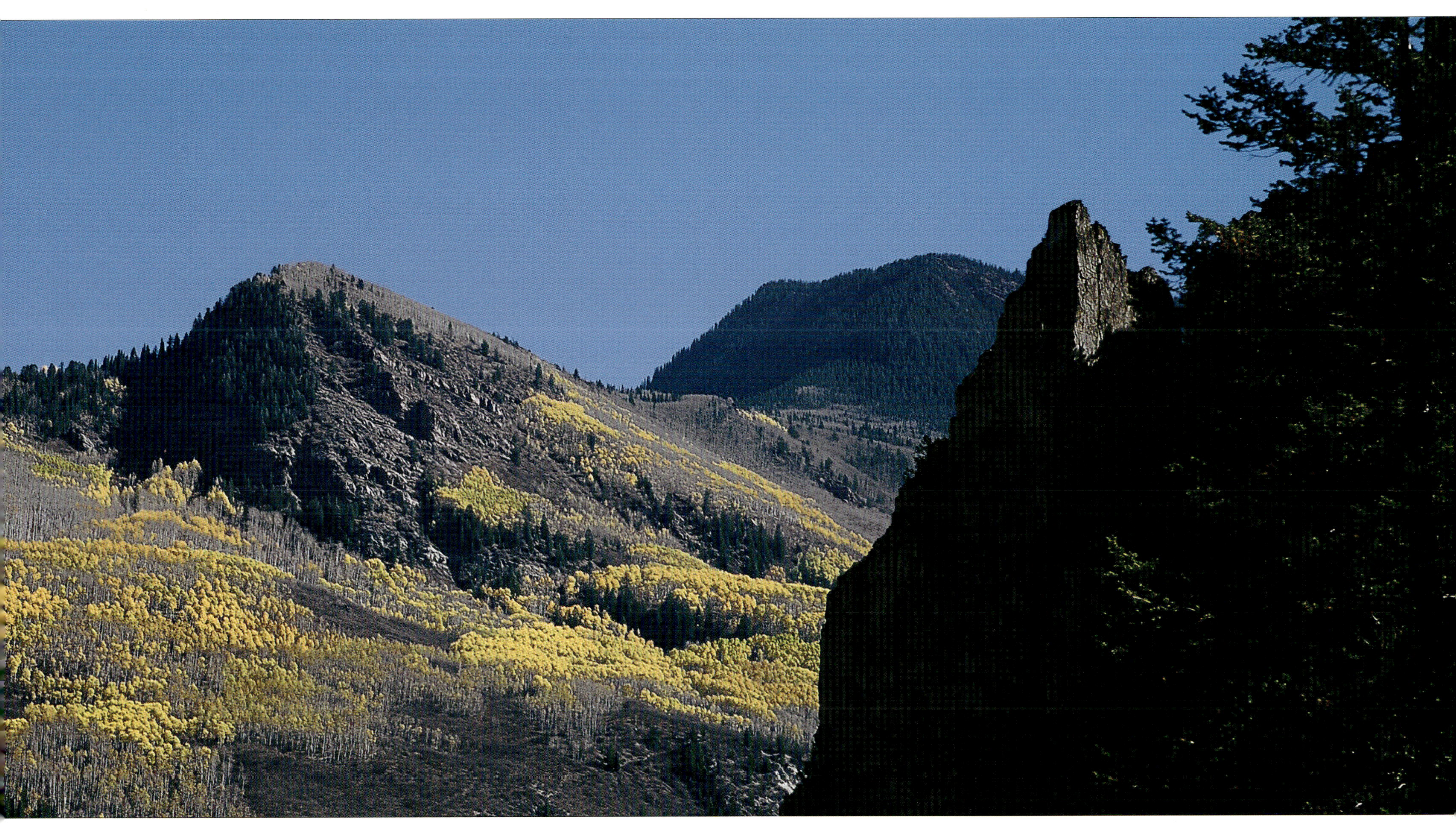

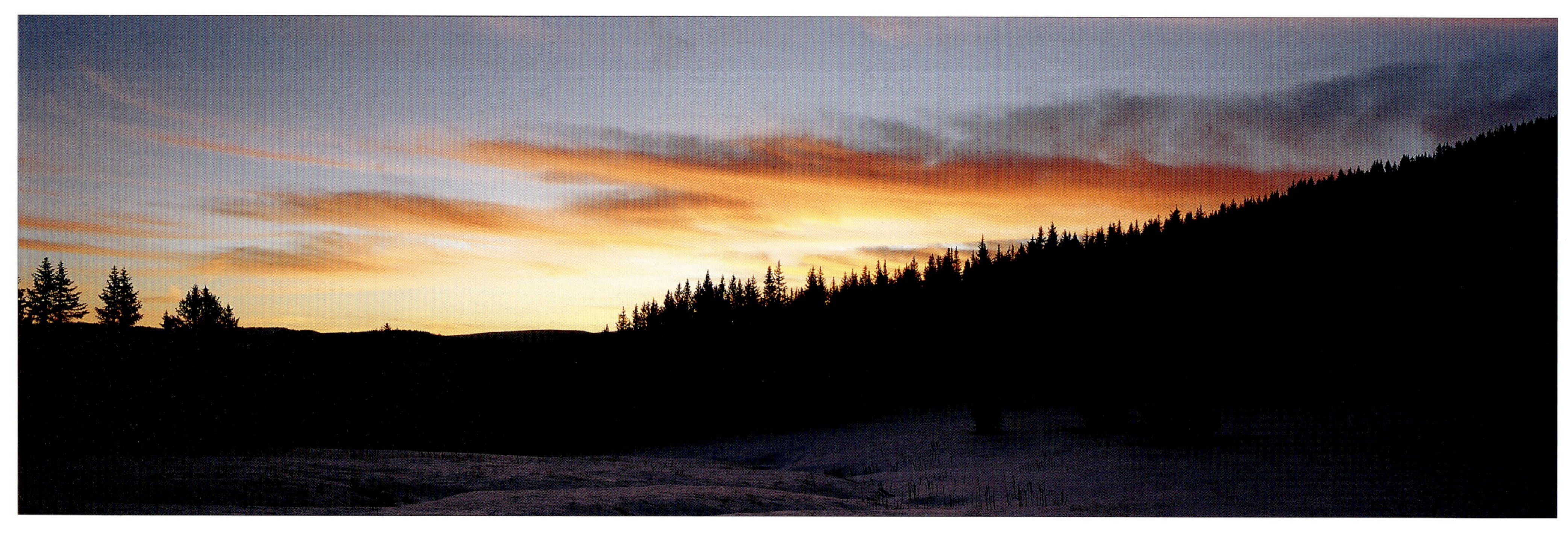

High in the San Juan Mountains of the Rio Grande National Forest

As the snow in this panographic image™ melts, it will flow east to the sunrise and pass through Texas as part of the Rio Grande River.

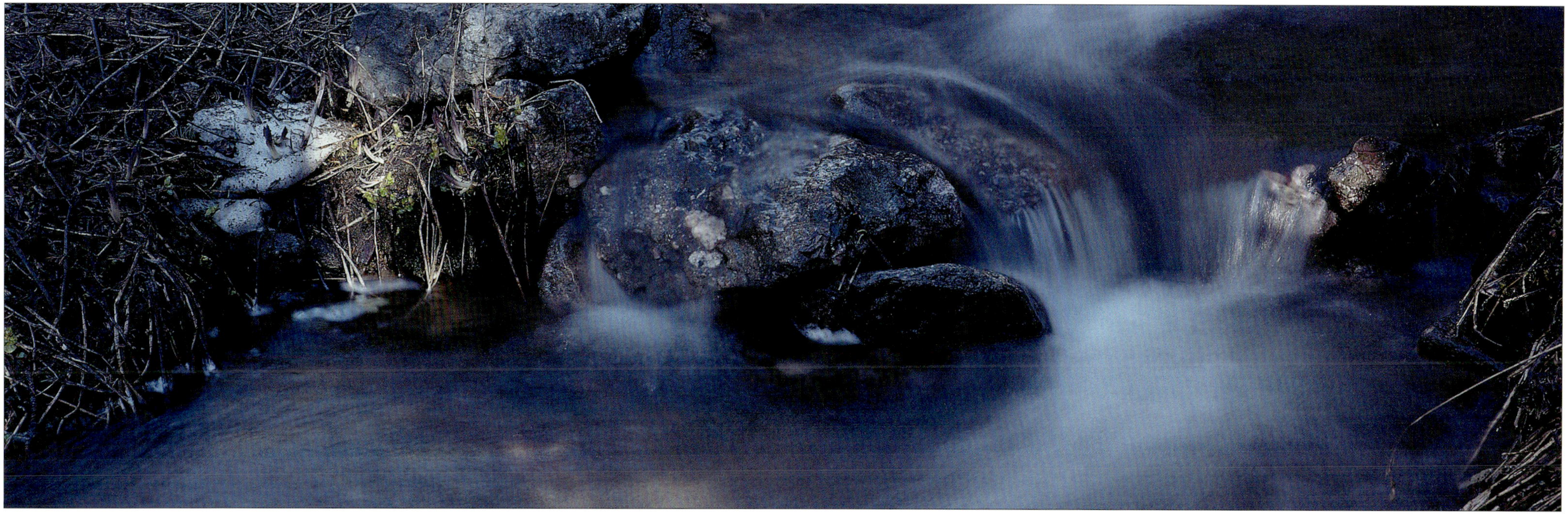

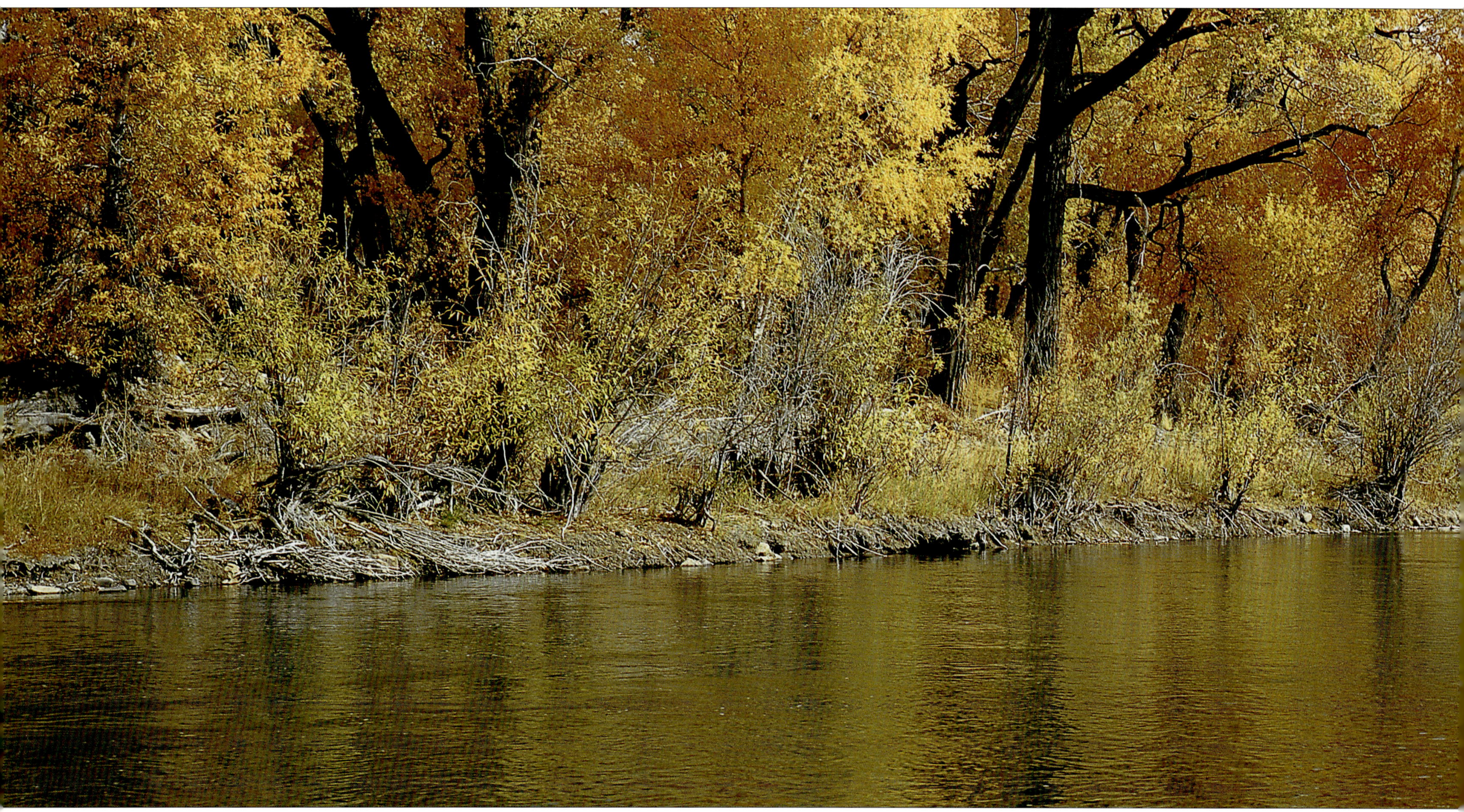

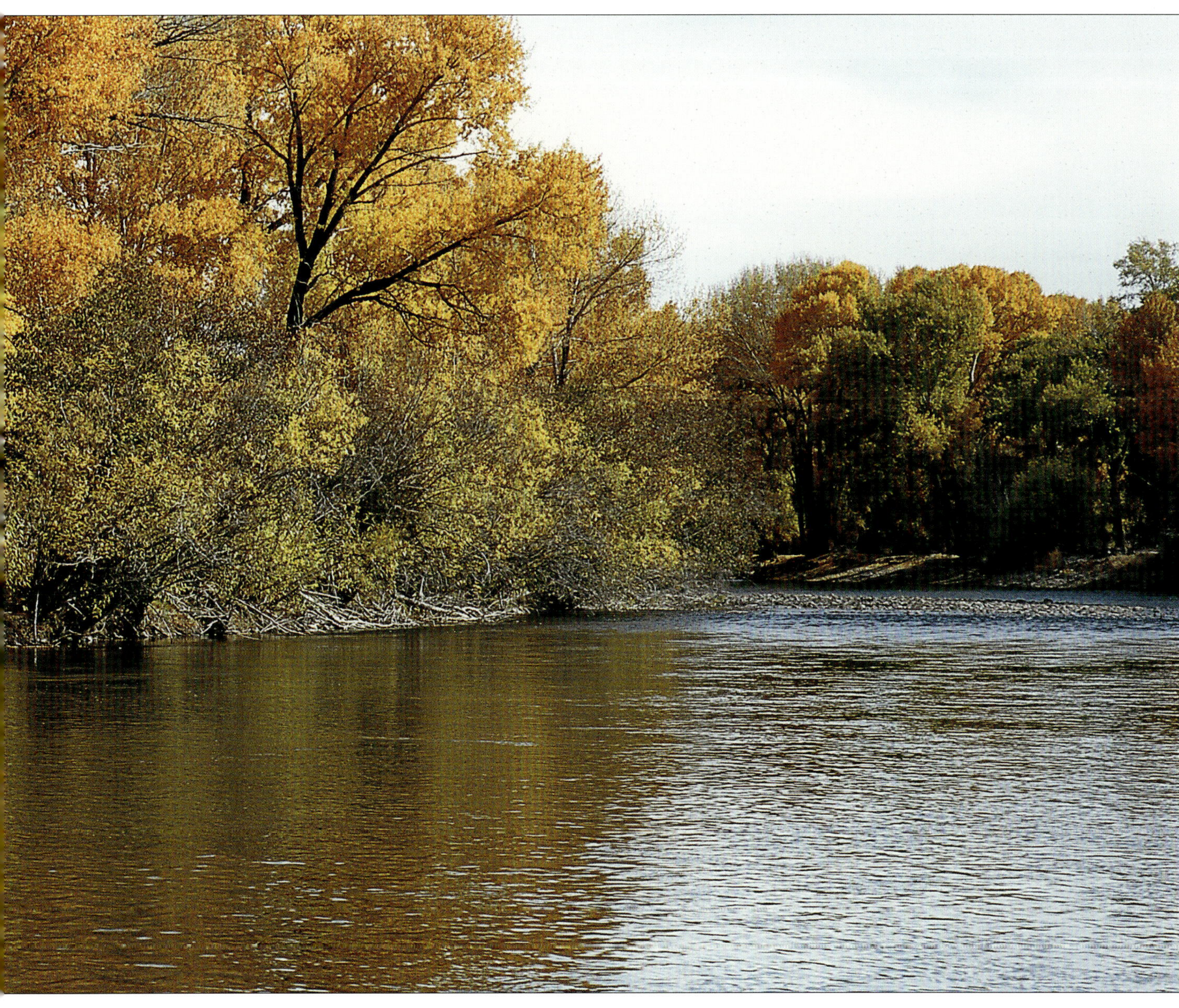

Near the headwaters of the Rio Grande River

The river will drop more than a mile in elevation from here before ending in the Gulf of Mexico.

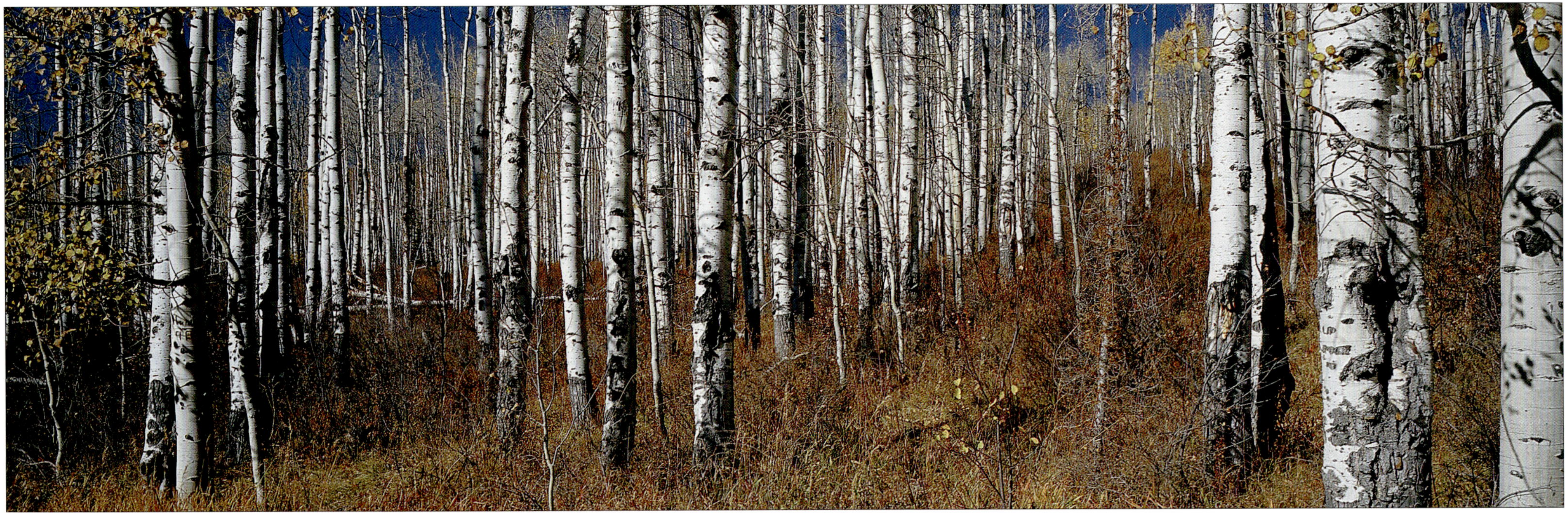

Aspen forest

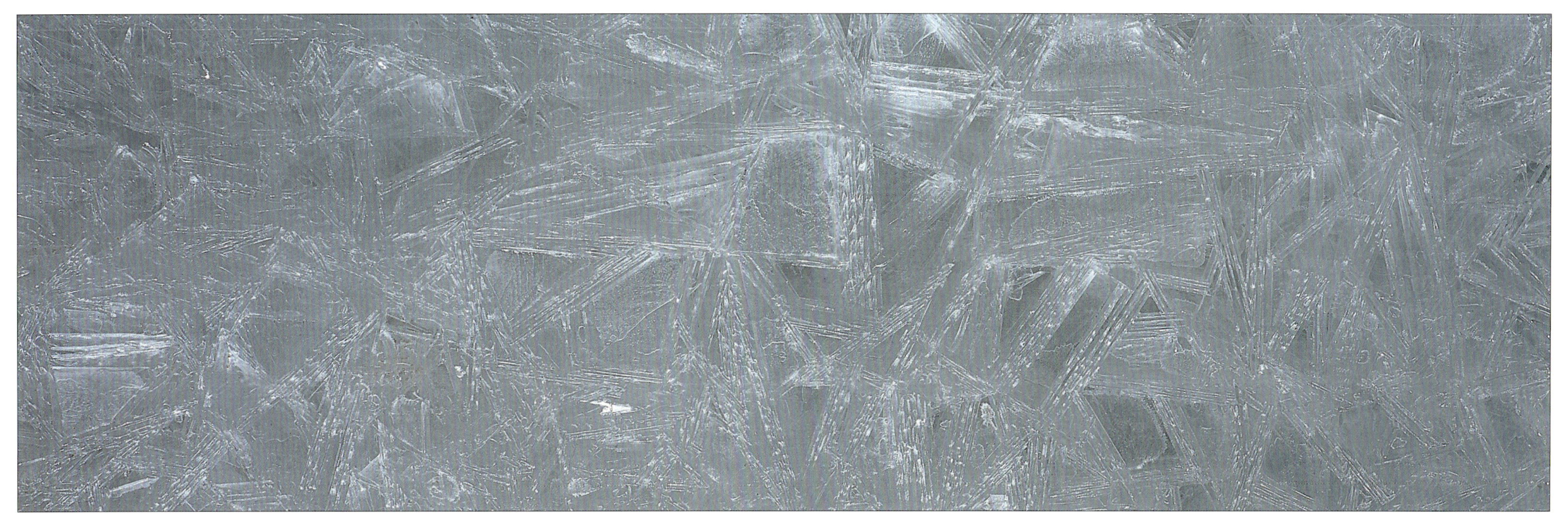

Closeup of a frozen stream

Bridal Veil Falls

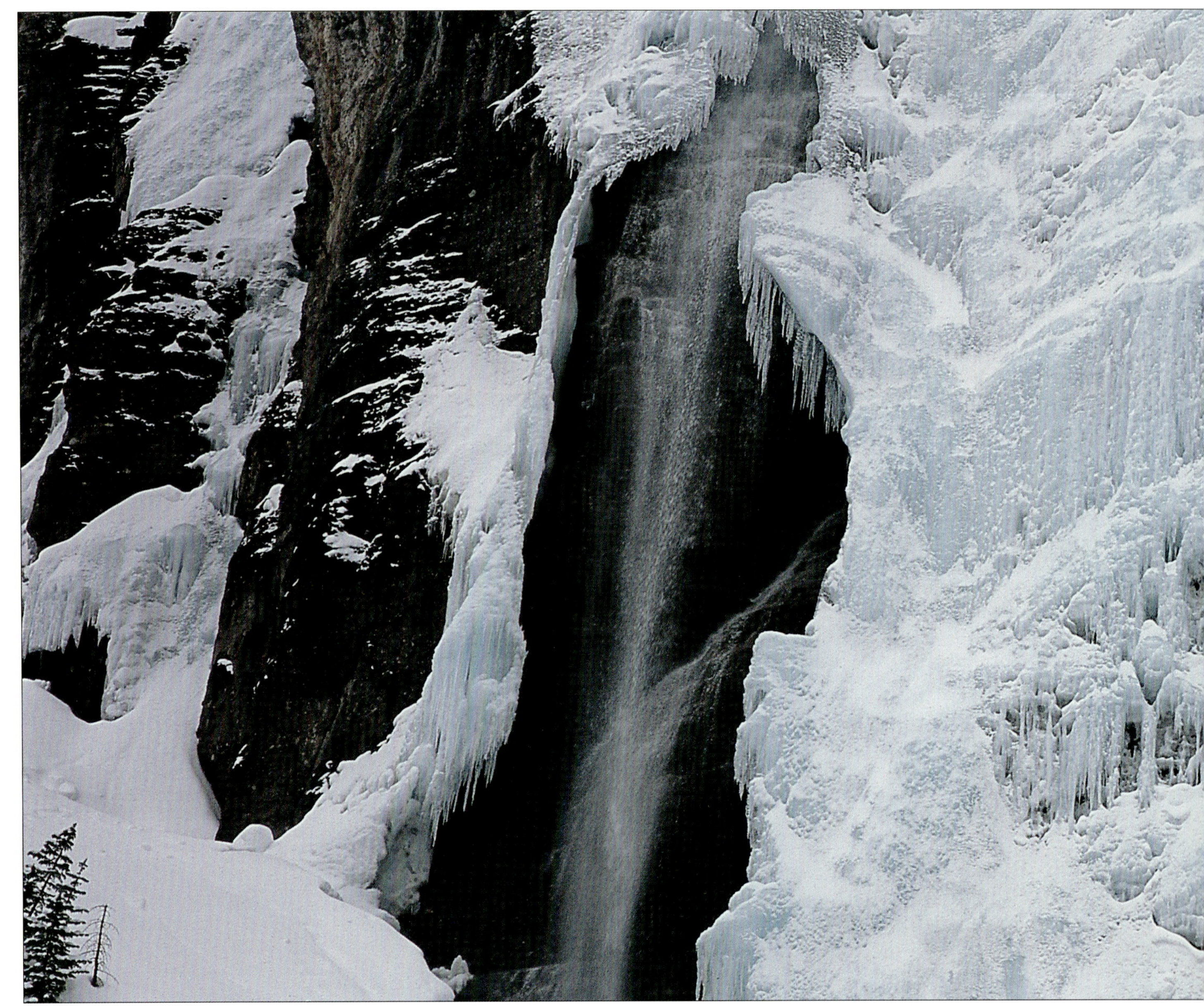

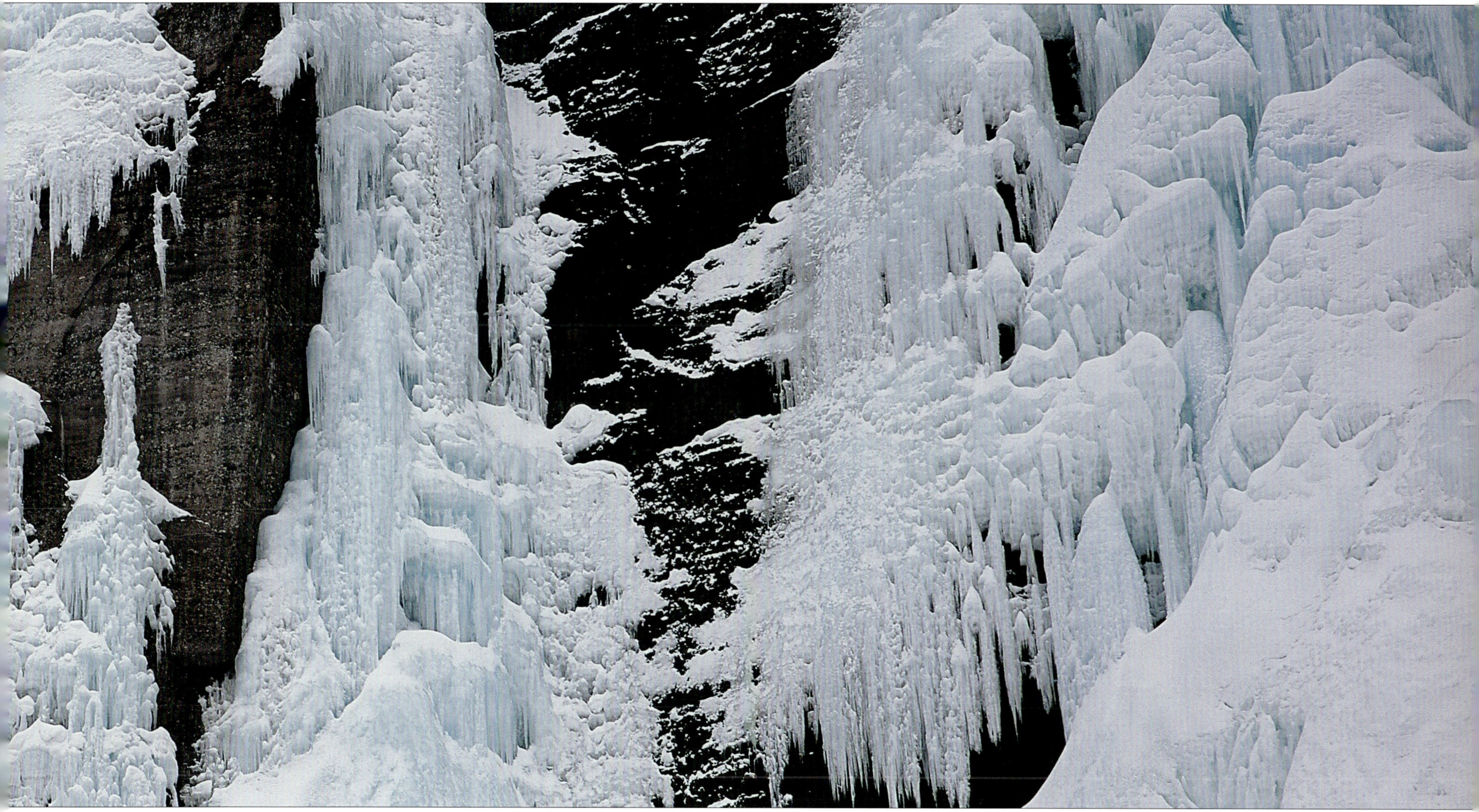

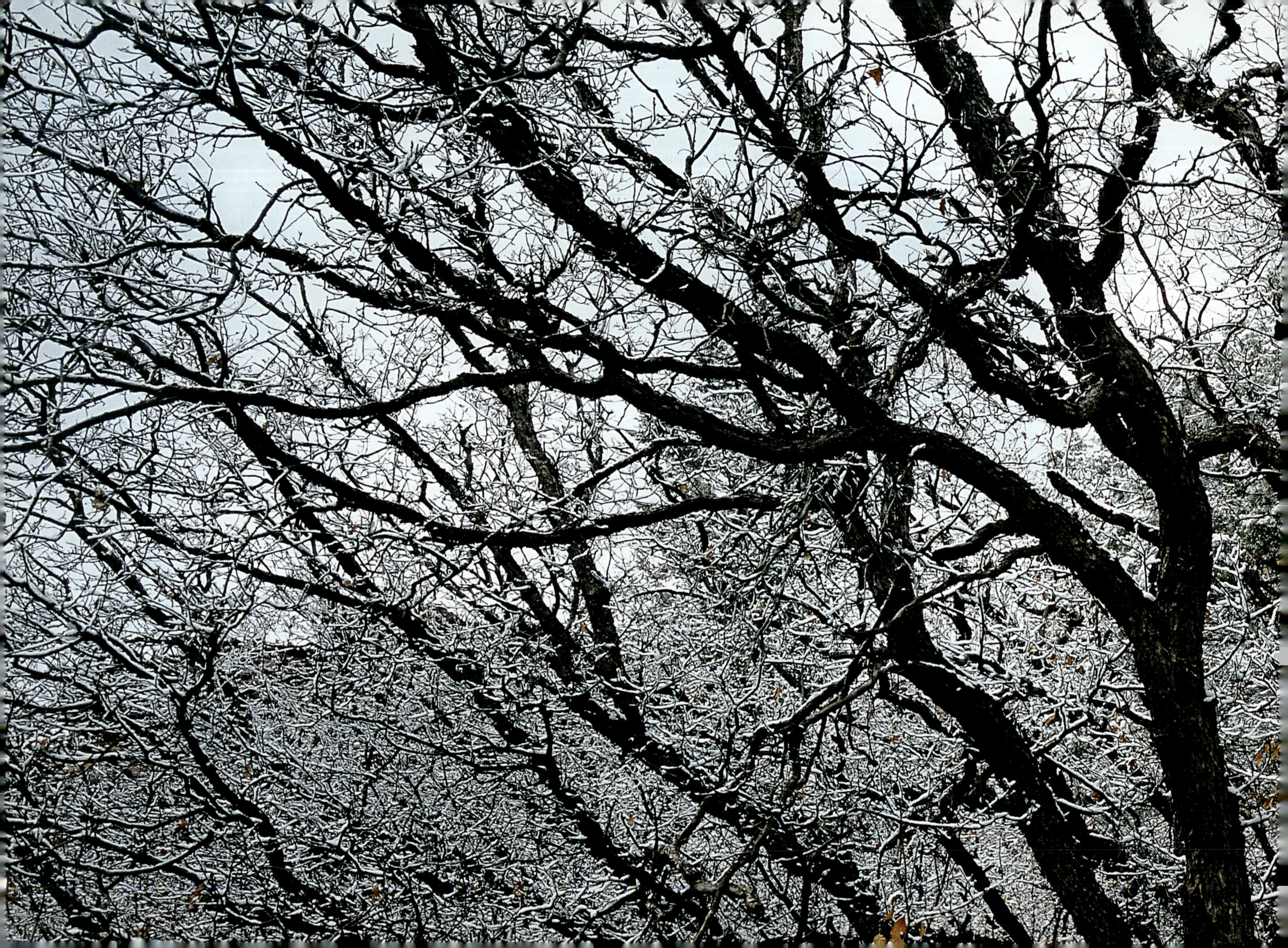

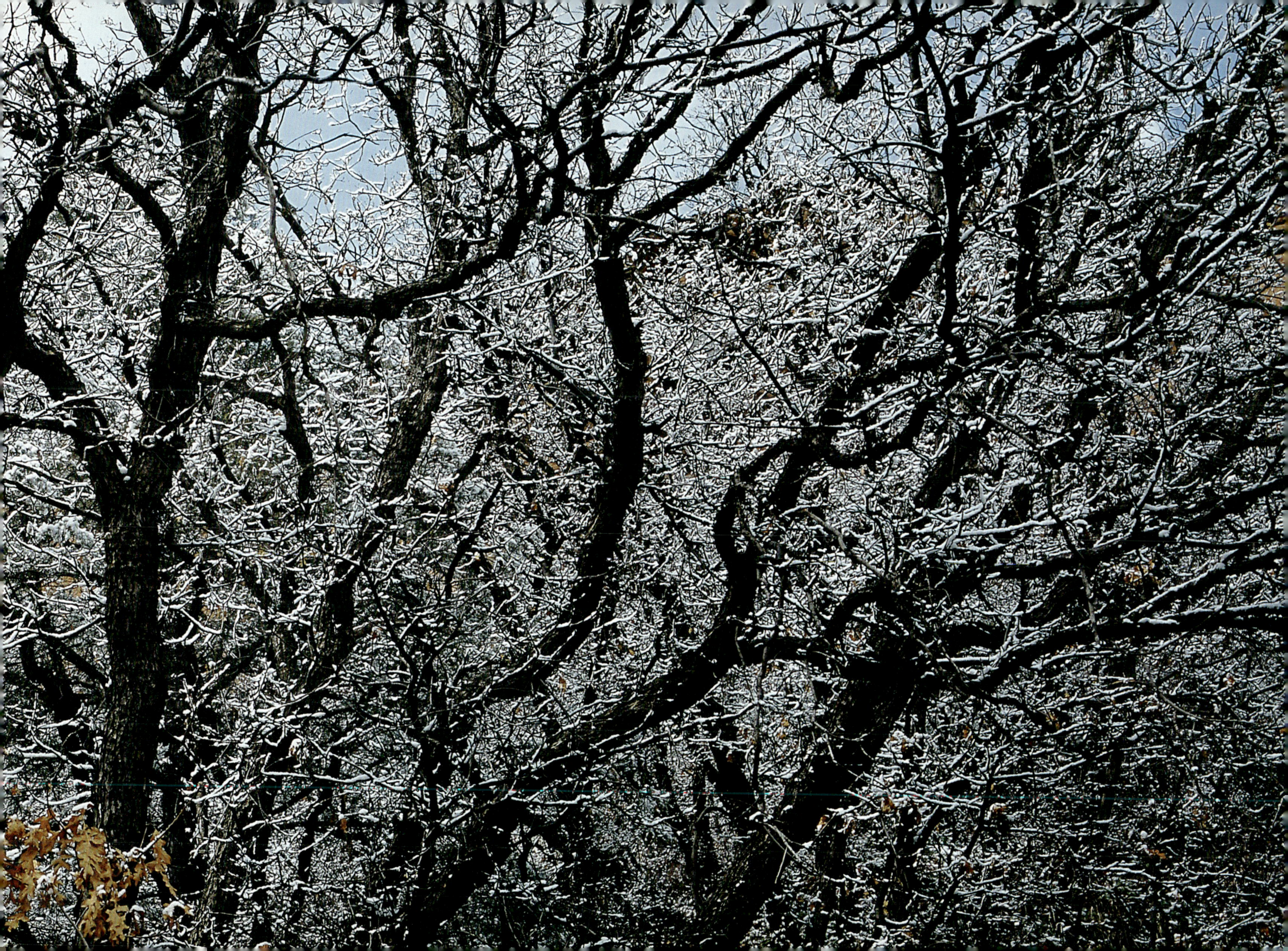

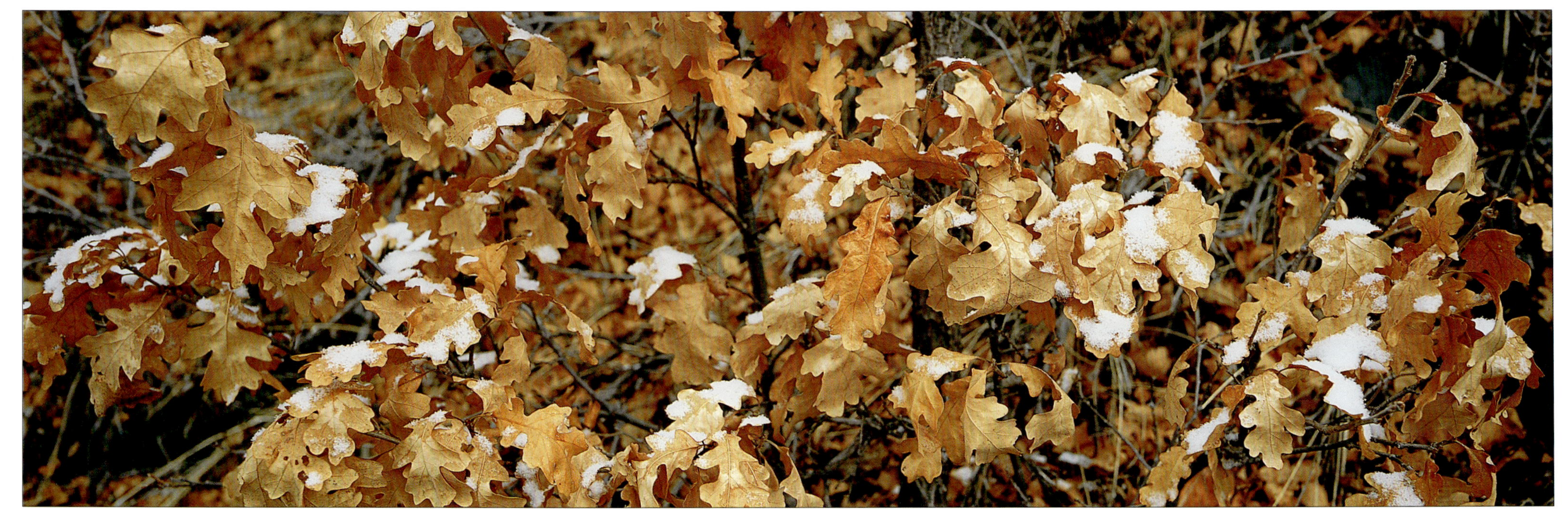

Above and Previous Spread: Snow-covered scrub oak

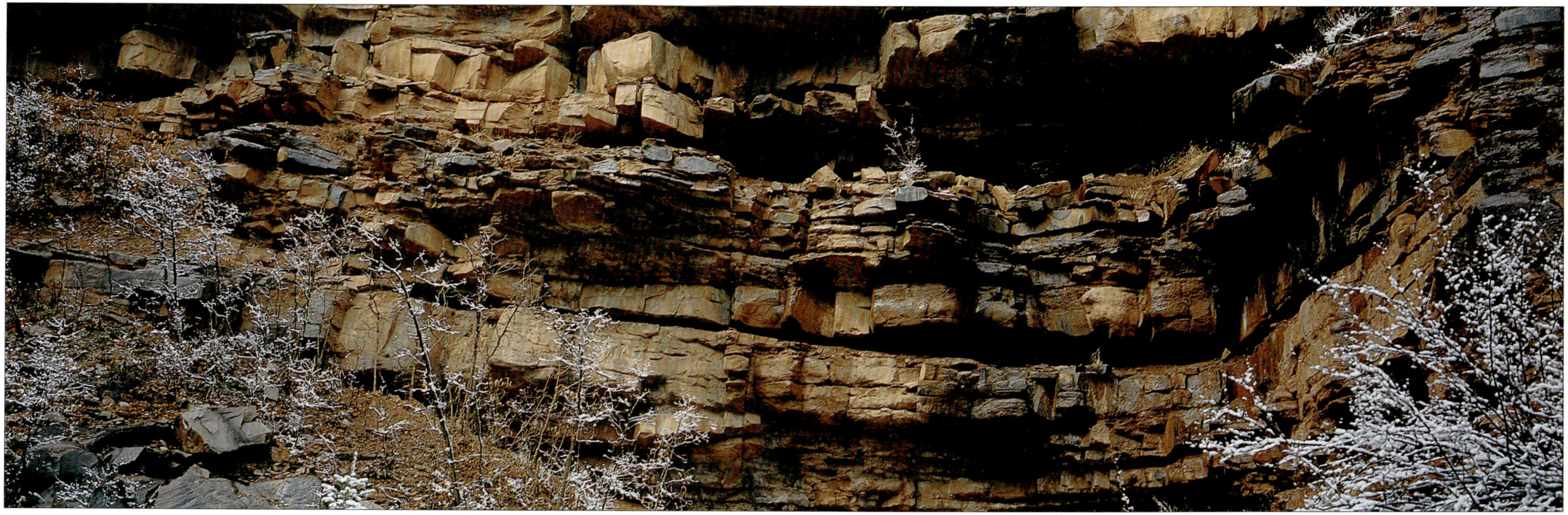

Red sandstone near Telluride

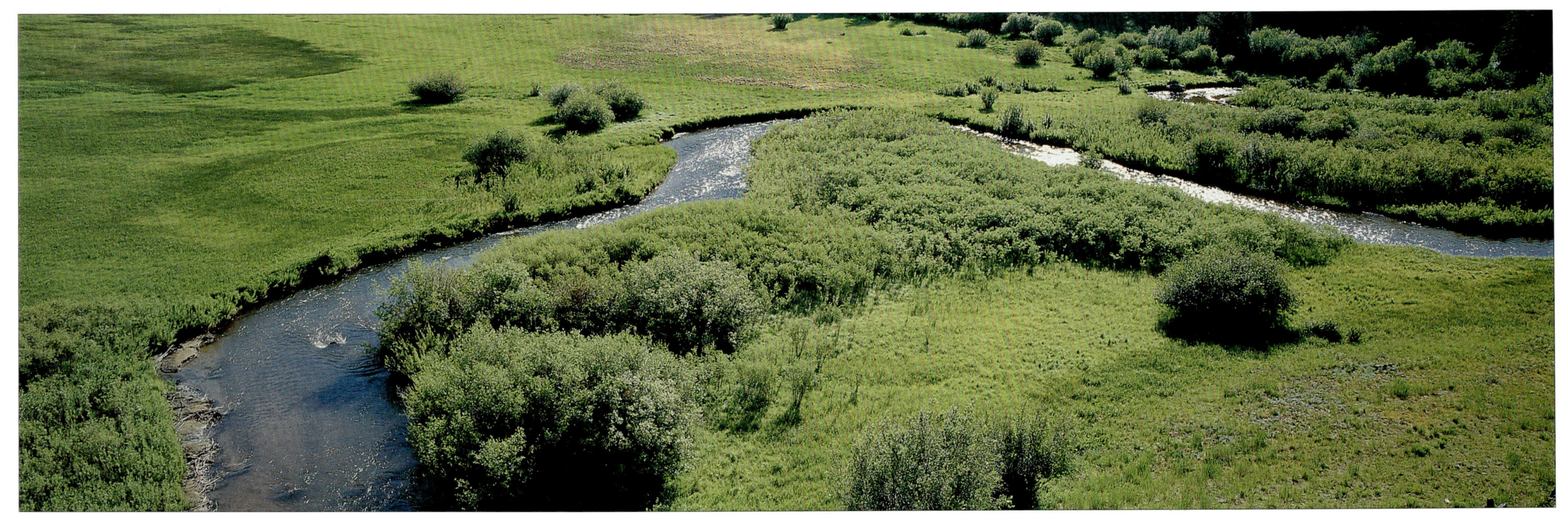

Springtime in the Rockies

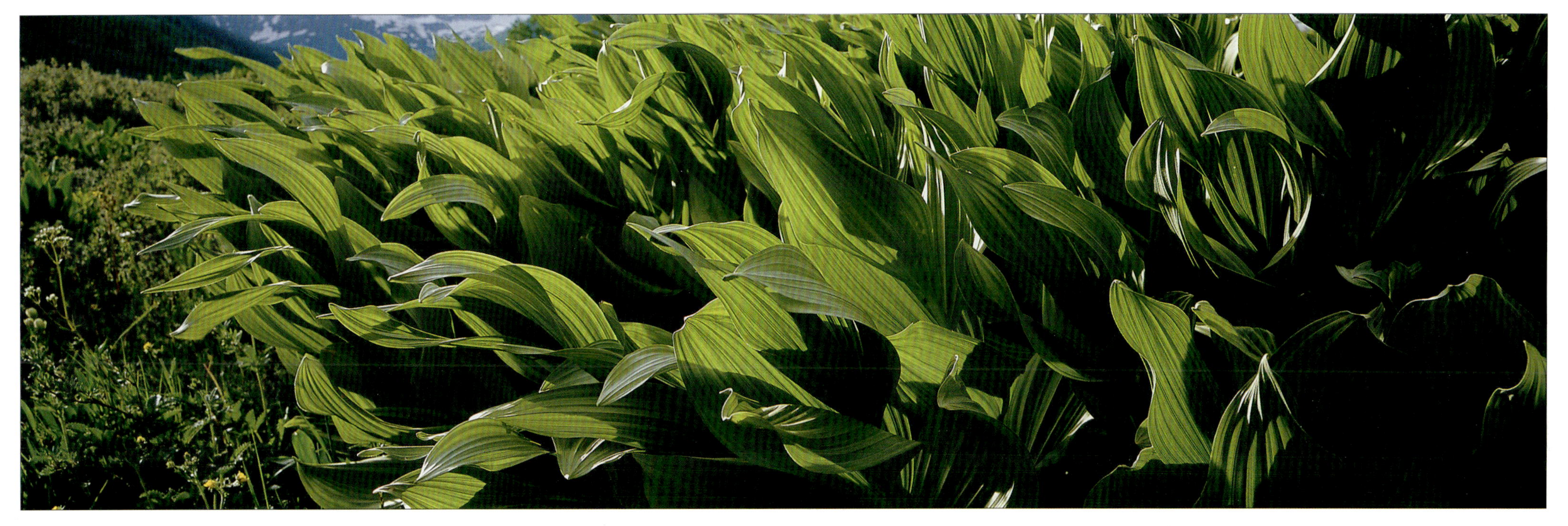

If you can name this plant, let us know at www.keenmedia.com.

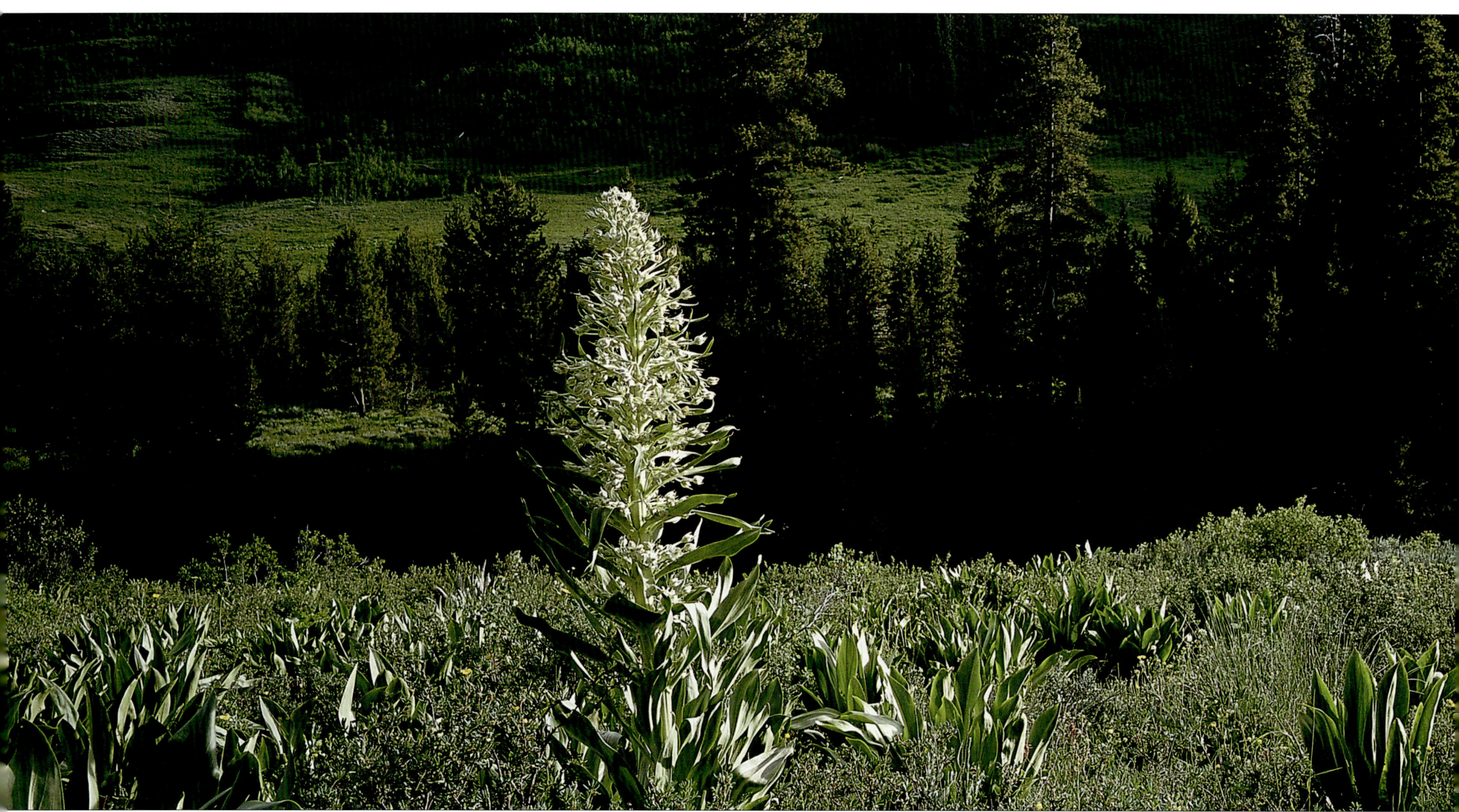

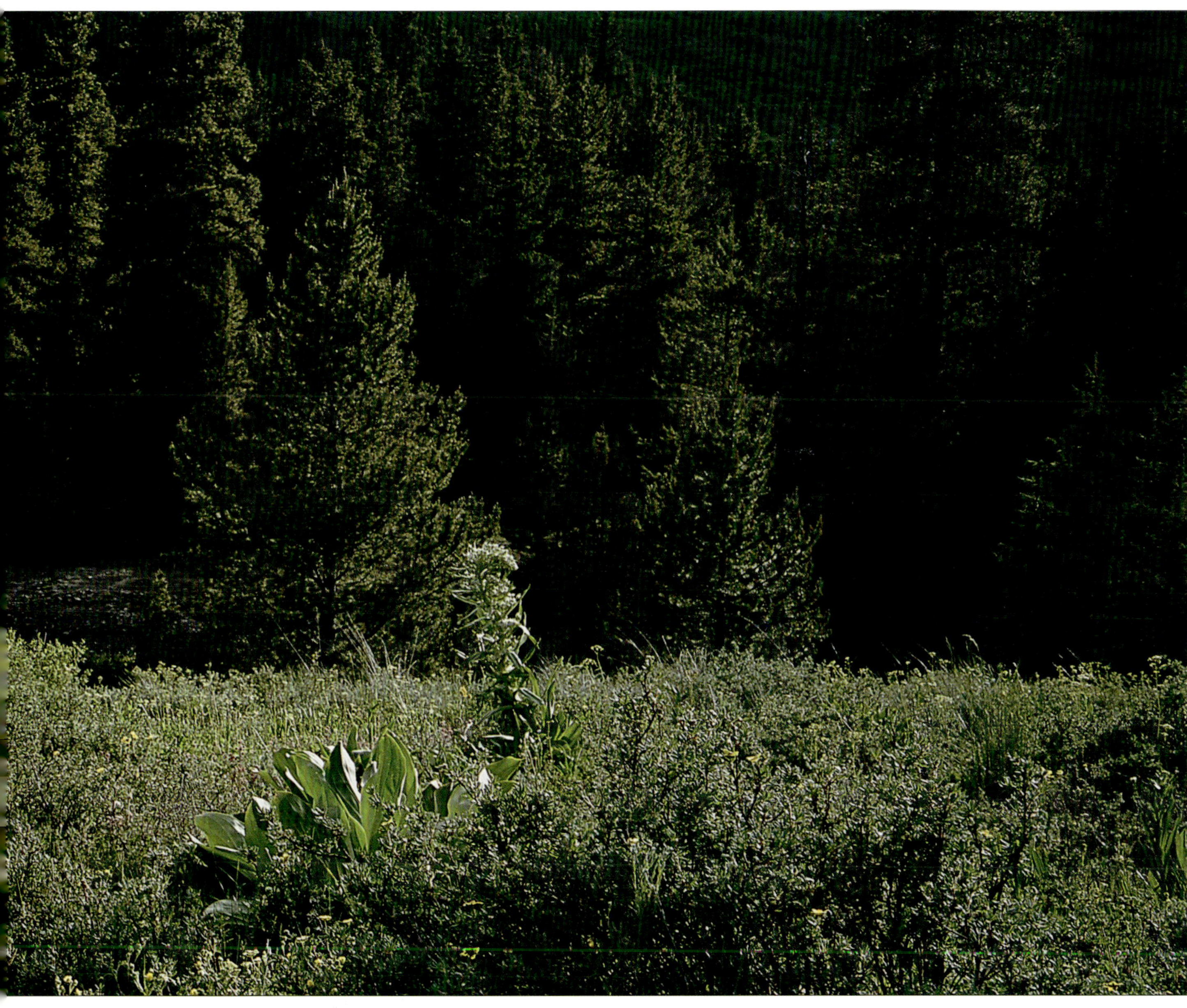

Monument Plant (Frasera speciosa) in Gunnison National Forest

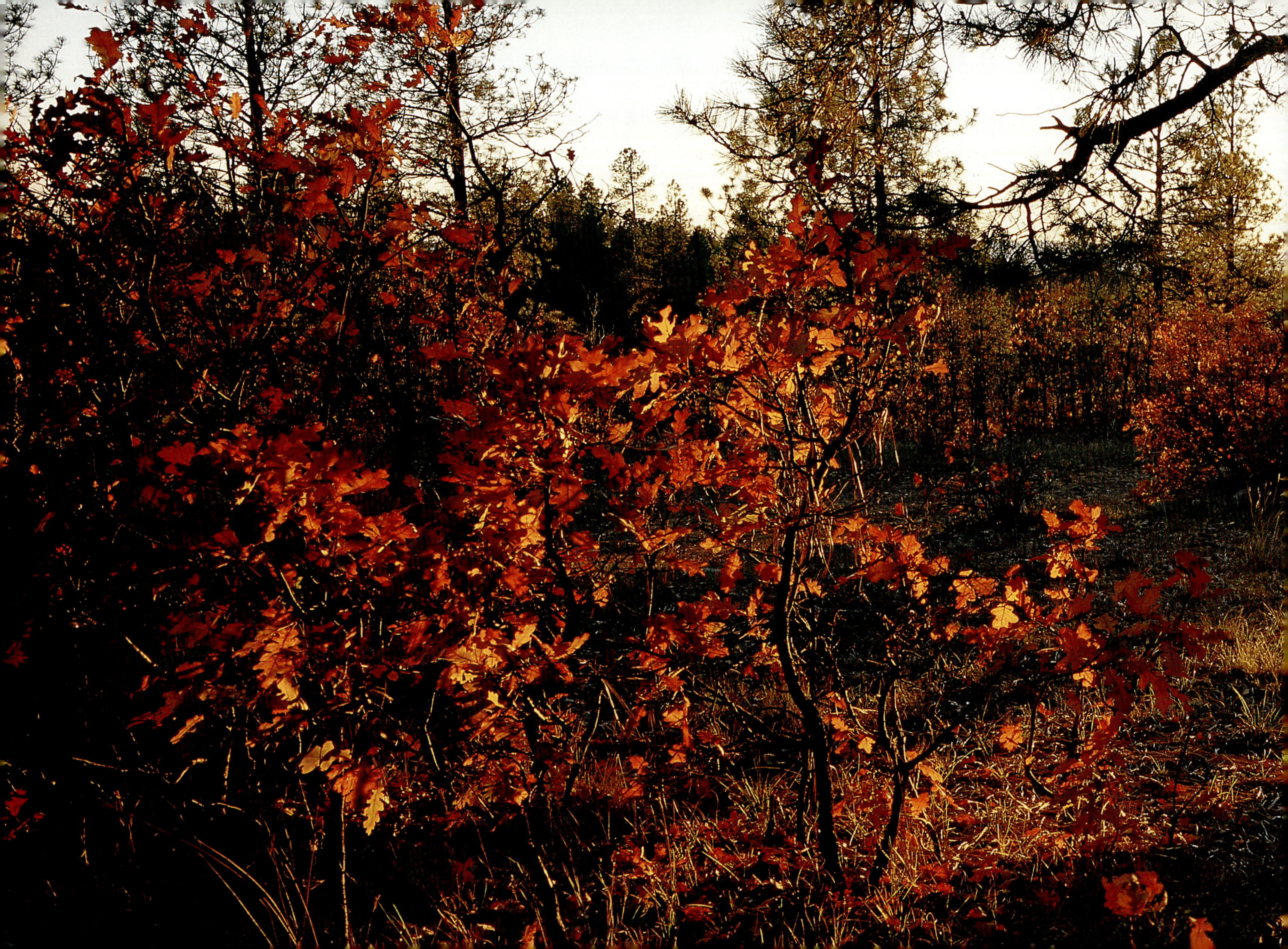

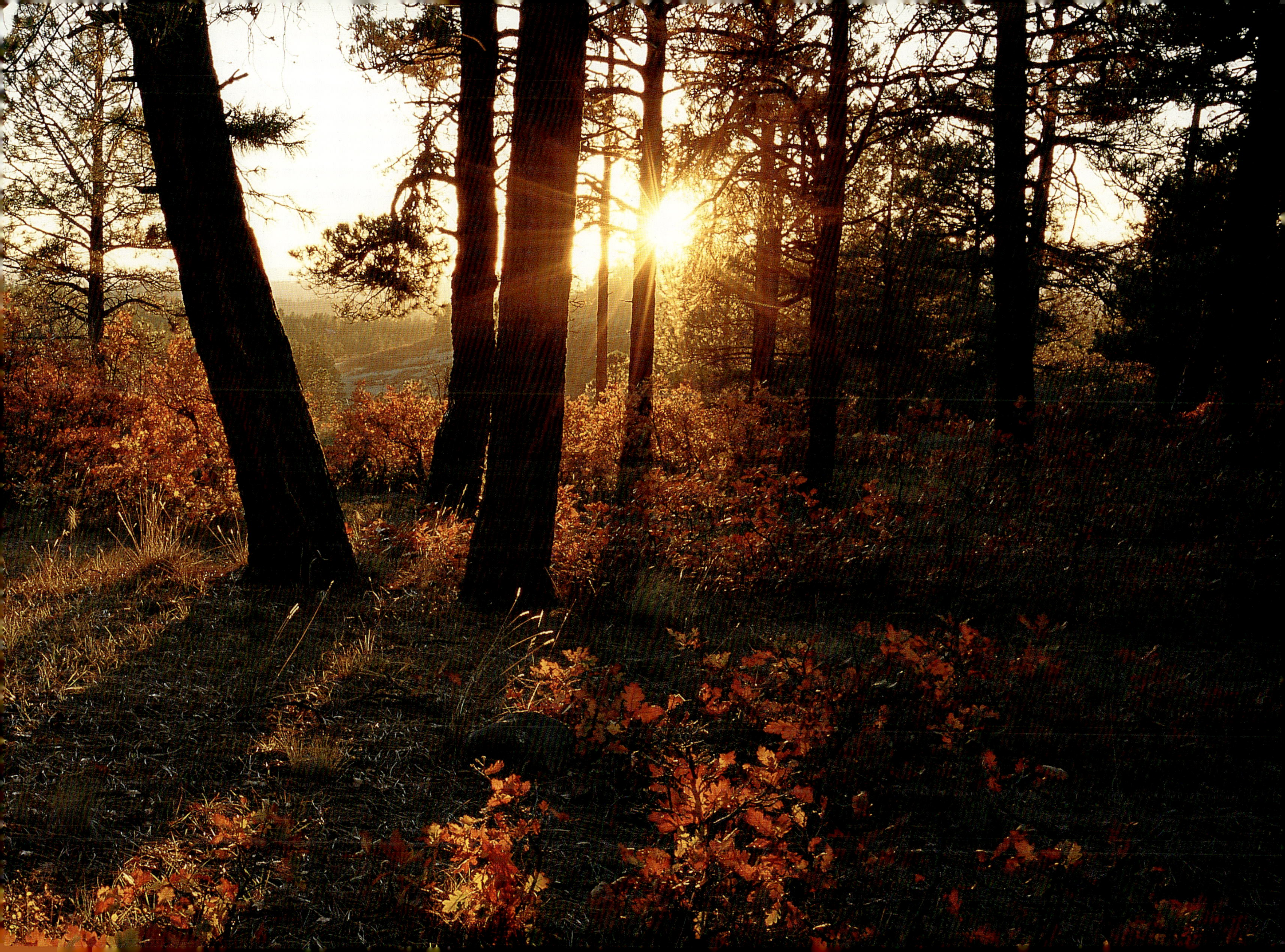

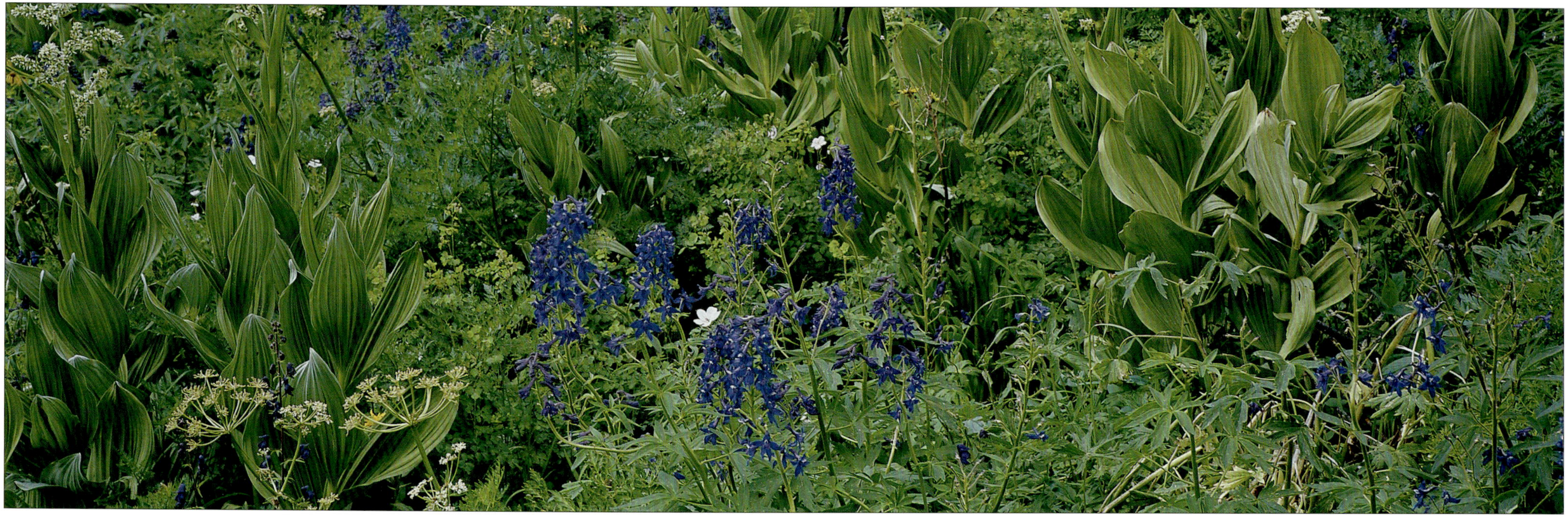

The blue wildflowers are Subalpine Larkspur (Delphinium barbei).

Previous Spread: Weminuche Wilderness, San Juan National Forest

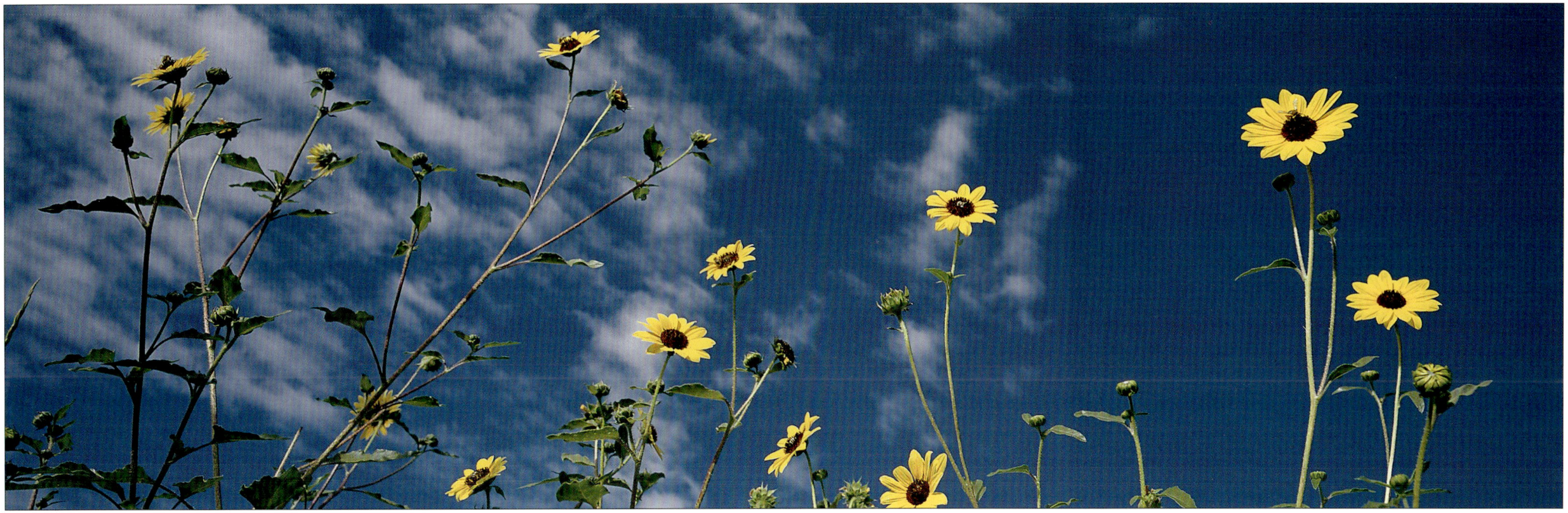

Little Sunflowers (Helianthus pumilus)

The Slate River,

Gunnison National Forest

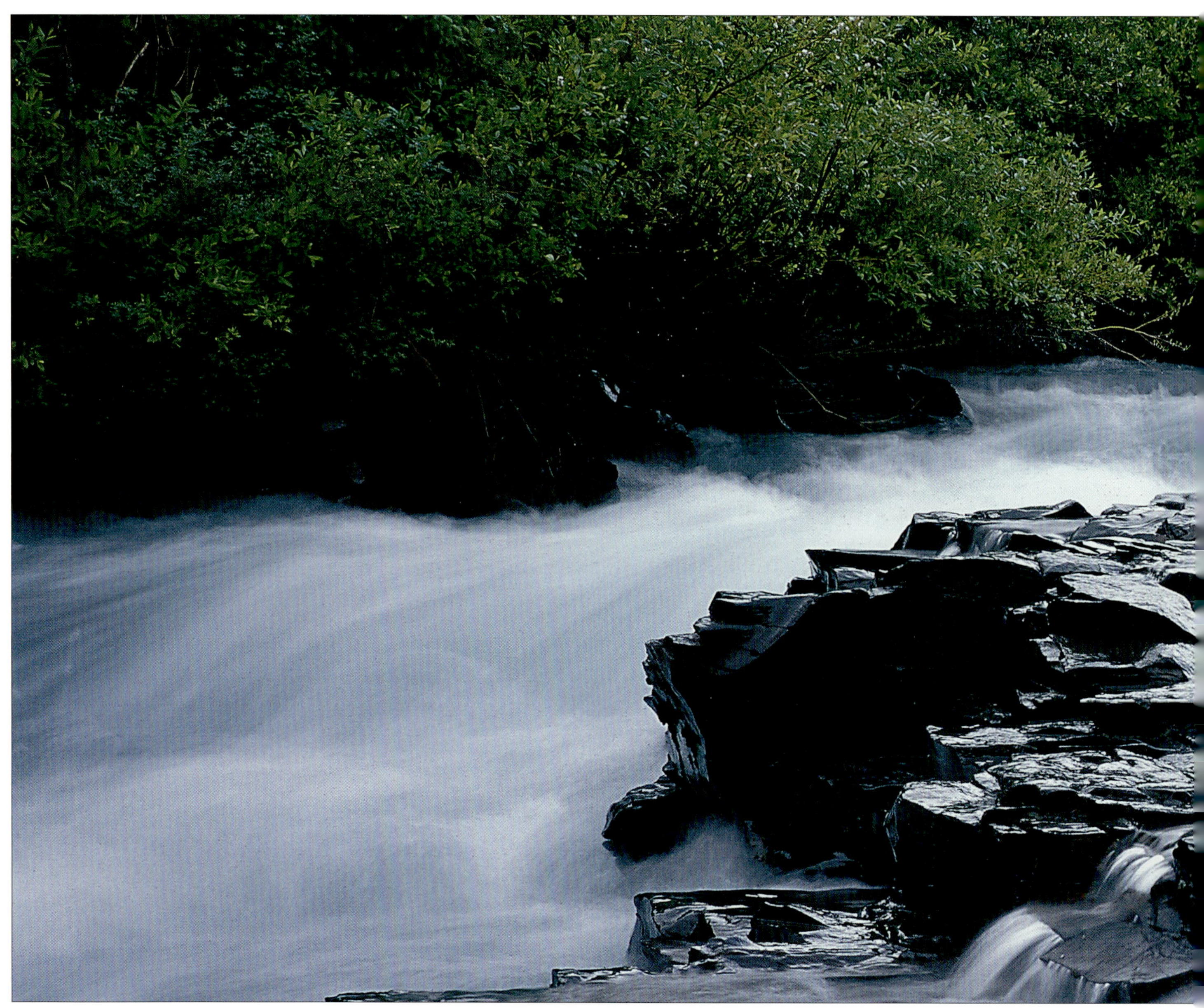

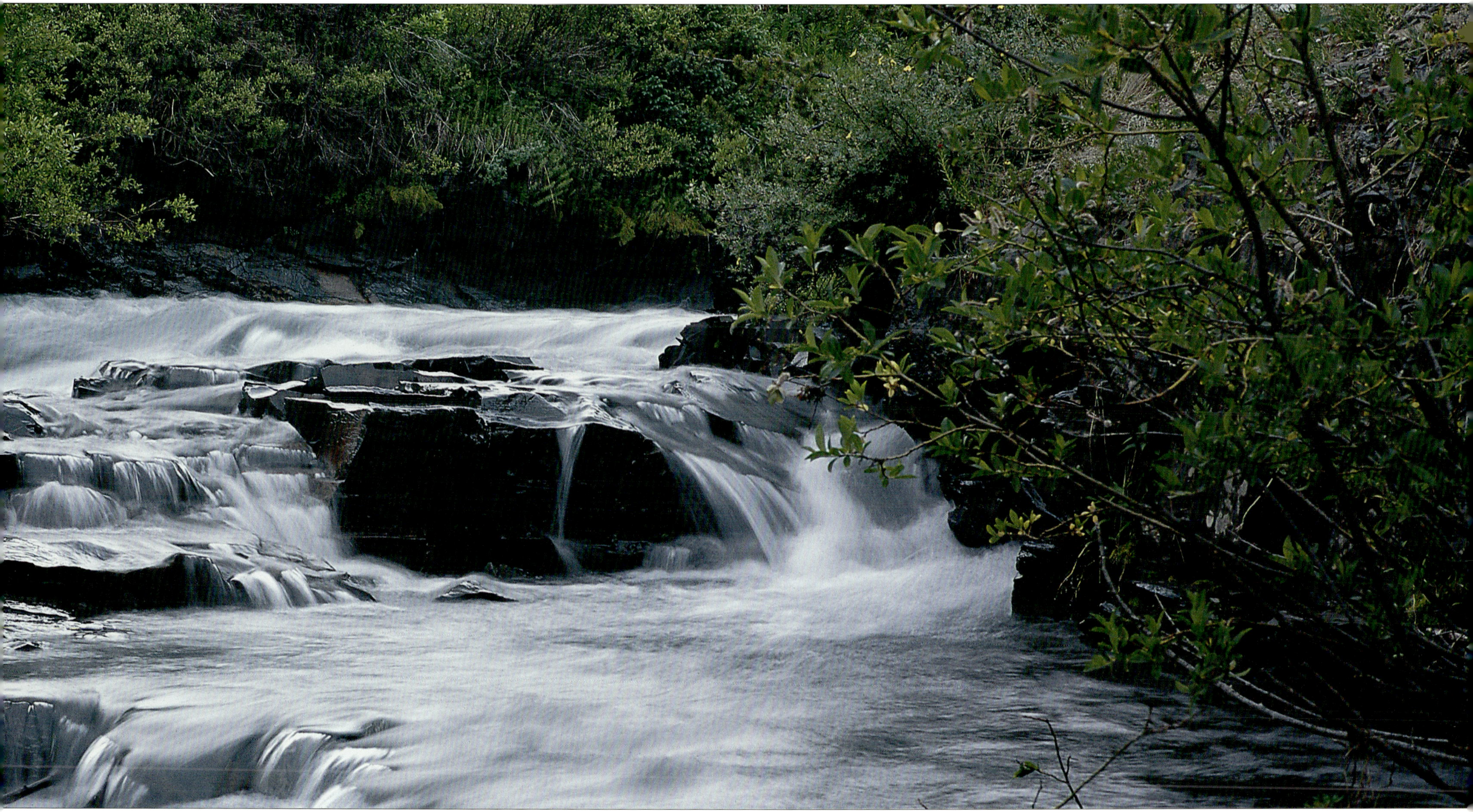

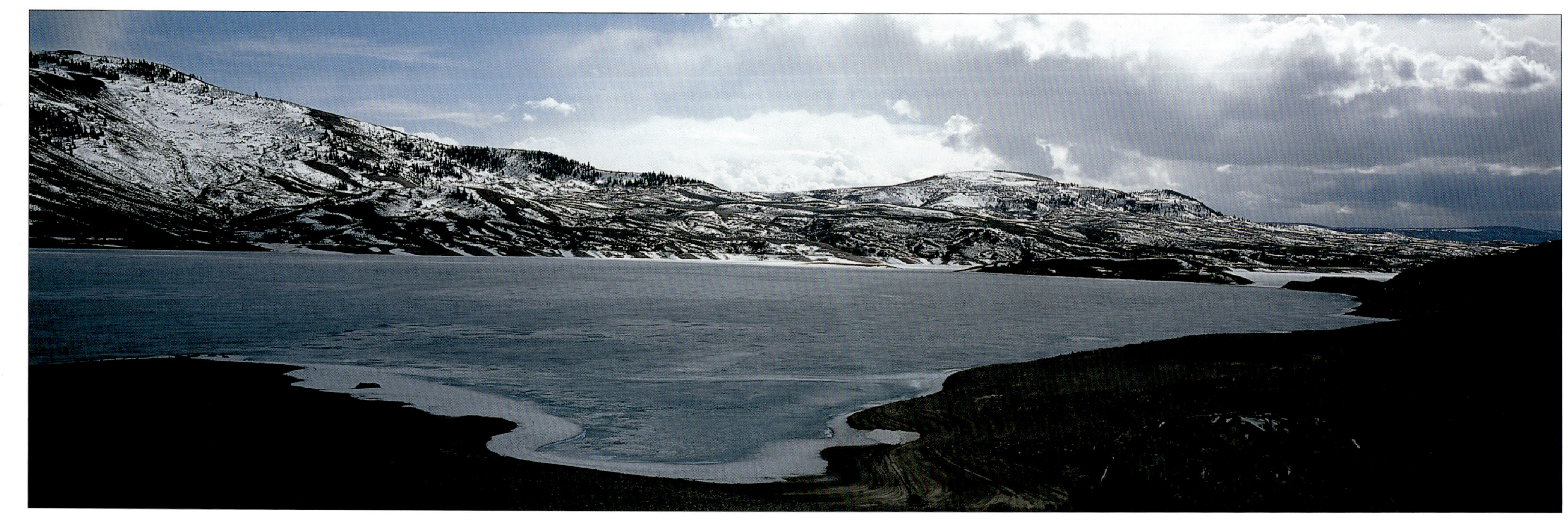

Blue Mesa Reservoir, a popular ice-fishing spot

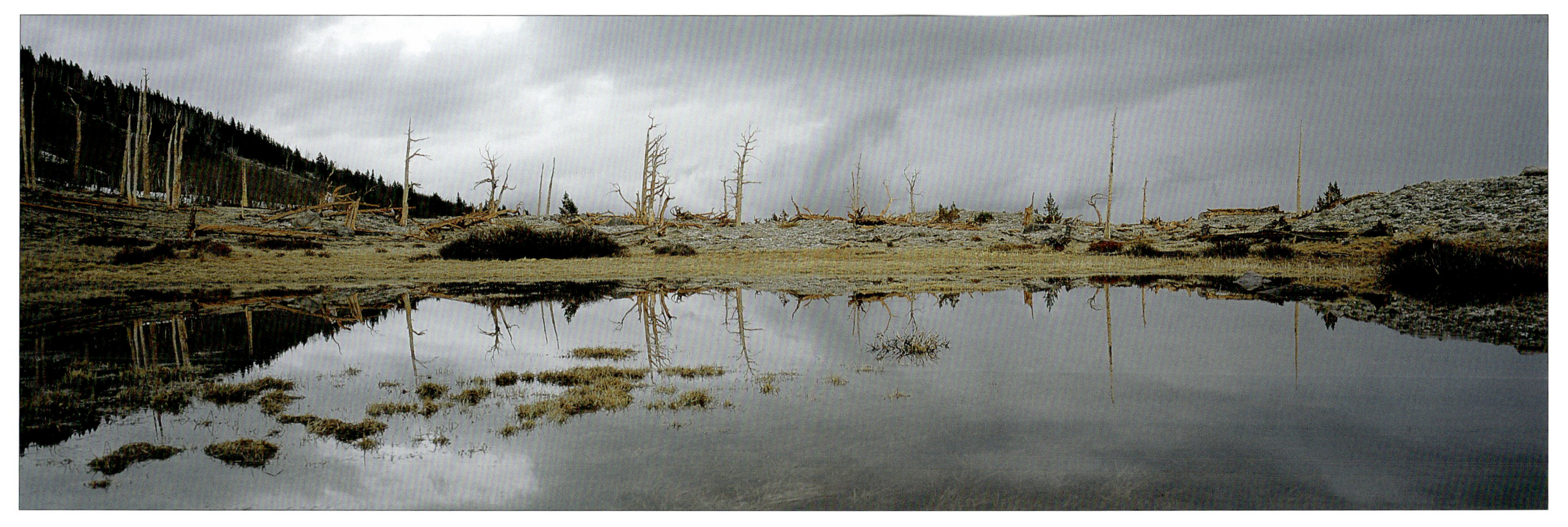

At tree line on Mount Columbia, San Isabel National Forest

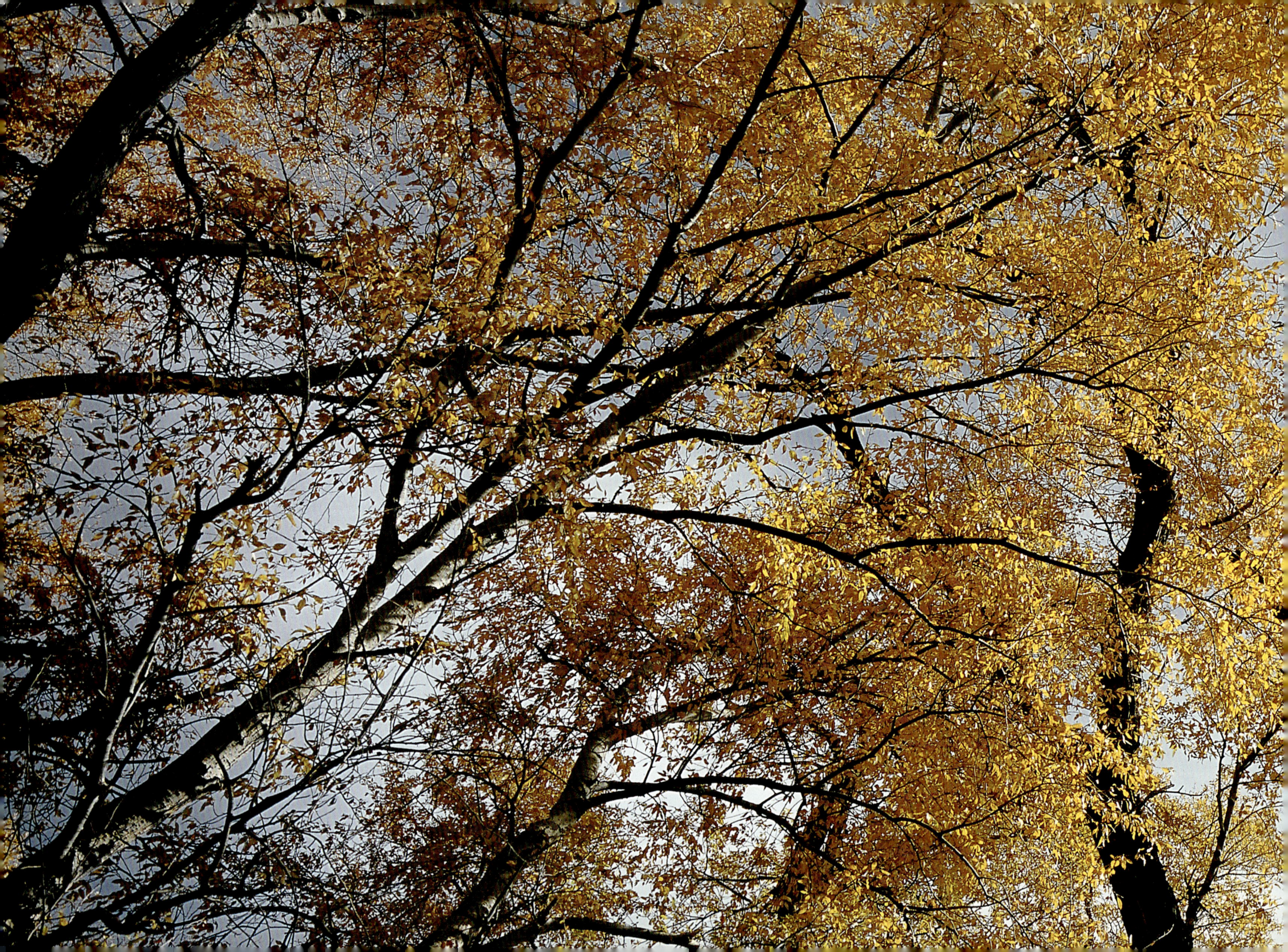

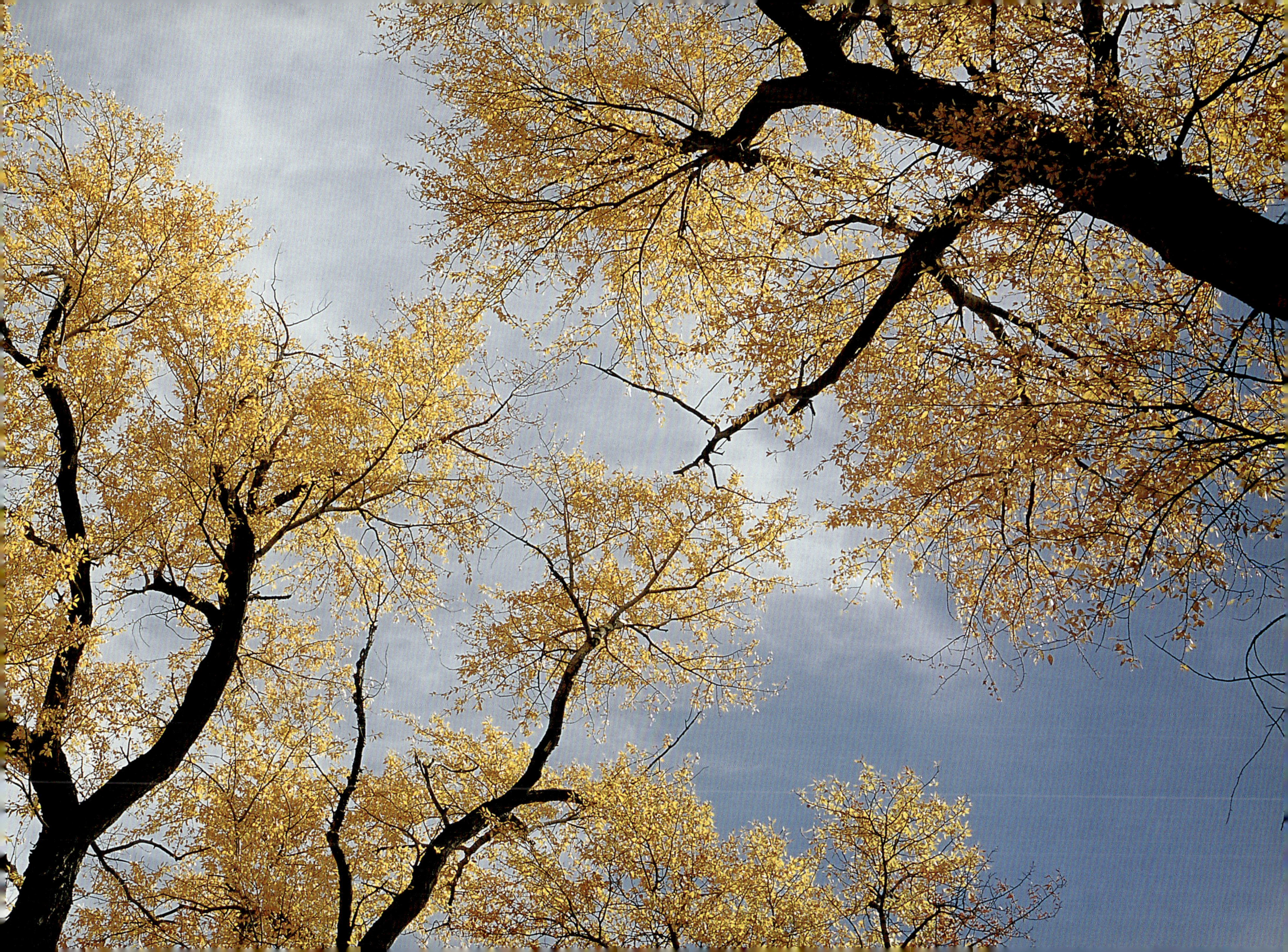

Arapaho National Forest

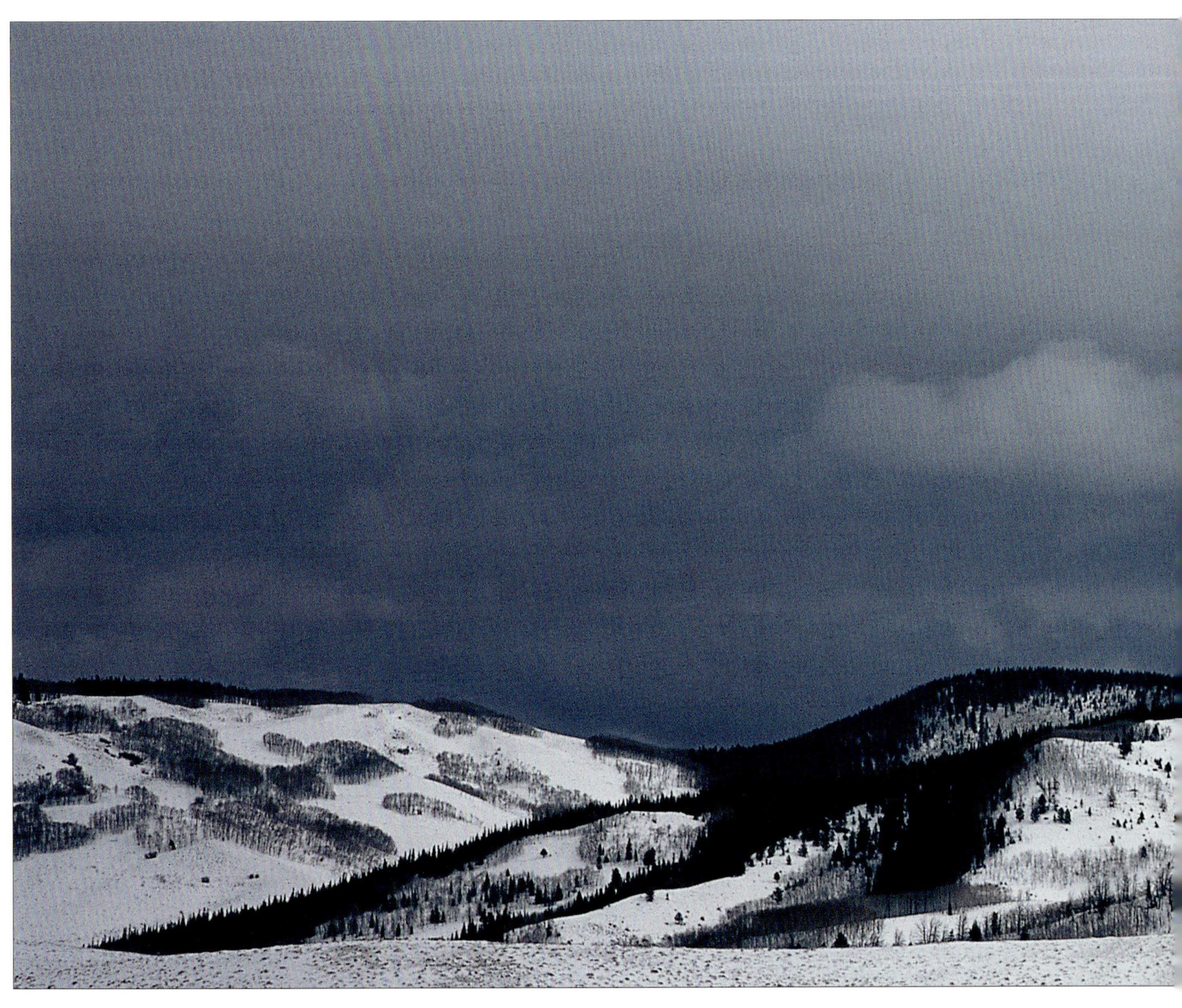

Previous Spread: Fall in the lower San Juan Mountains

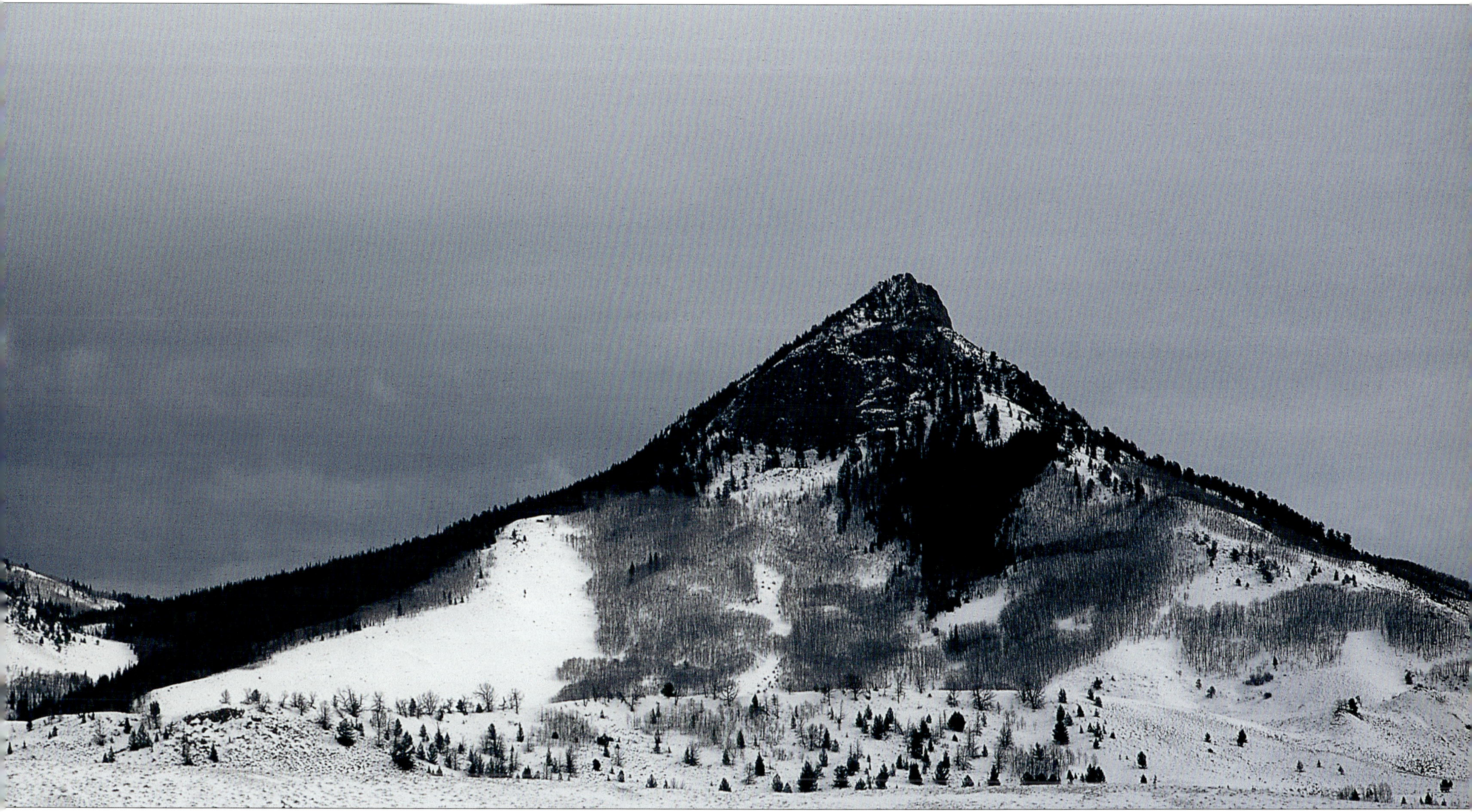

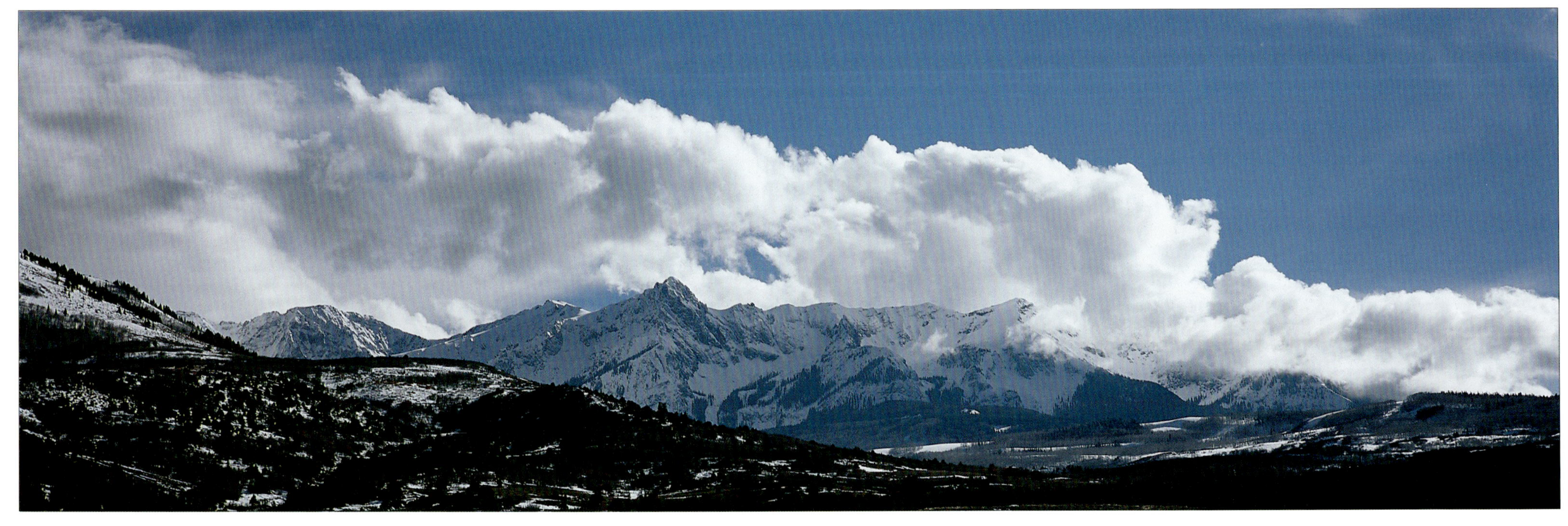

The Sneffels Range

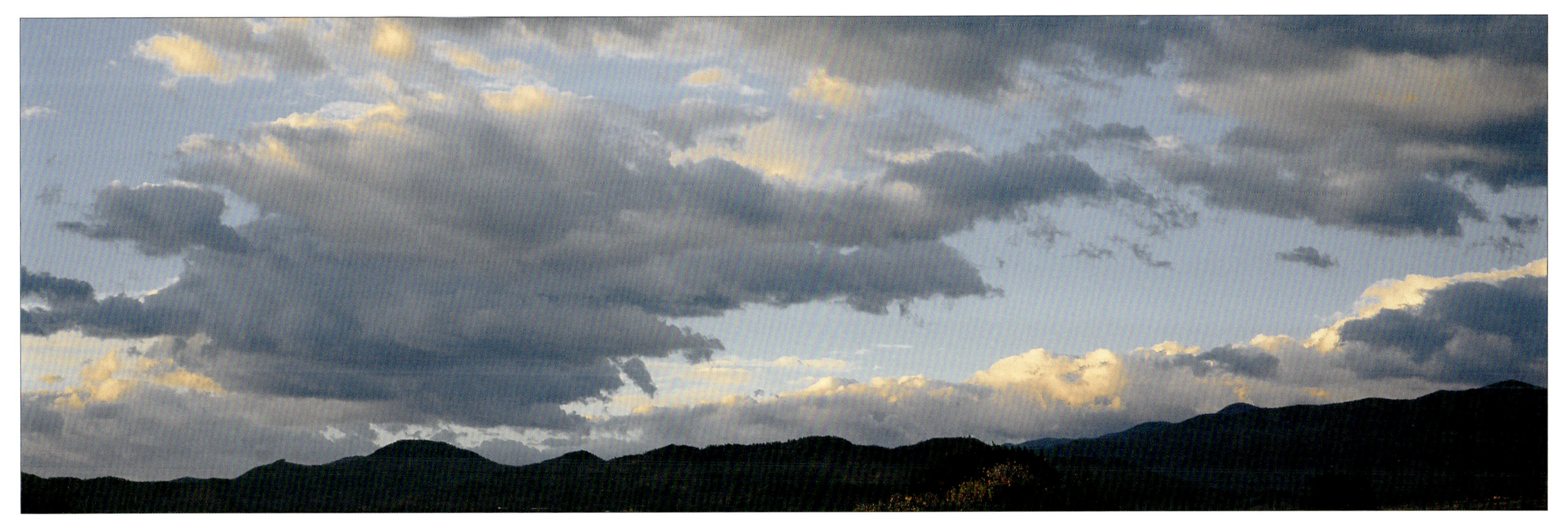

The Wet Mountains, San Isabel National Forest

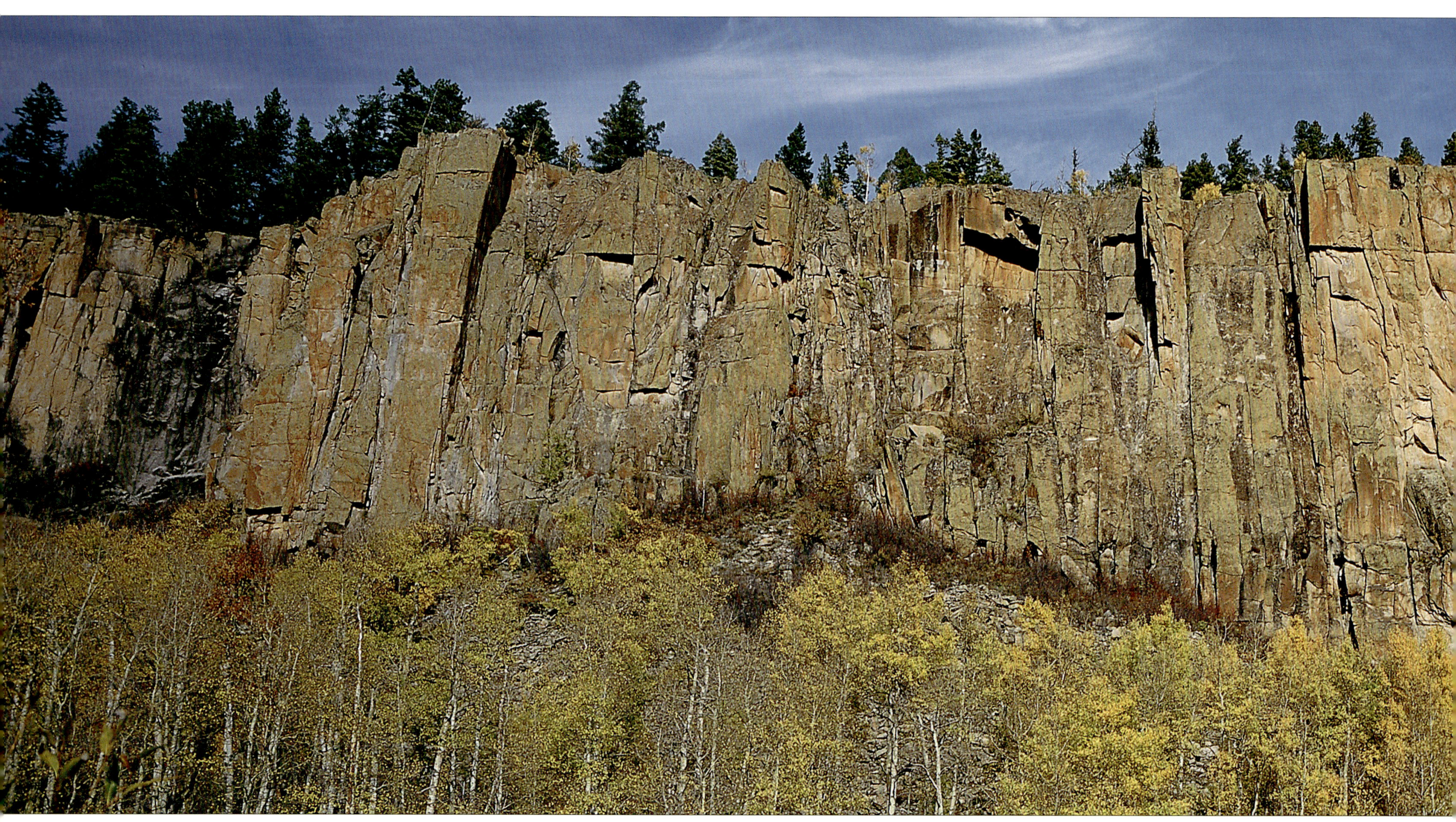

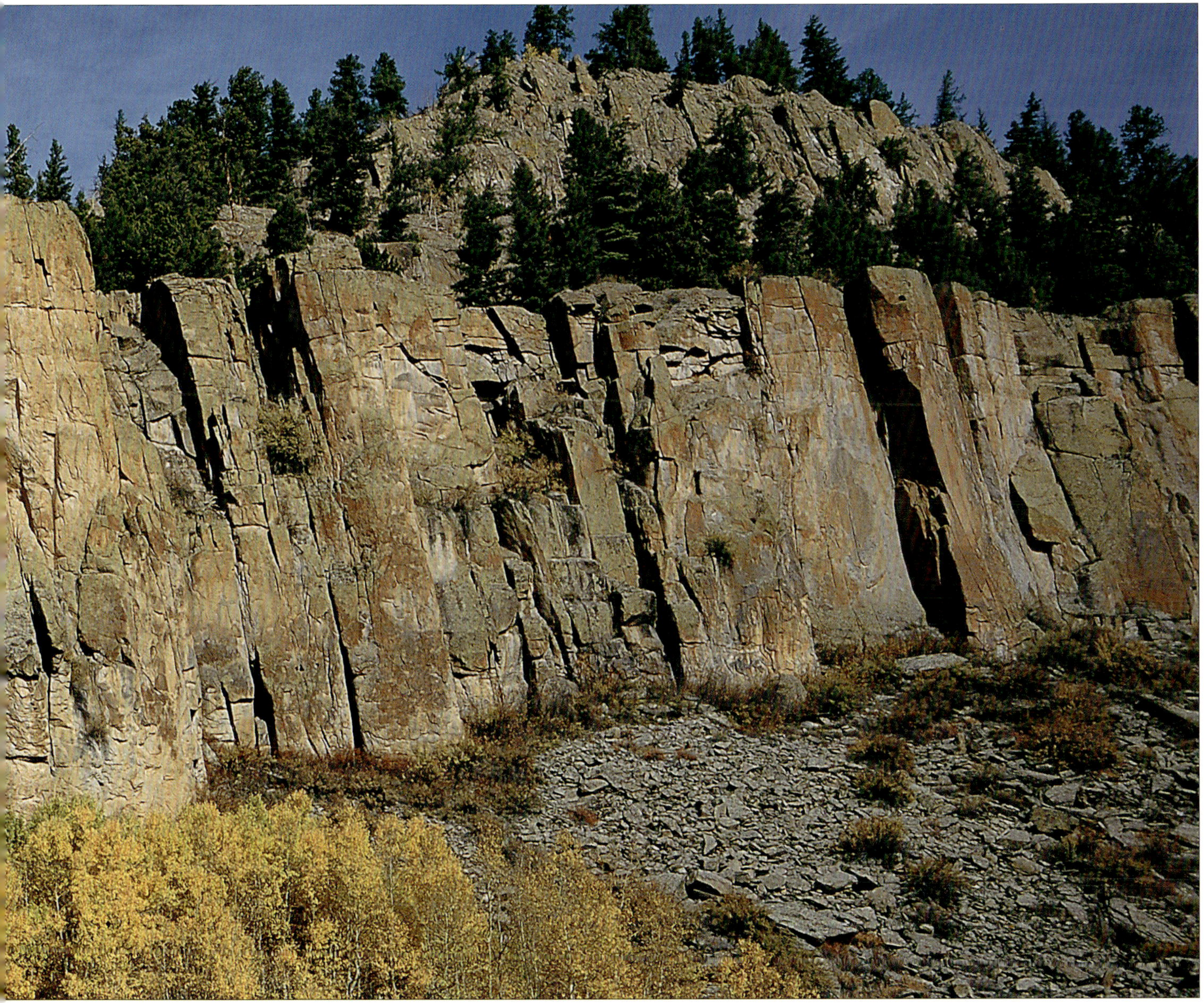

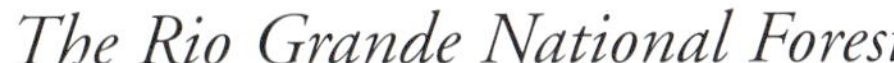

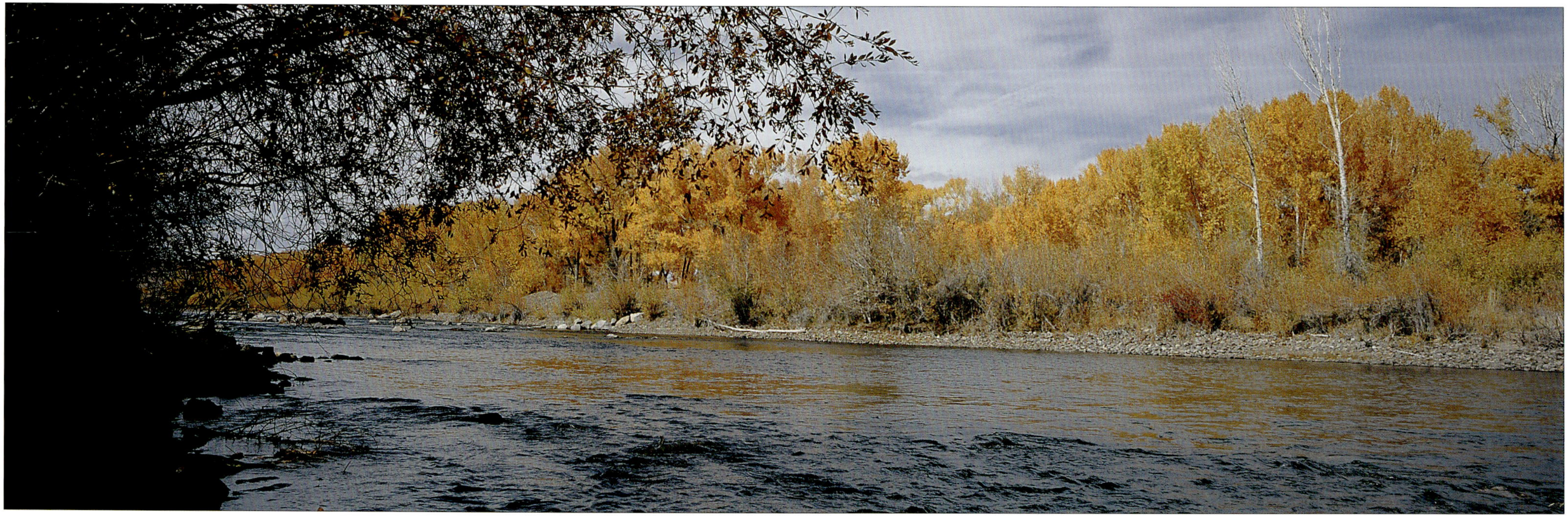

The Rio Grande River

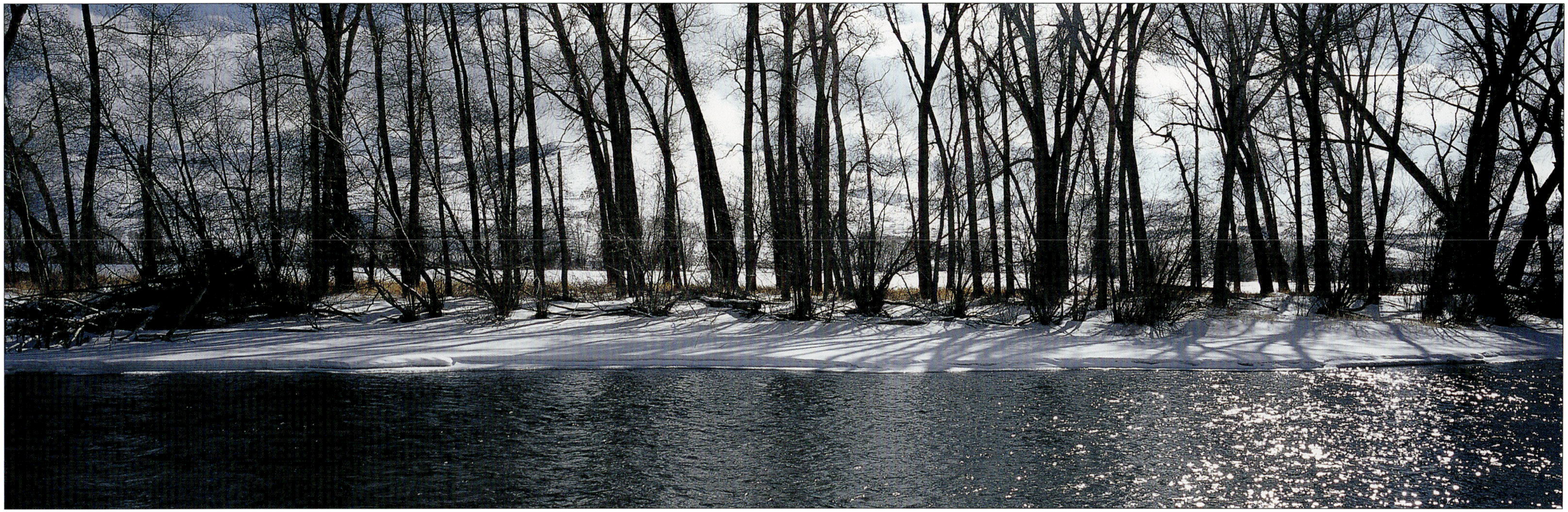

The Colorado River

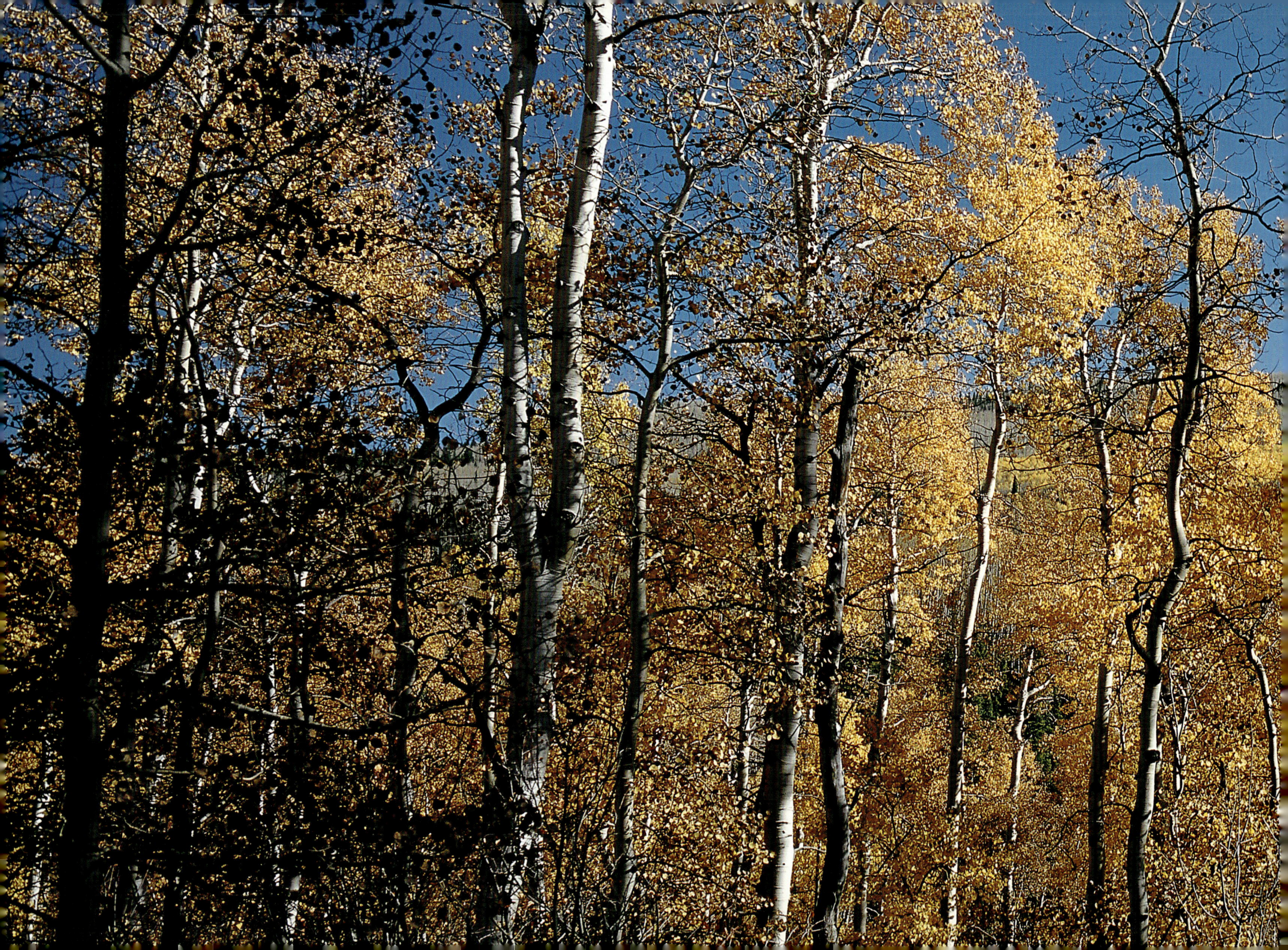

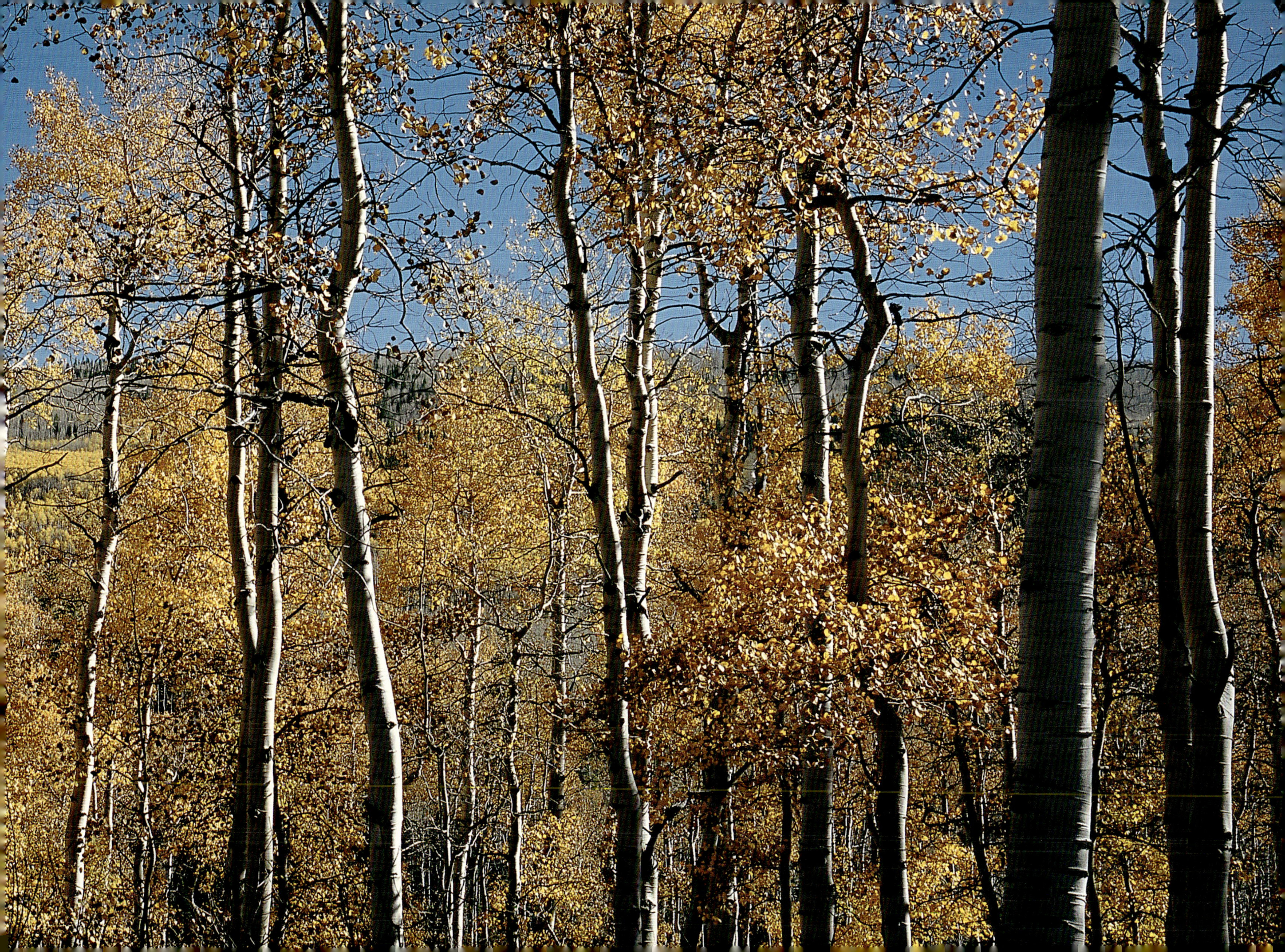

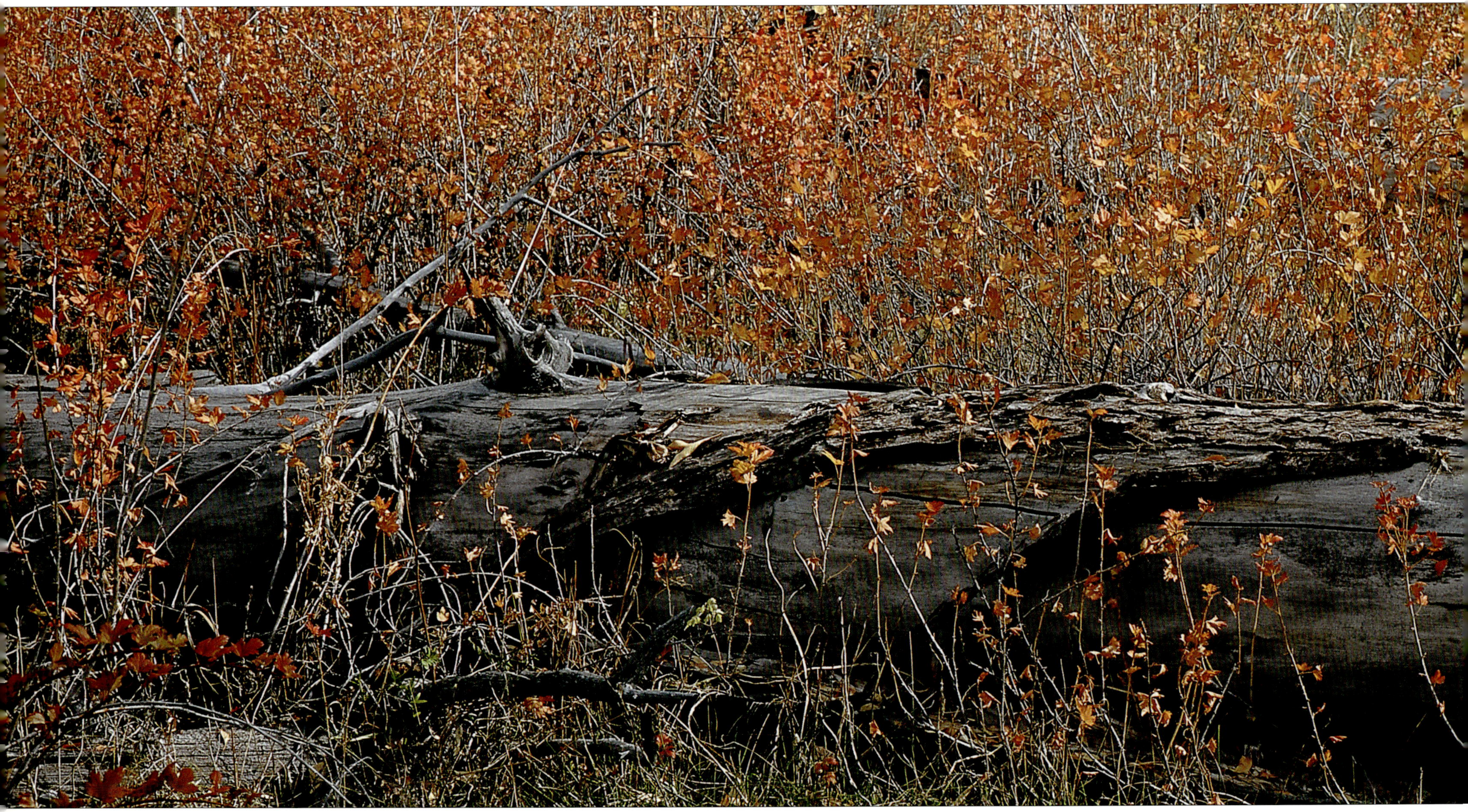

Previous Spread: The Gunnison National Forest

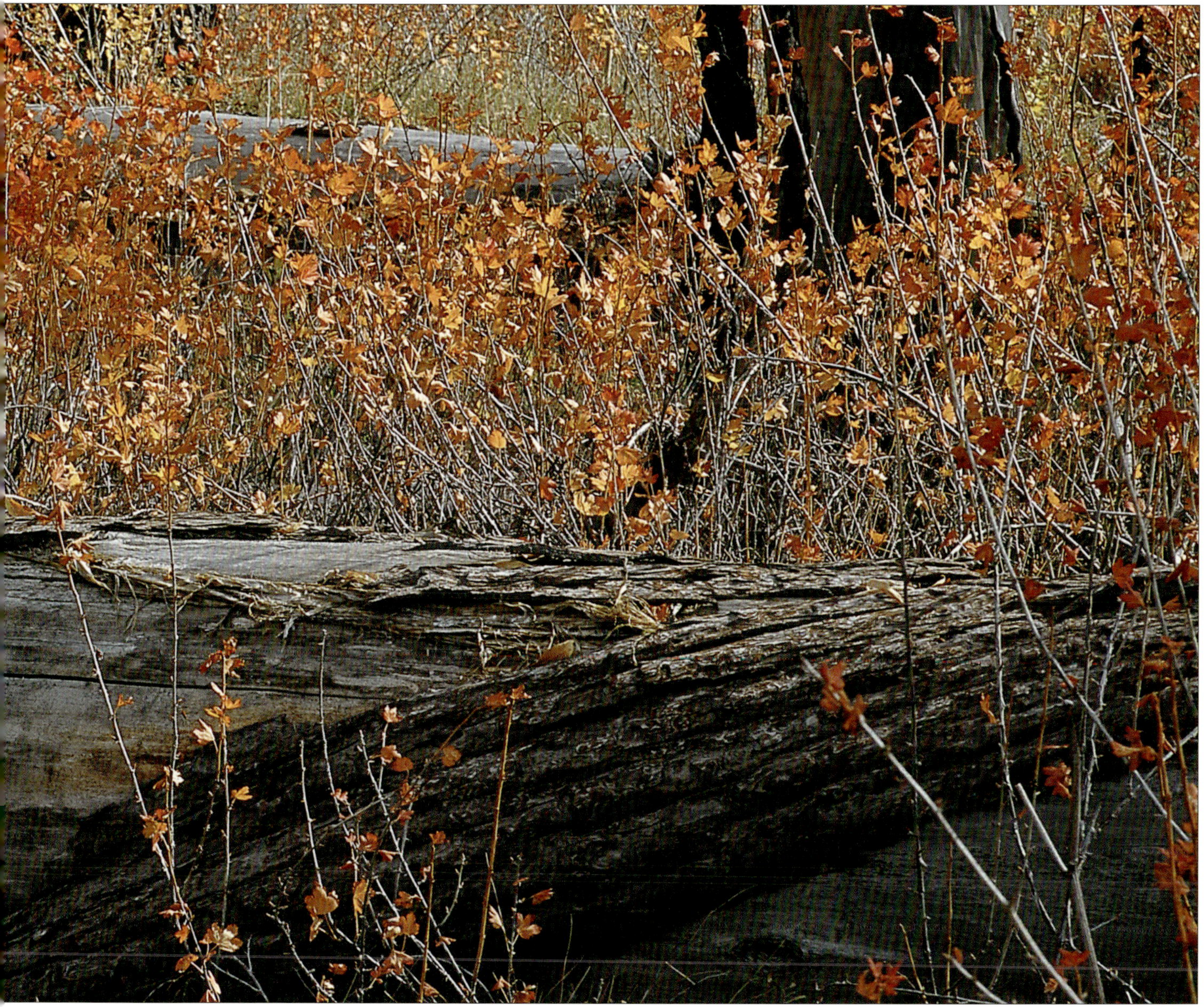

The Raggeds Wilderness,
Gunnison National Forest

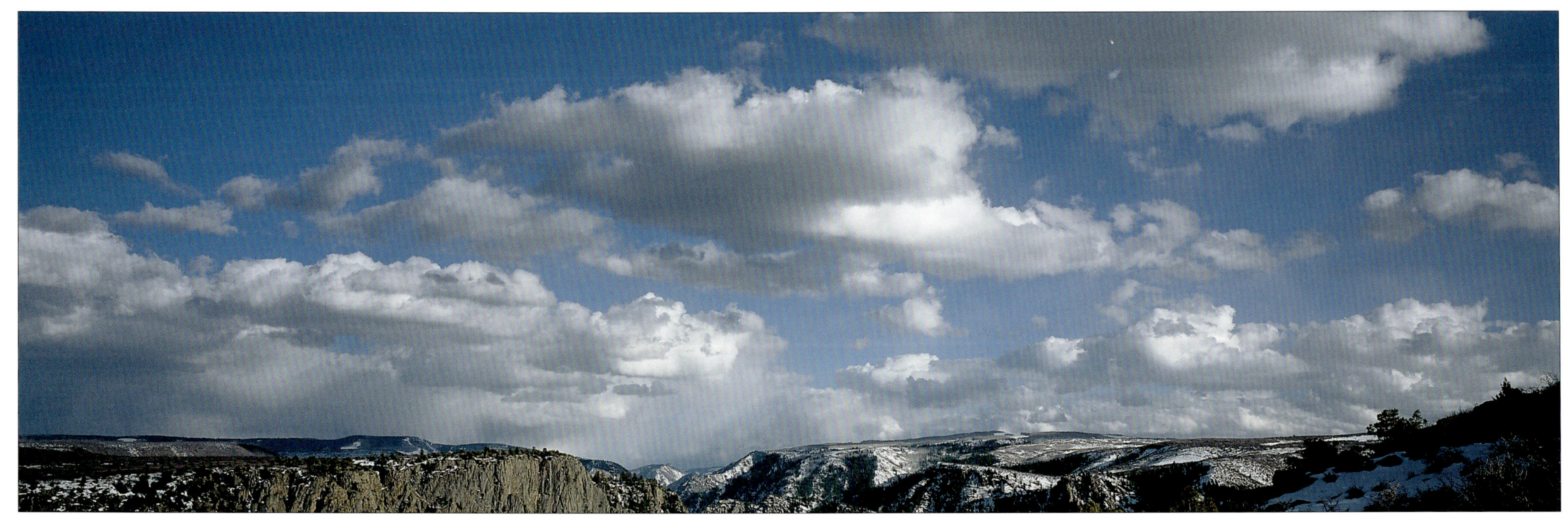

Black Canyon of the Gunnison National Park

Only a couple of hours separated the creation of these two panographic images™. They were made from the same place, yet the use of a different focal-length lens and the change in lighting make them look like two different places.

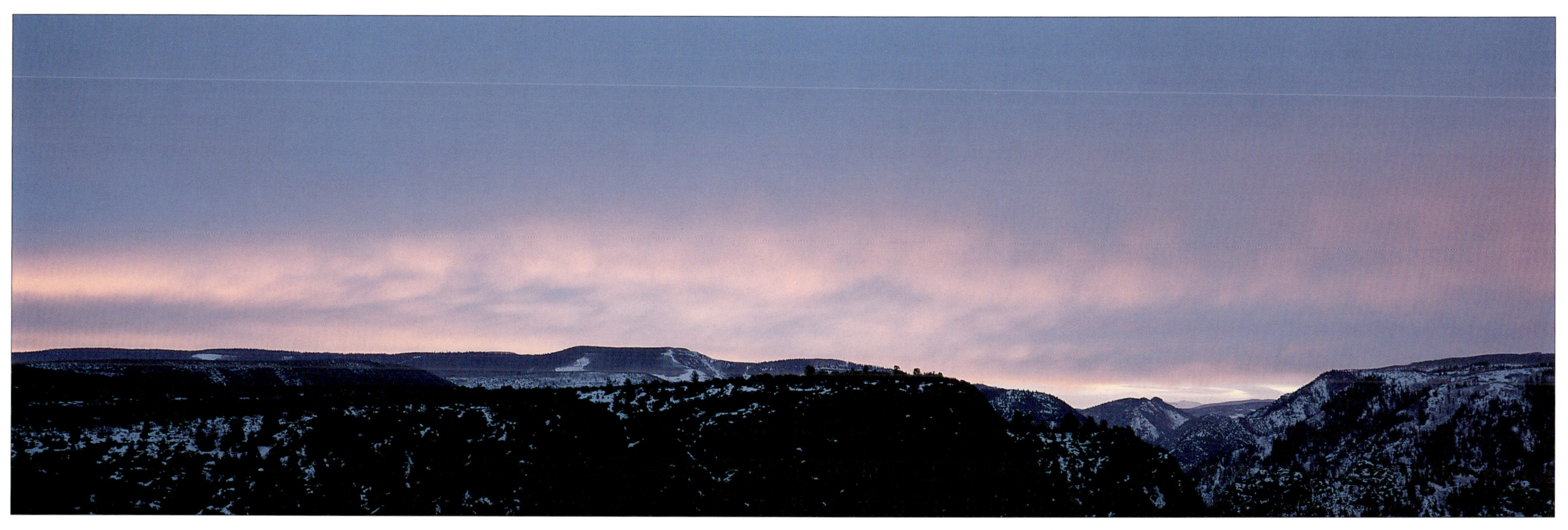

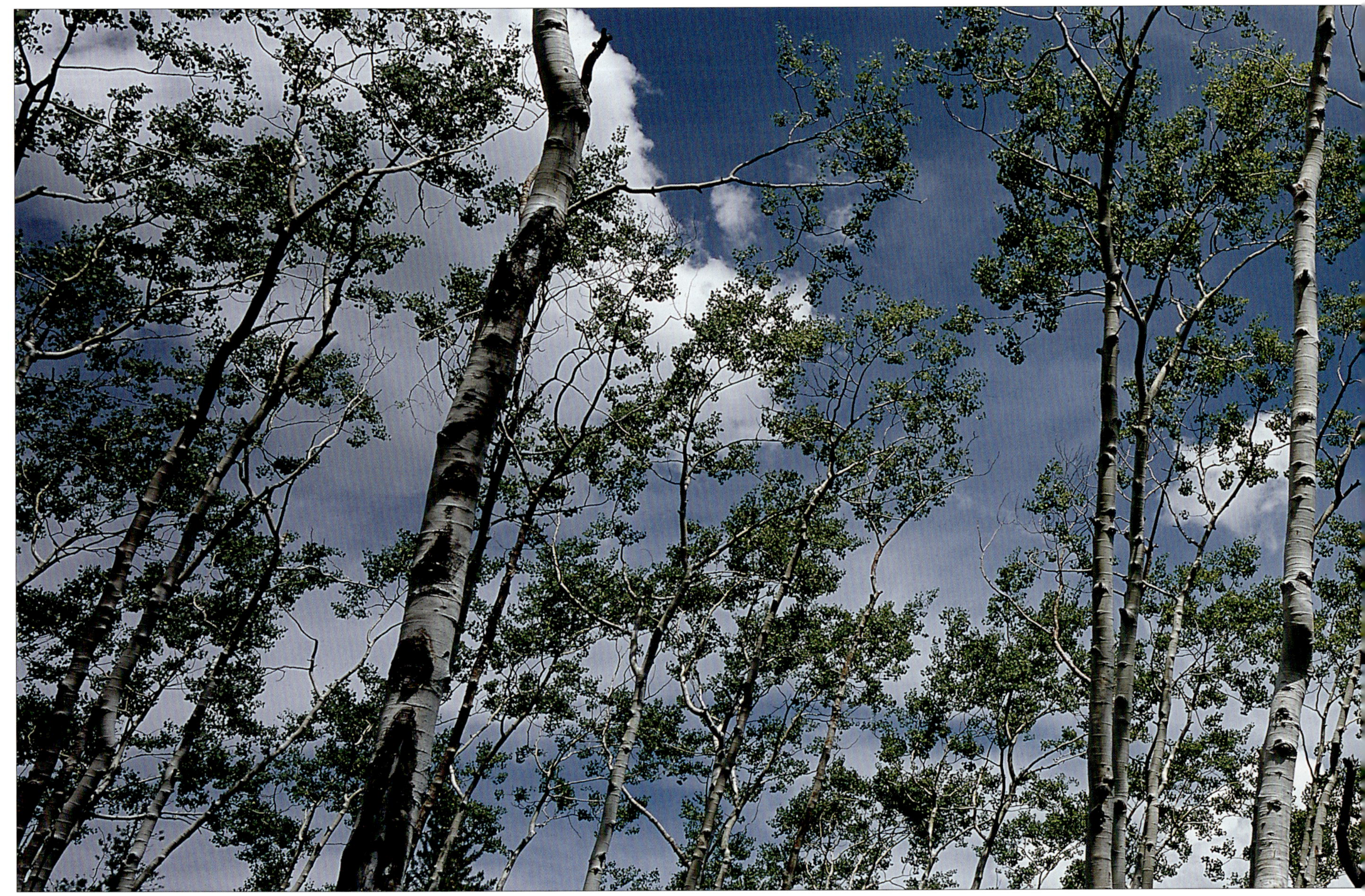

Black Sage Pass

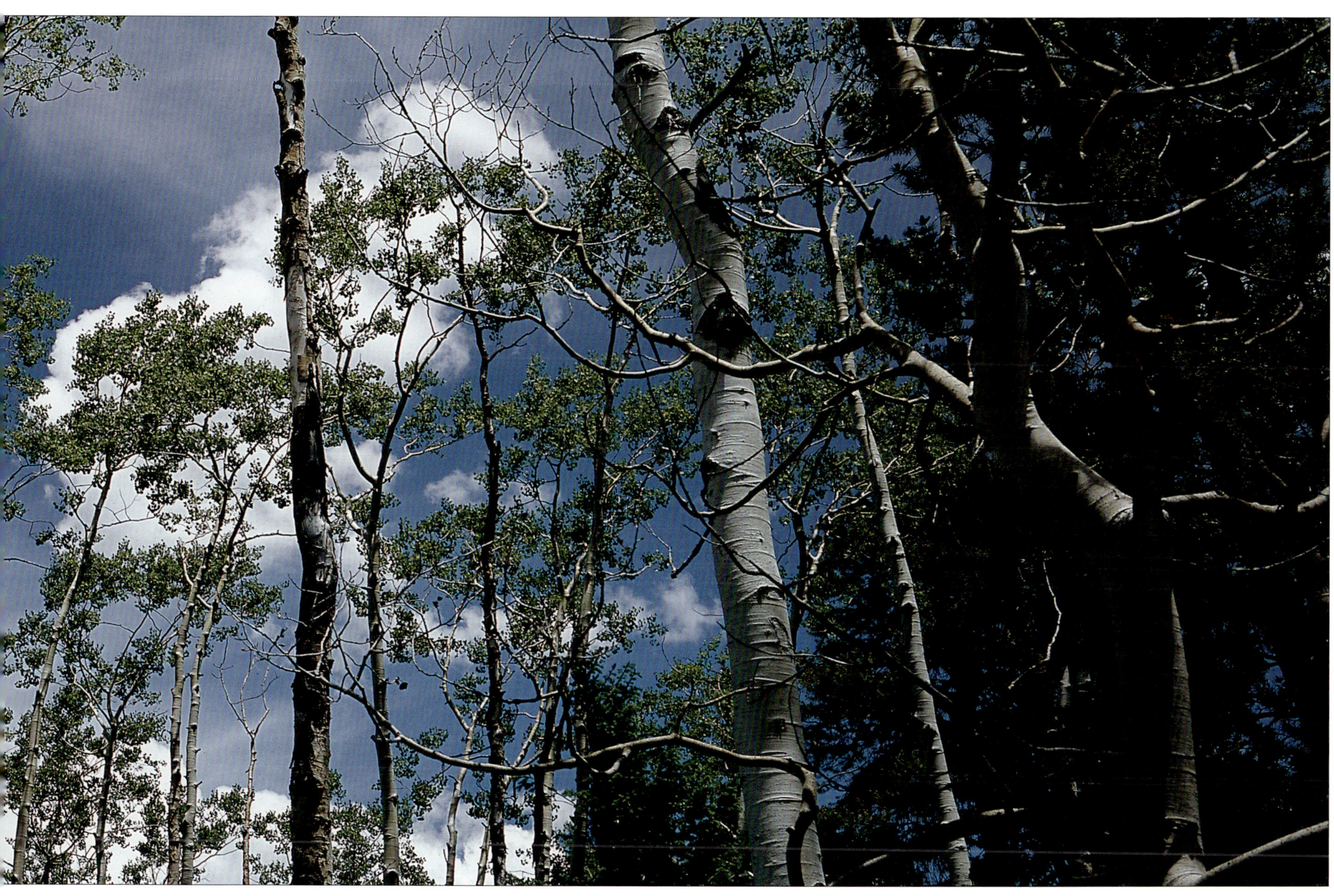

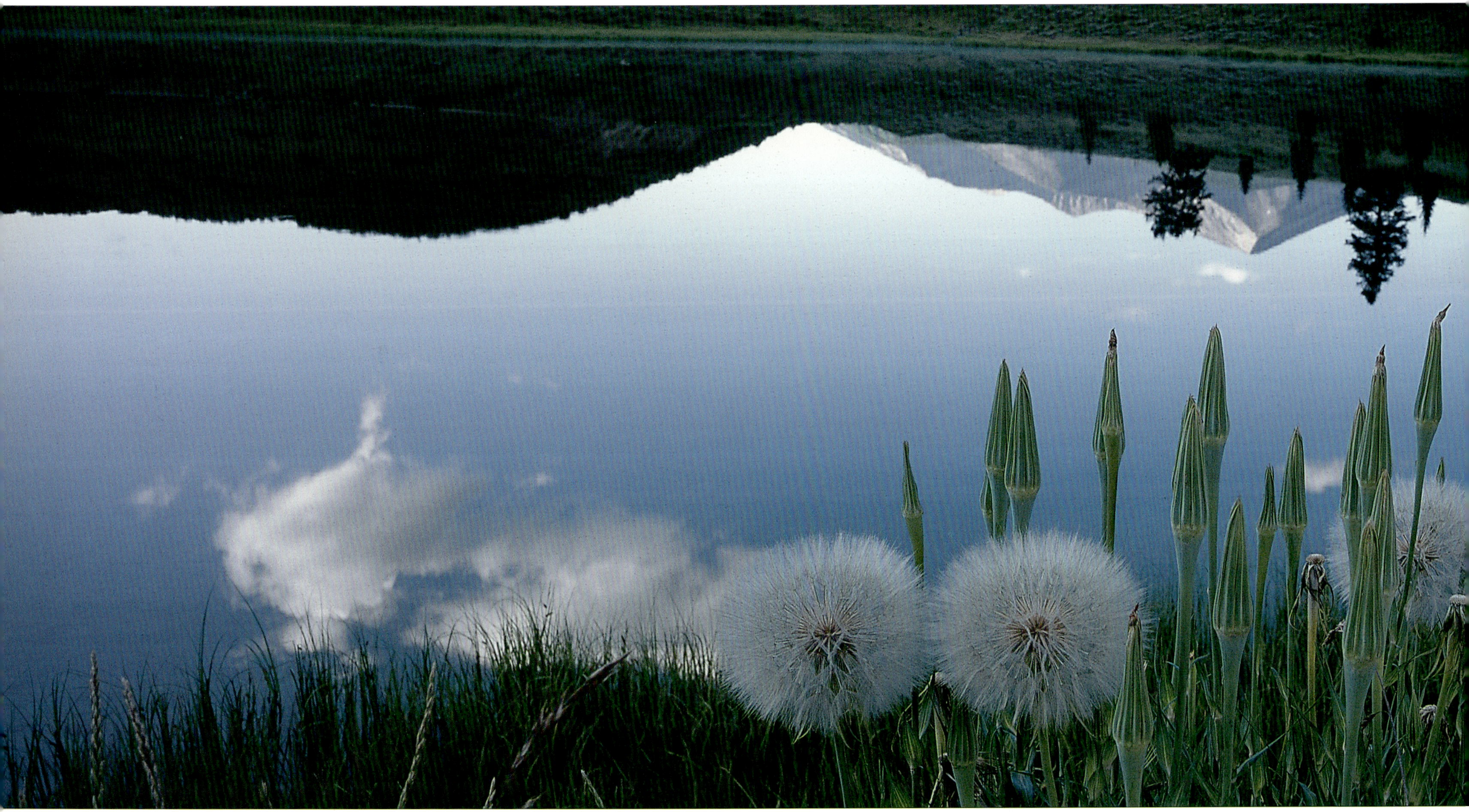

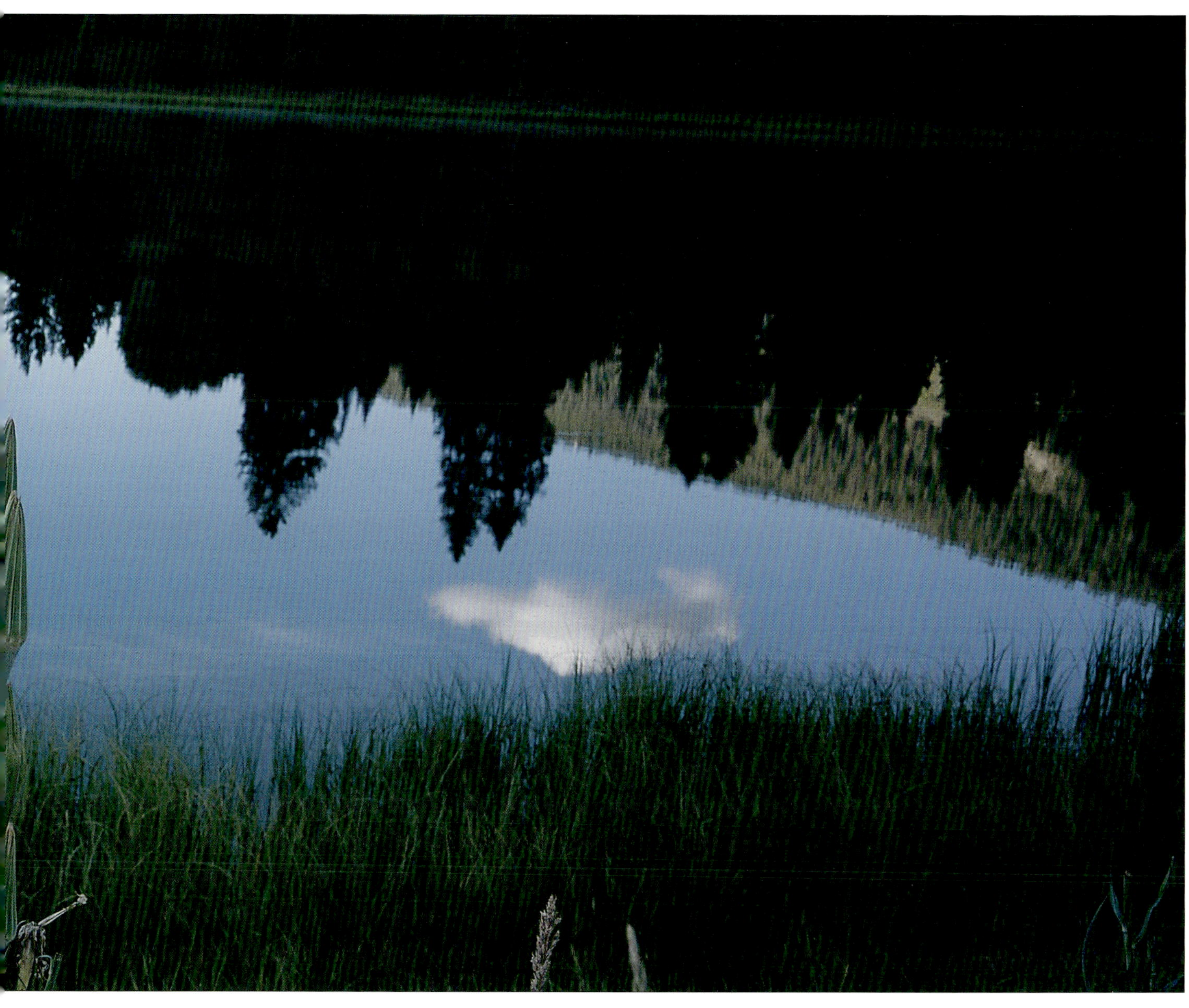

Early morning reflections with Salsify (Tragopogon dubius) in the Gunnison National Forest

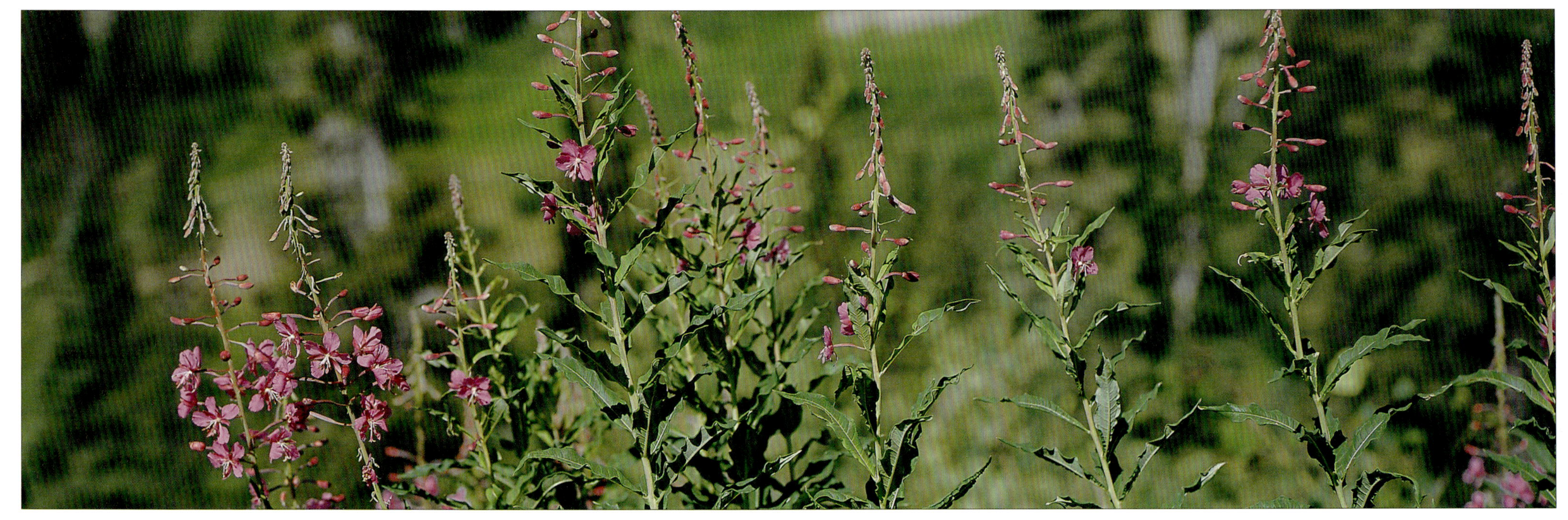

Fireweed (Epilobium angustifolium)

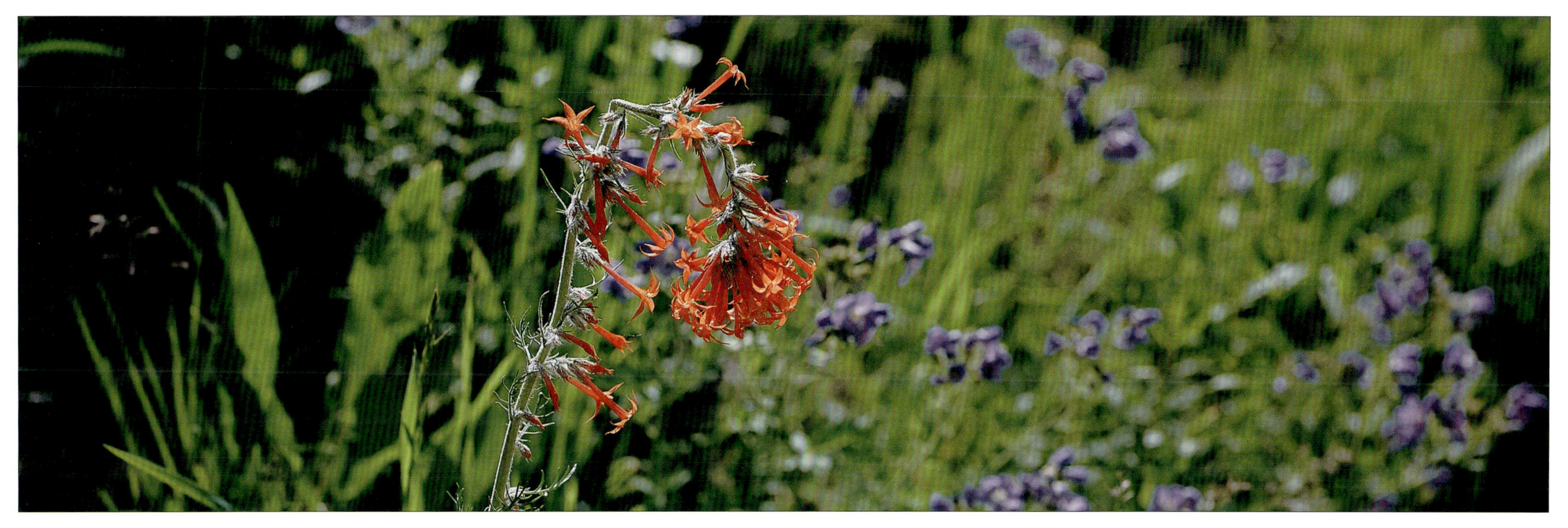

Scarlet Gilia (Ipomopsis aggregata) damaged by the storms of life but still blooming

The warmth of the sun will soon rise above the frozen Mosquito Range.

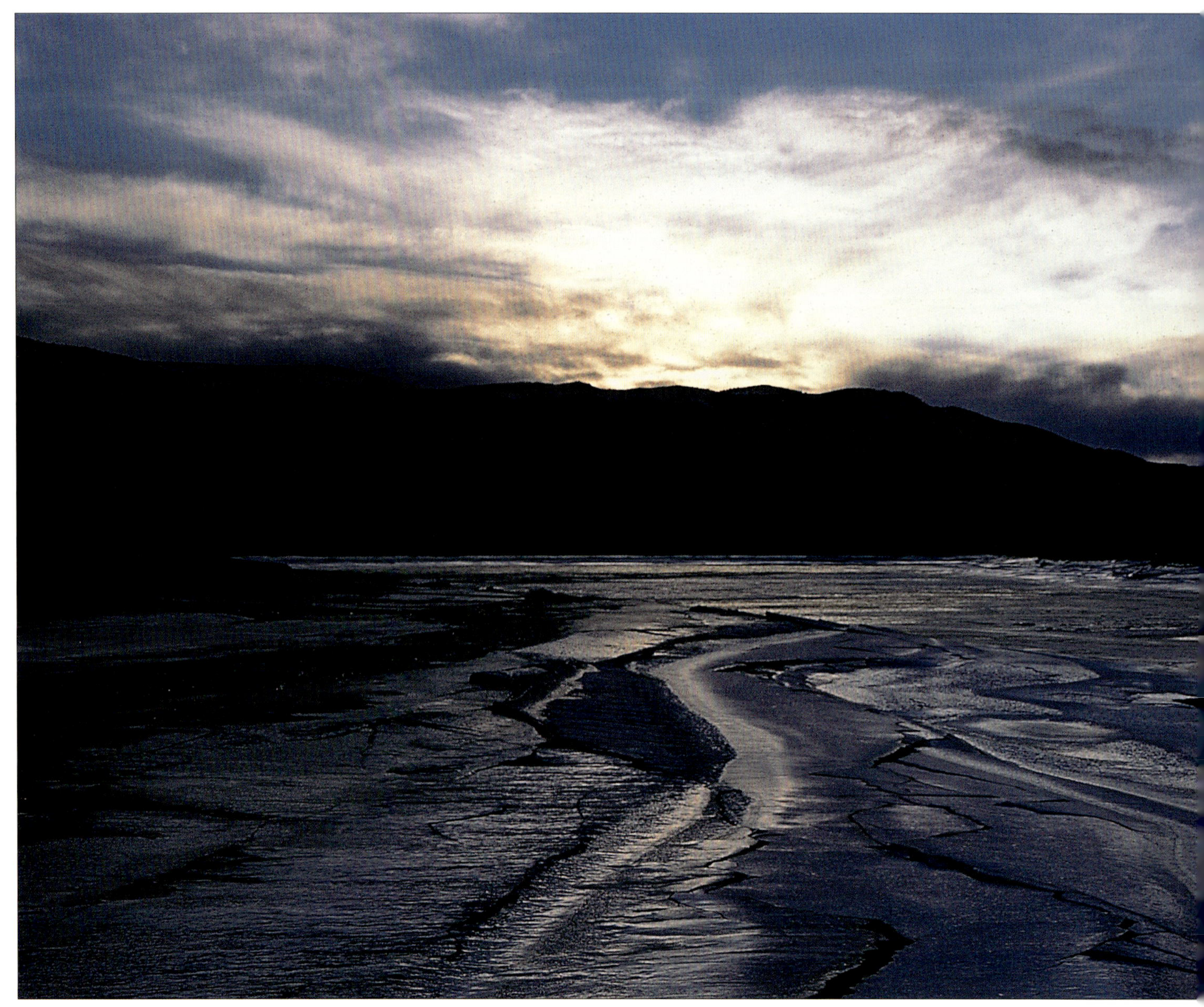

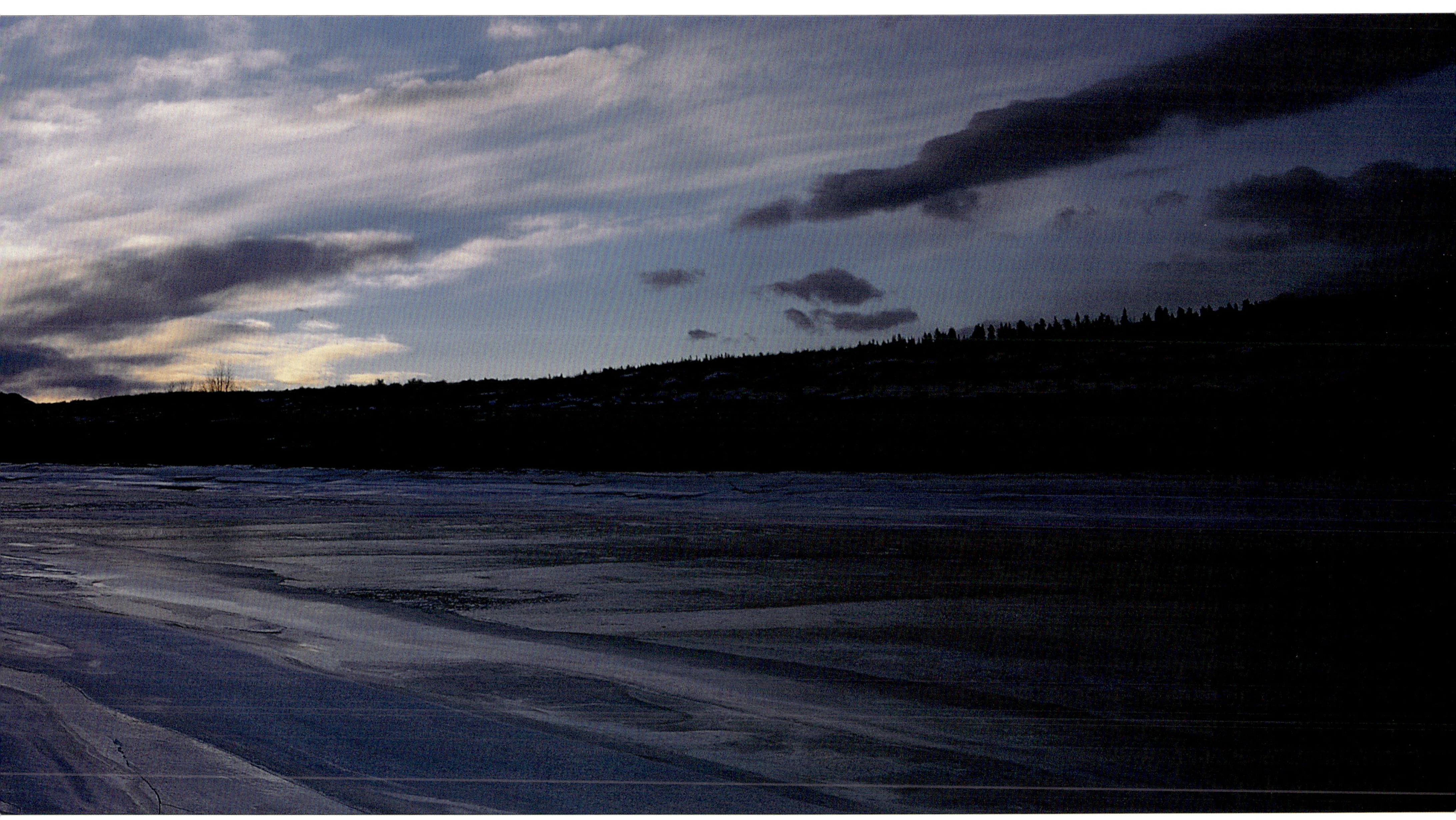

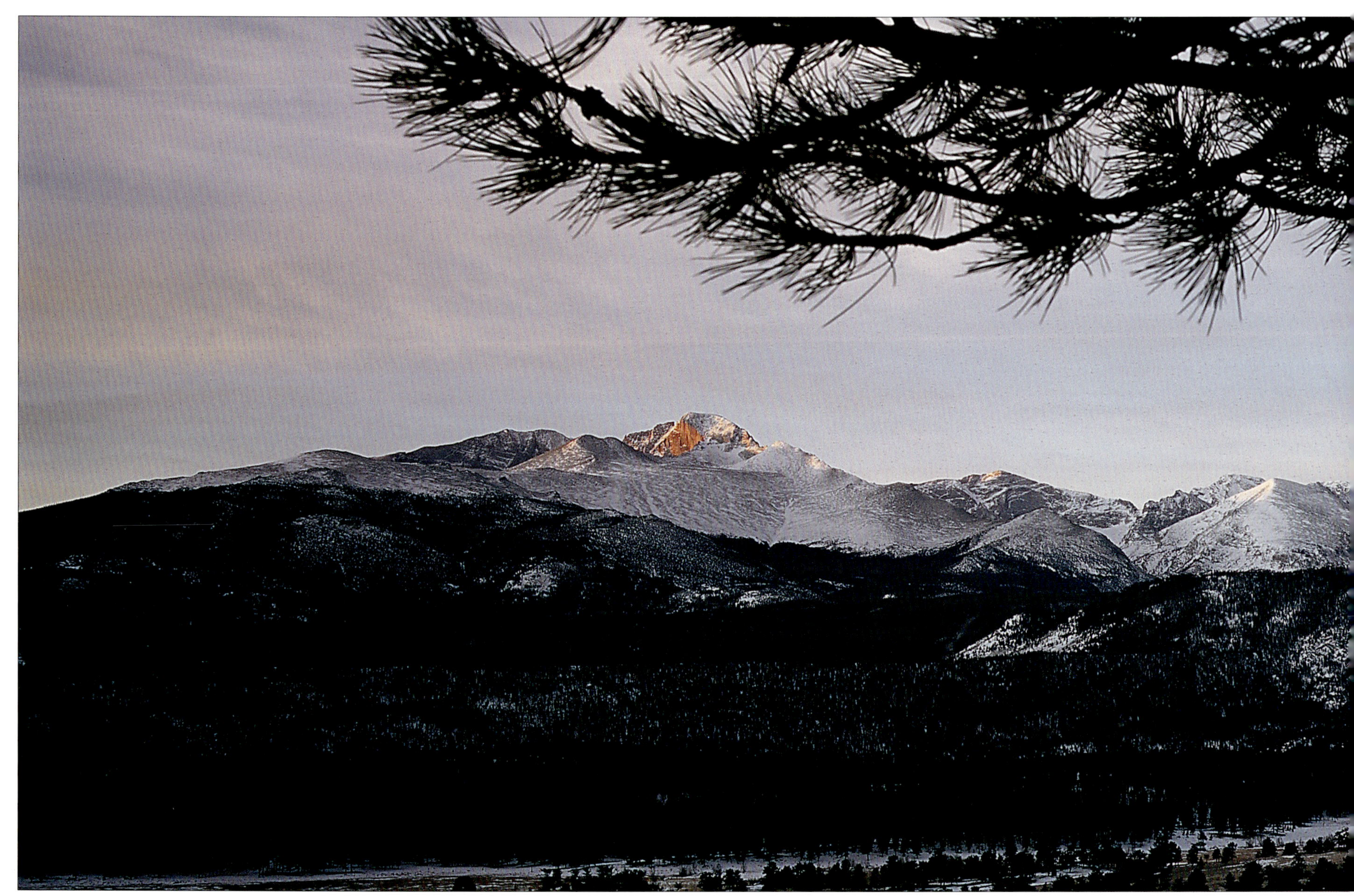

The first light of dawn in Rocky Mountain National Park

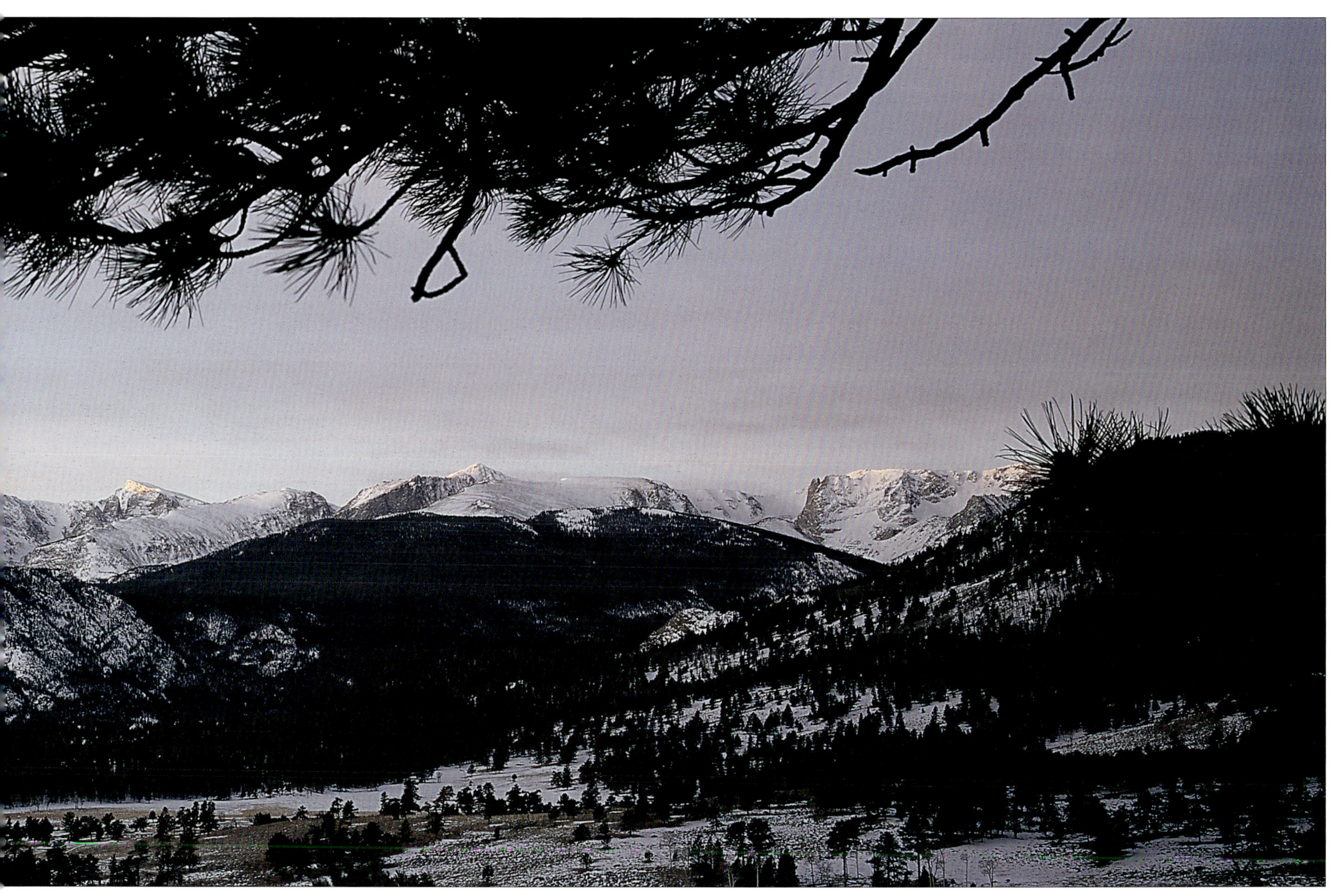

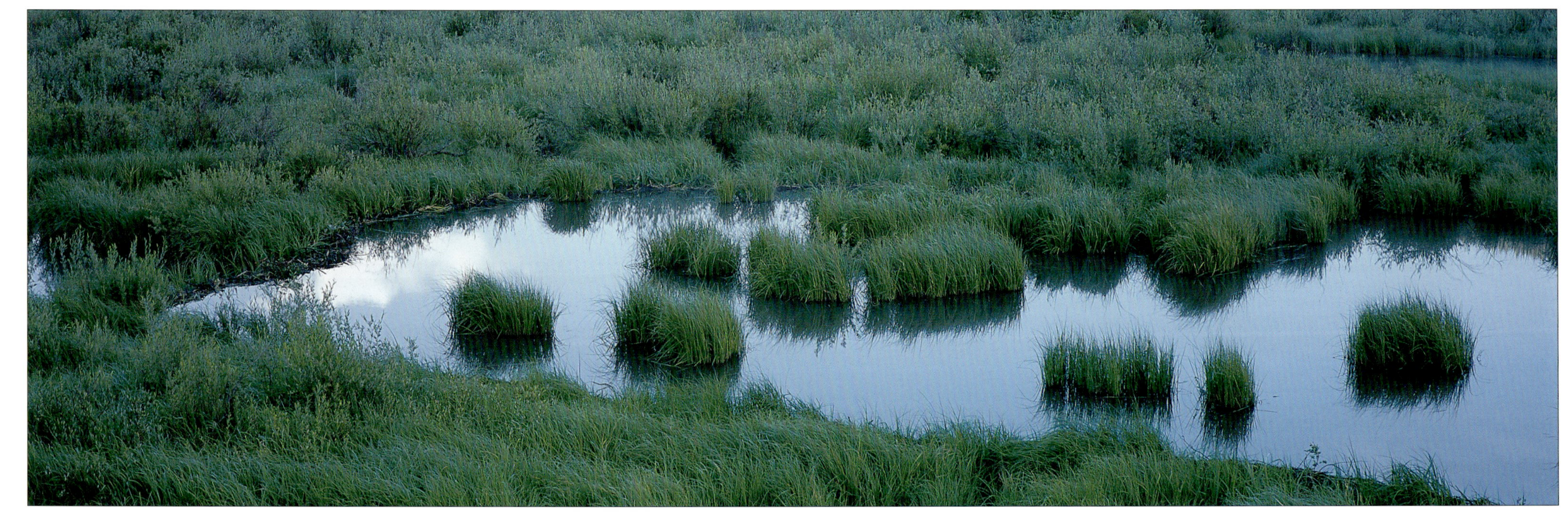

Gunnison National Forest

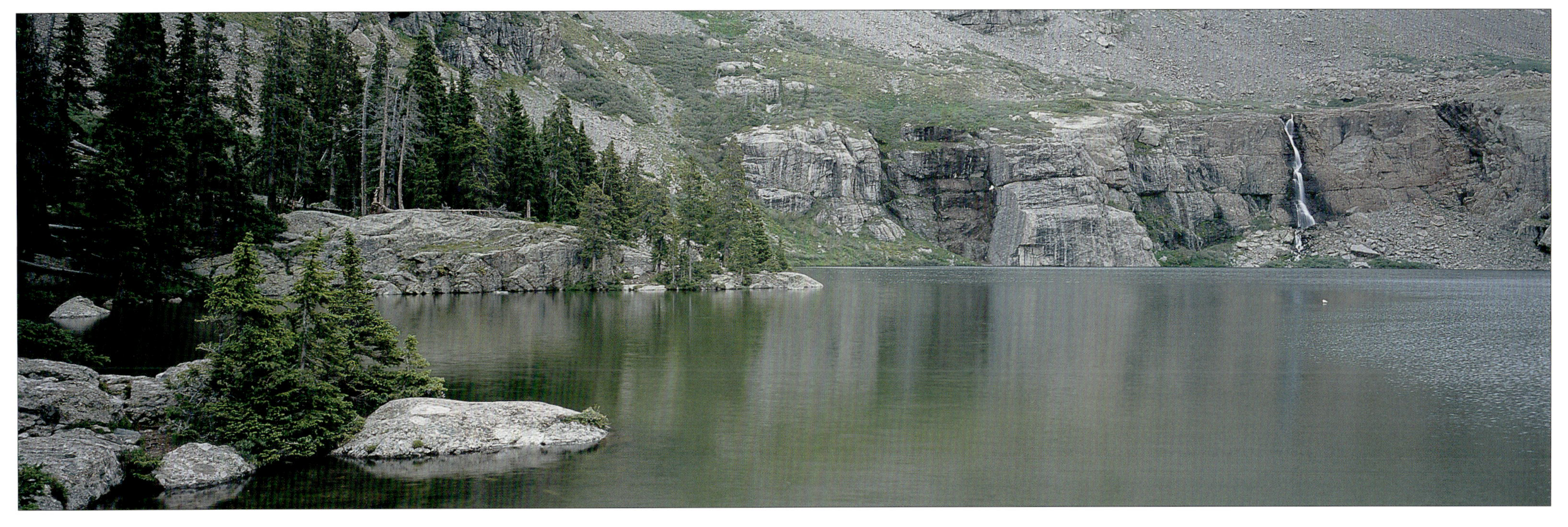

Willow Lake, Sangre de Cristo Mountains

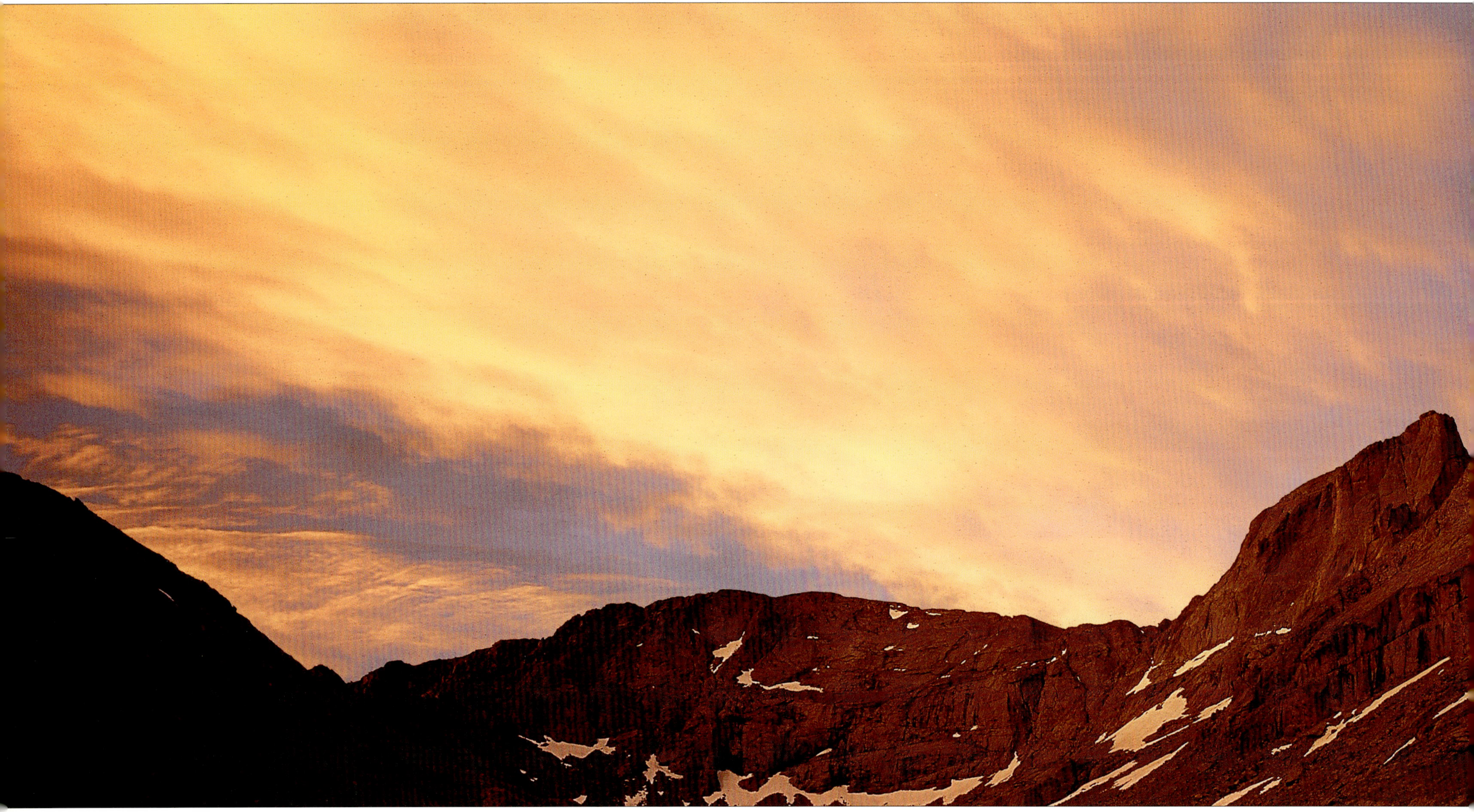

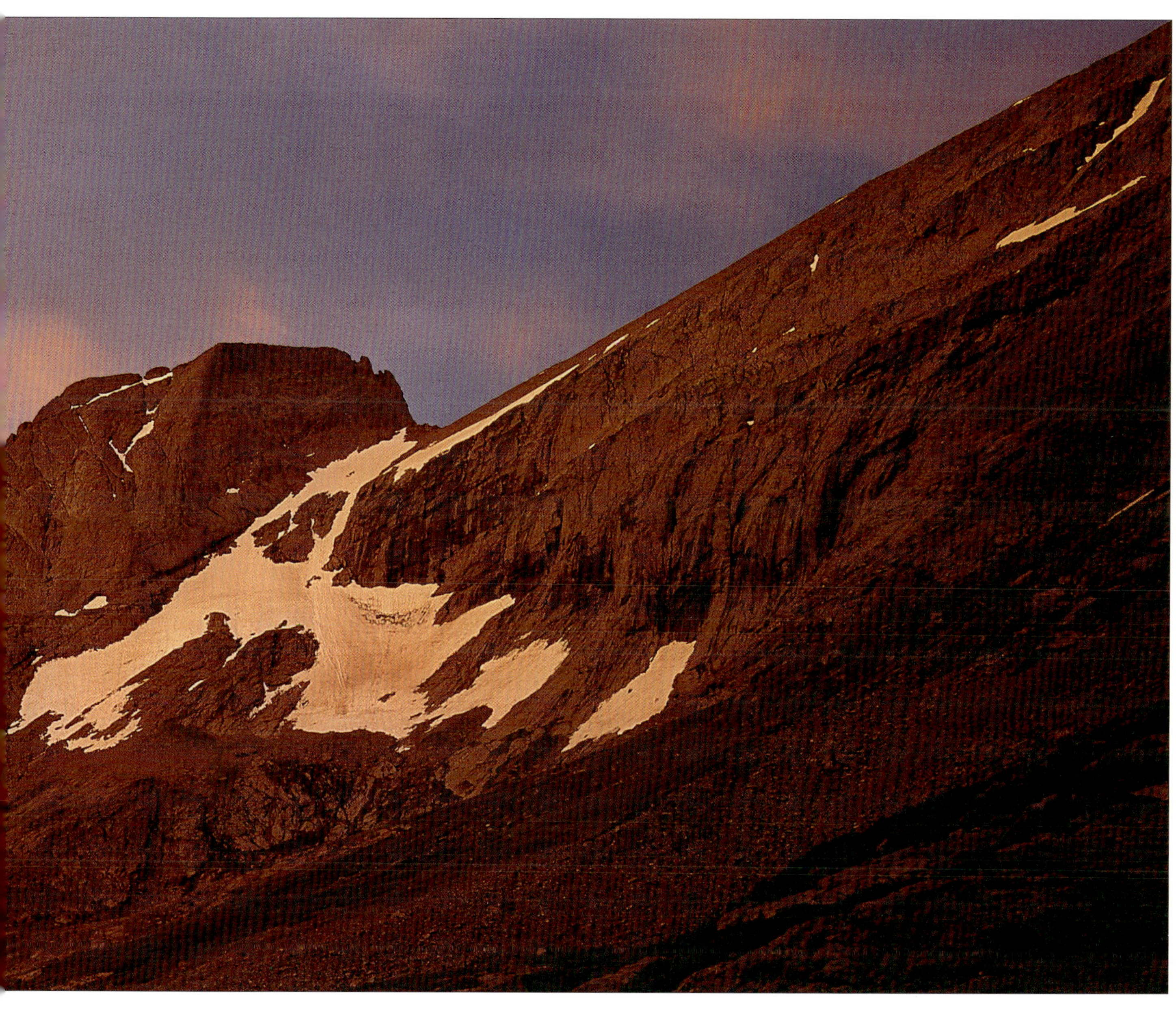

Kit Carson is the pointed peak in the background, and Challenger Peak is the one just in front of it. They are both over 14,000 feet high, but Challenger is not considered a separate mountain in the listing of Colorado's 54 "Fourteeners"—peaks over 14,000 feet.

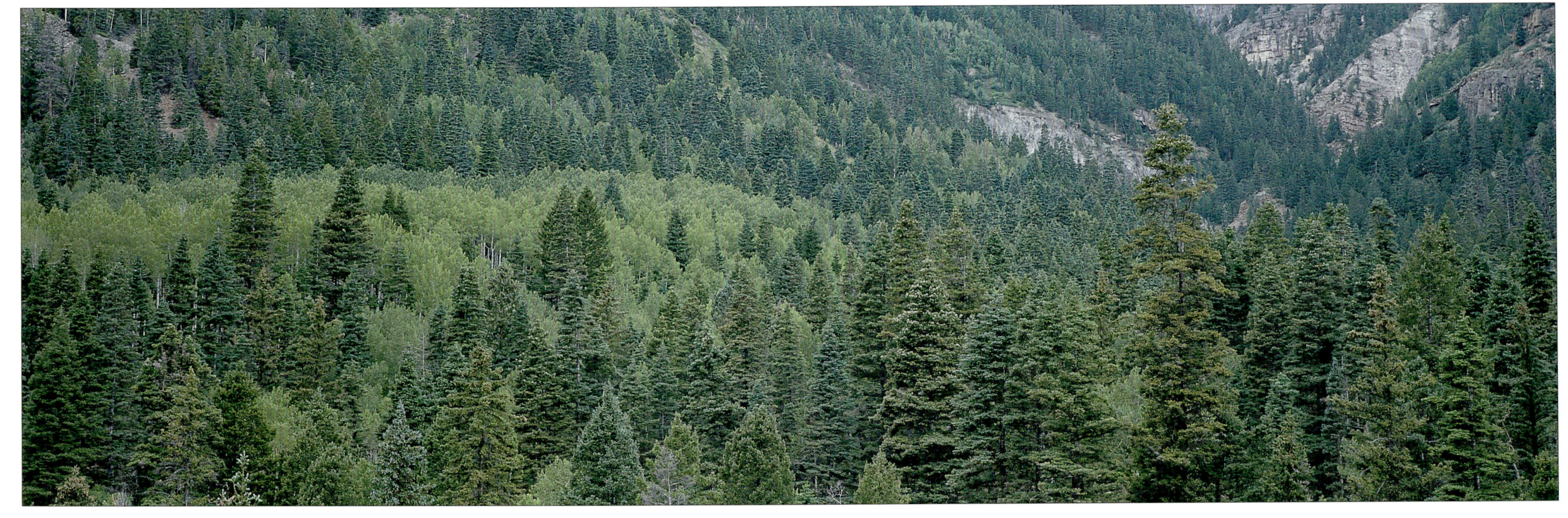

Mount Sneffels Wilderness

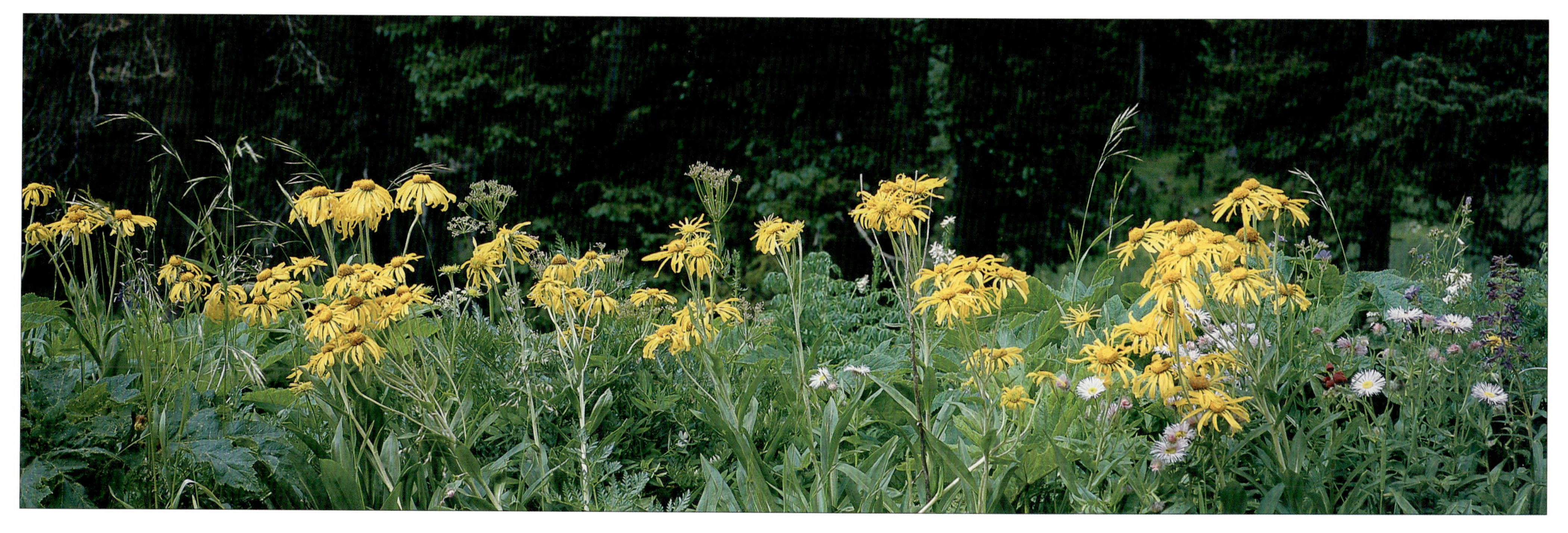

Coneflower (Rudbeckia ampla), Ohio Pass, Gunnison National Forest

Twilight clouds

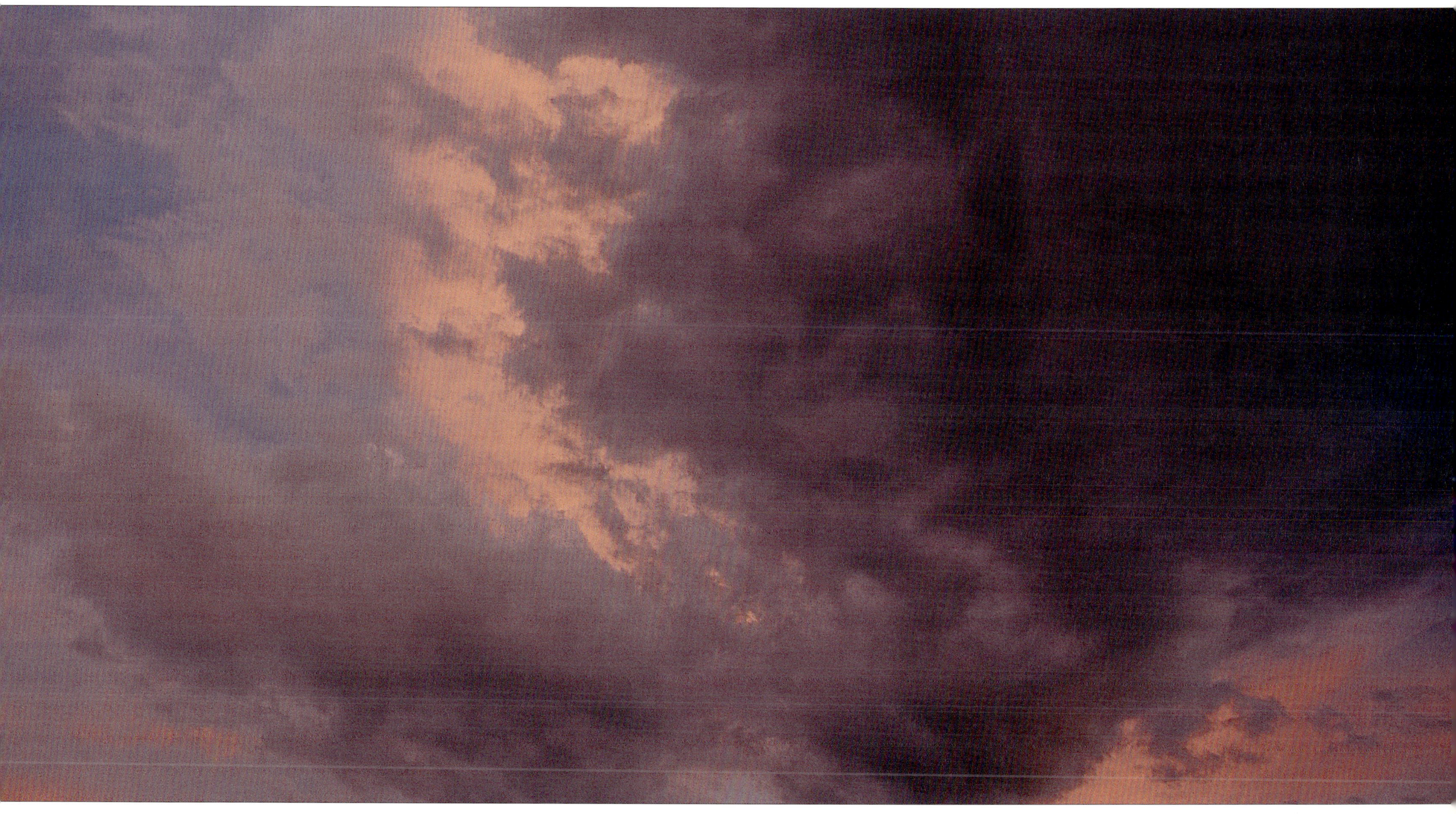

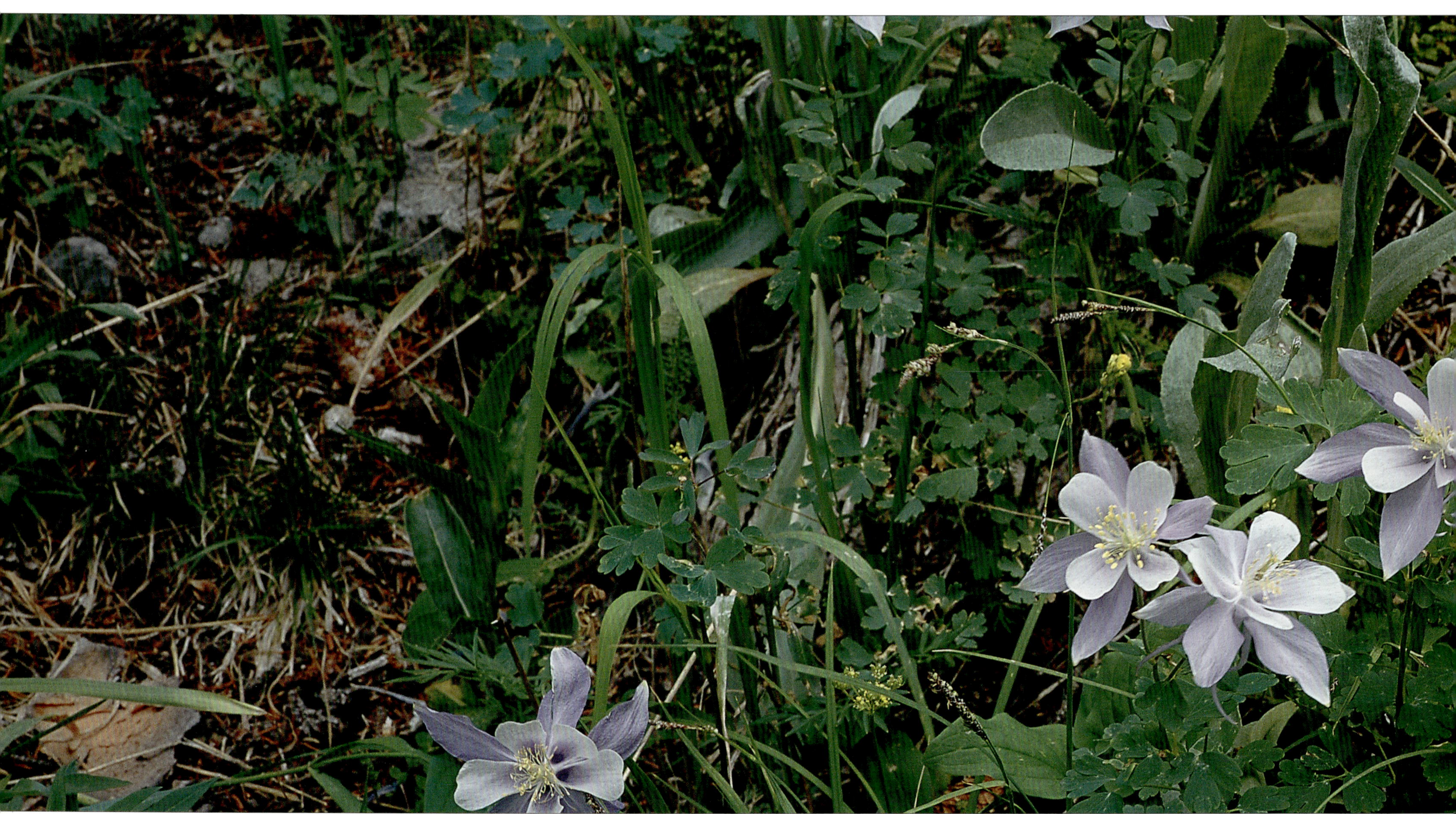

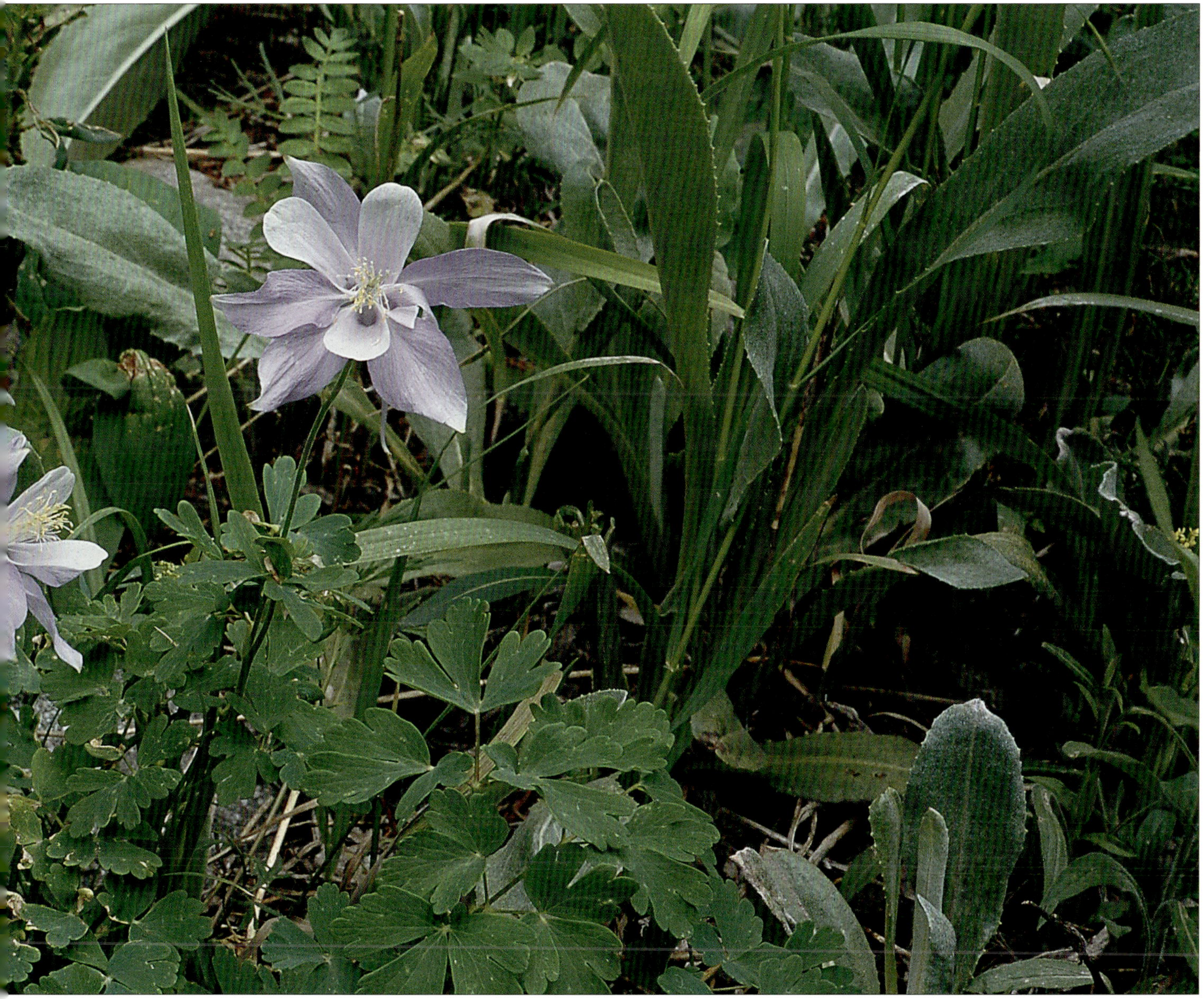

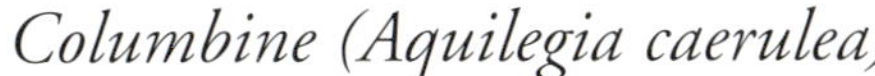

Columbine (Aquilegia caerulea)

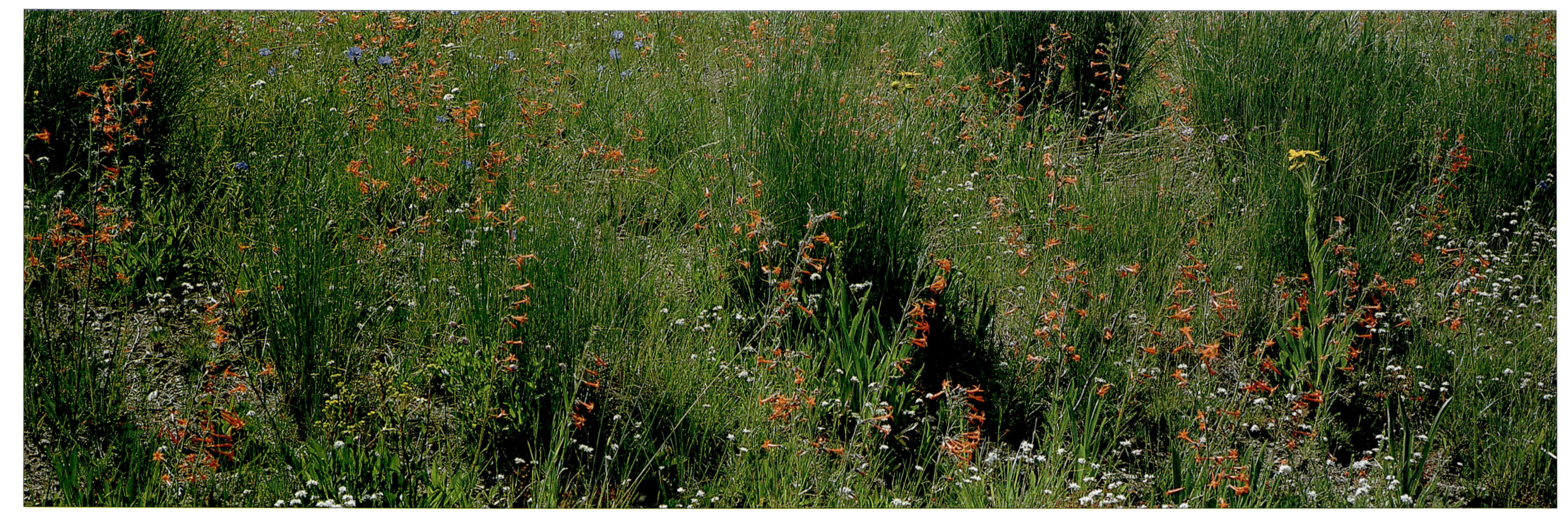

Scarlet Gilia (also known as Fairy Trumpet) near Lake Irwin, Gunnison National Forest

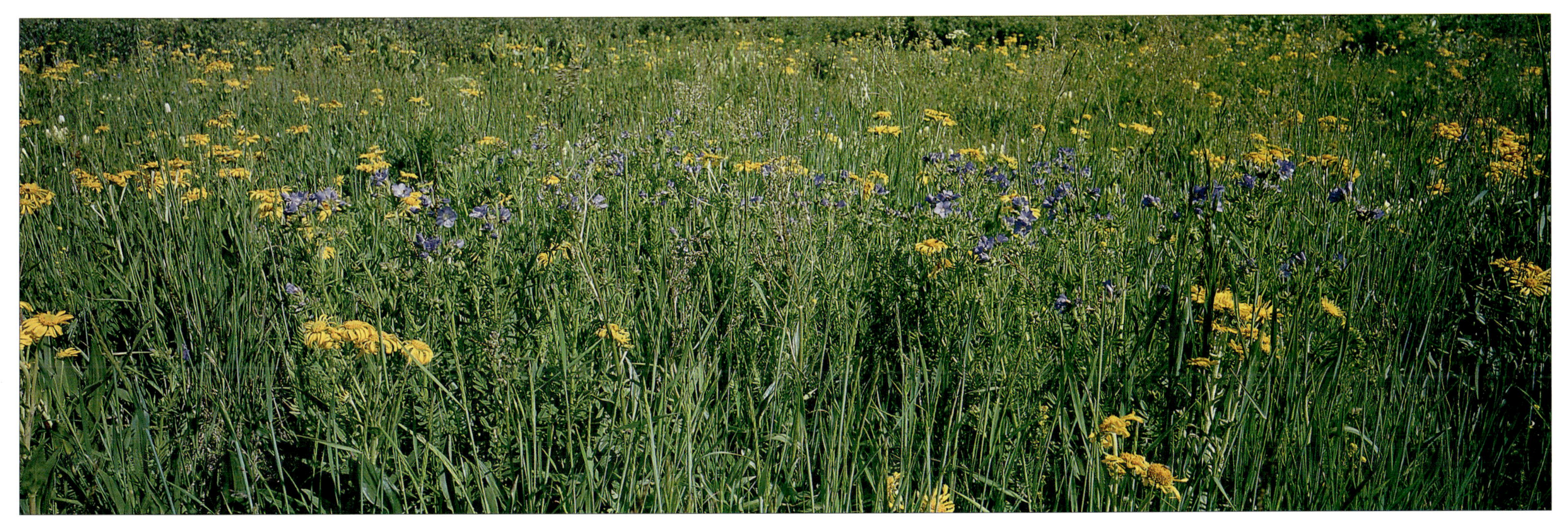

Blanket Flower (Gaillardia aristata)

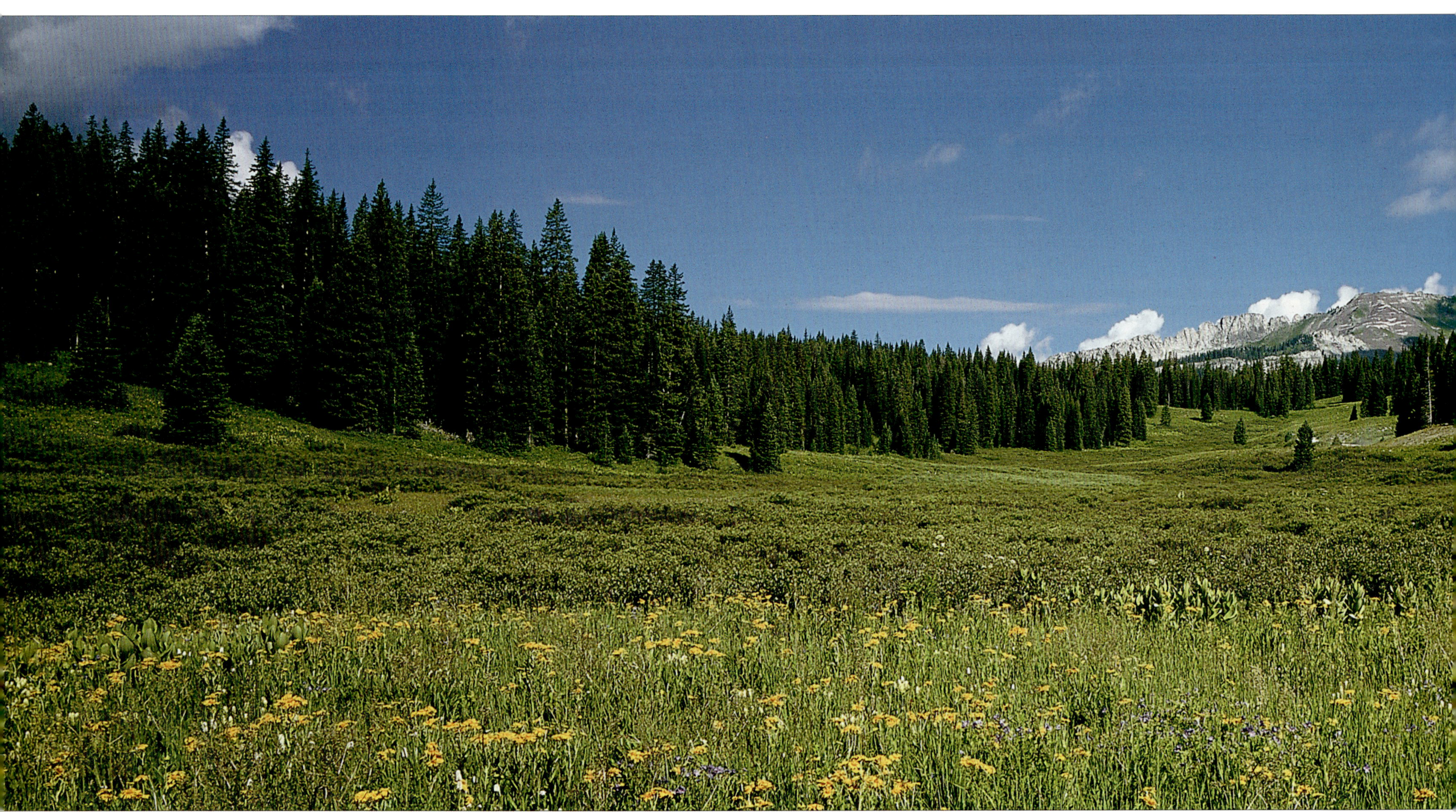

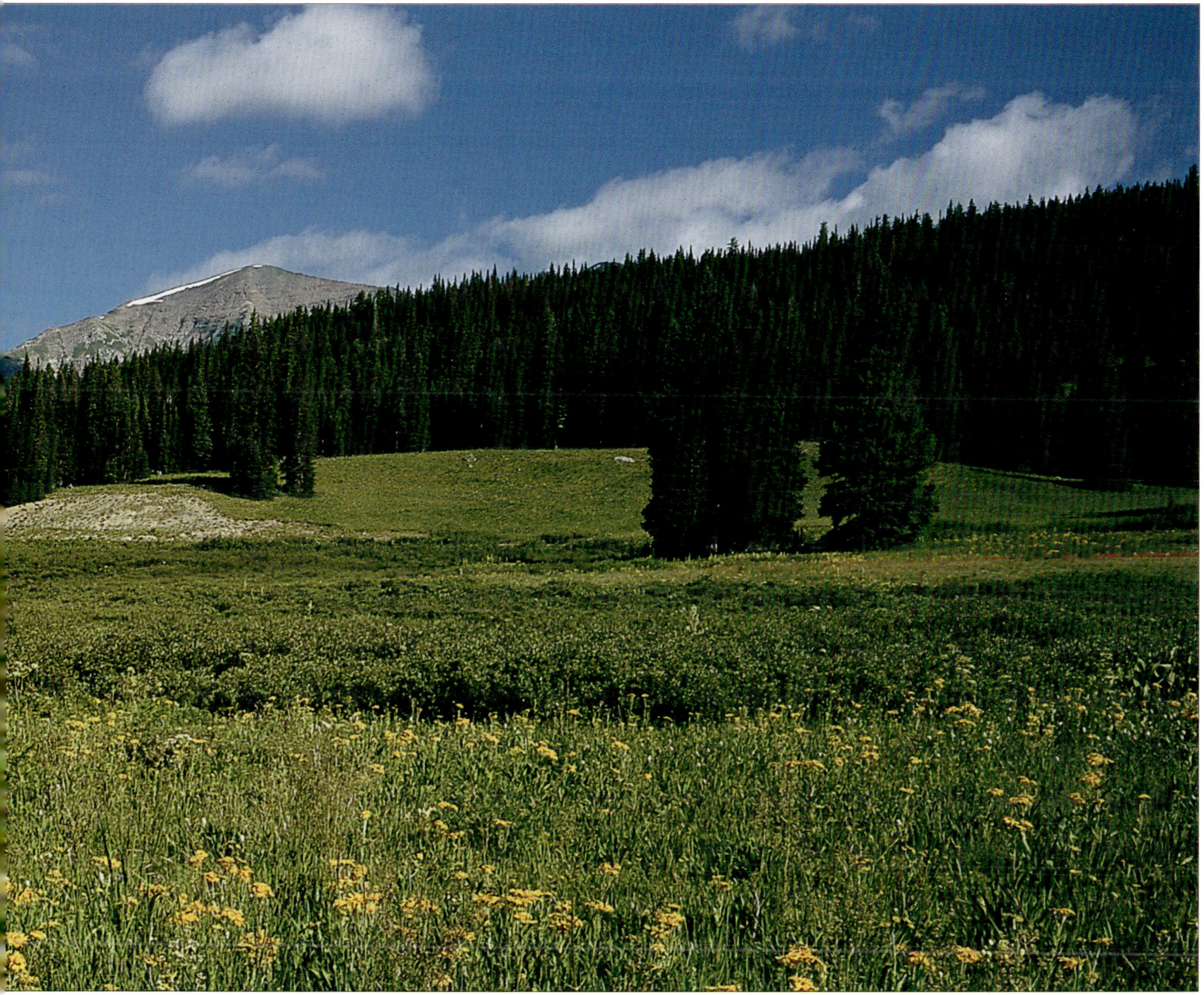

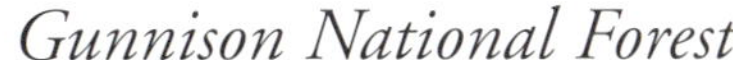

Gunnison National Forest

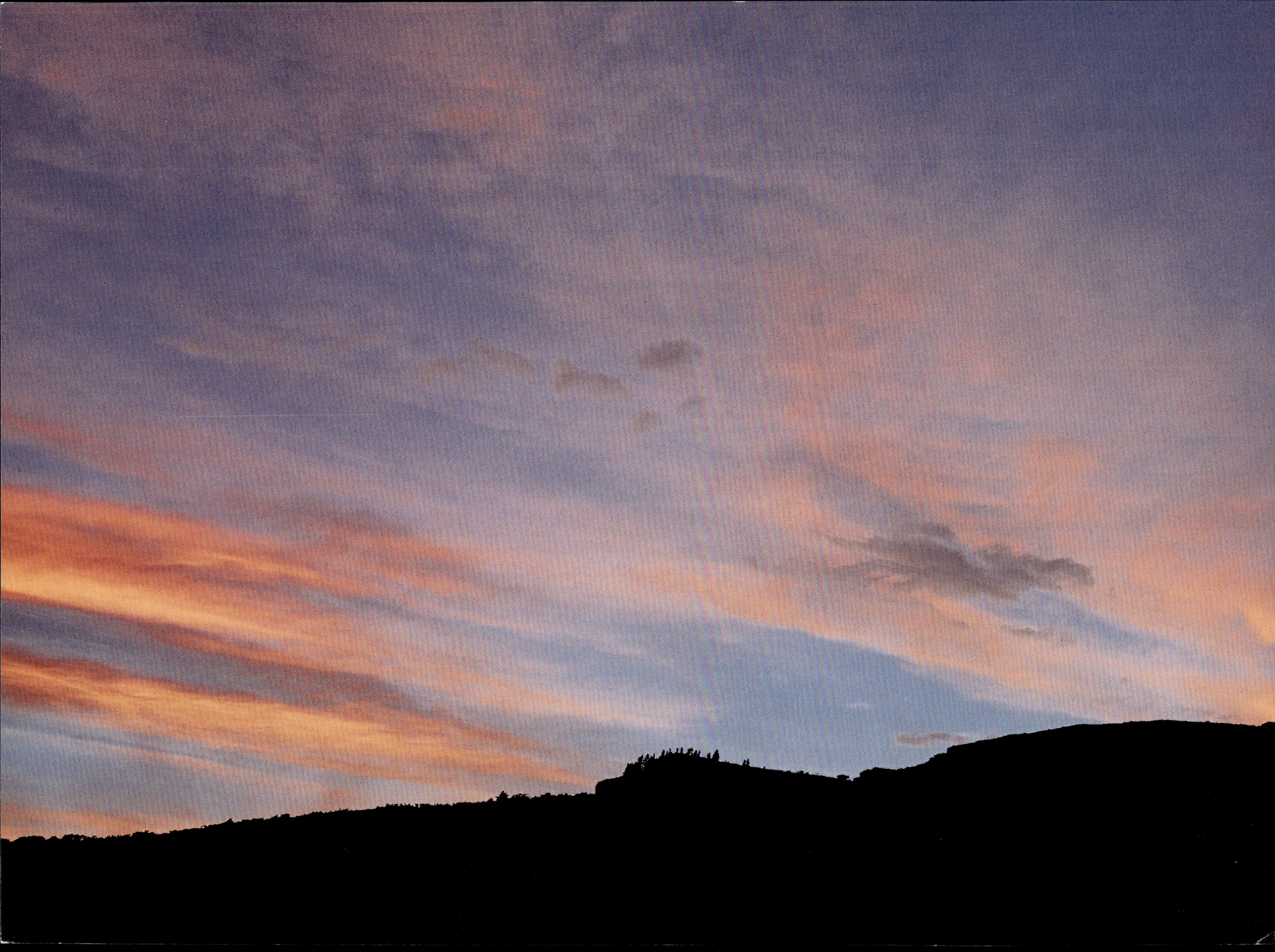

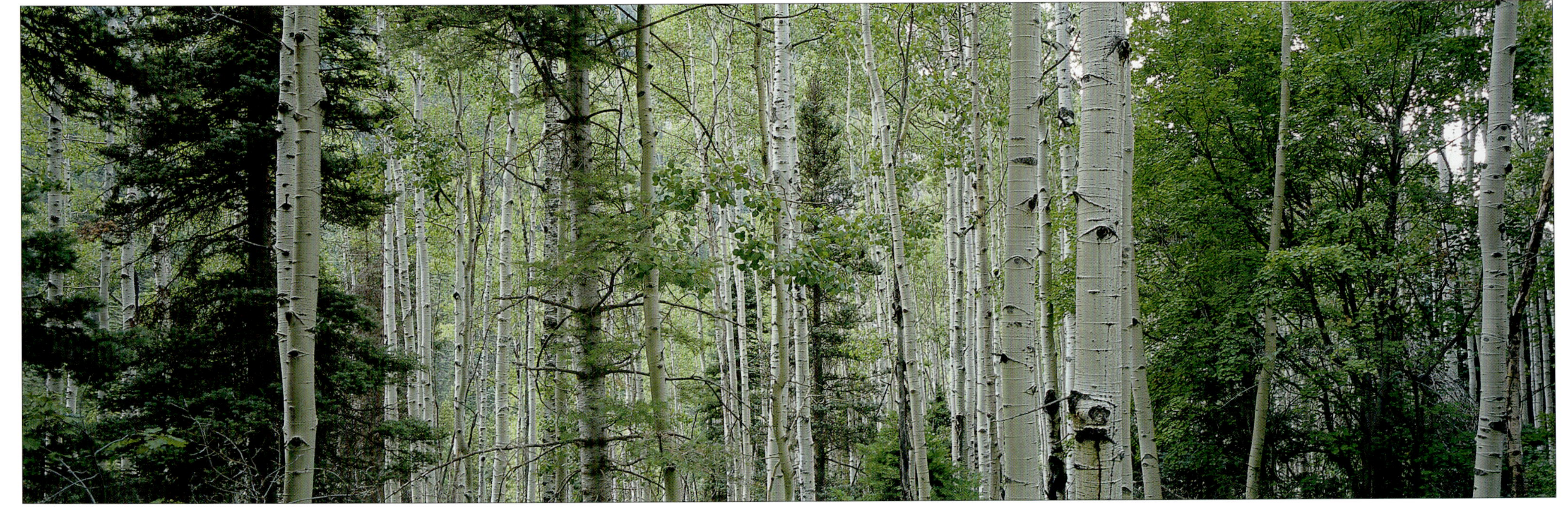

Aspen trees at the base of Potosi Peak, Mount Sneffels Wilderness

Previous Spread: Soap Mesa, Gunnison National Forest

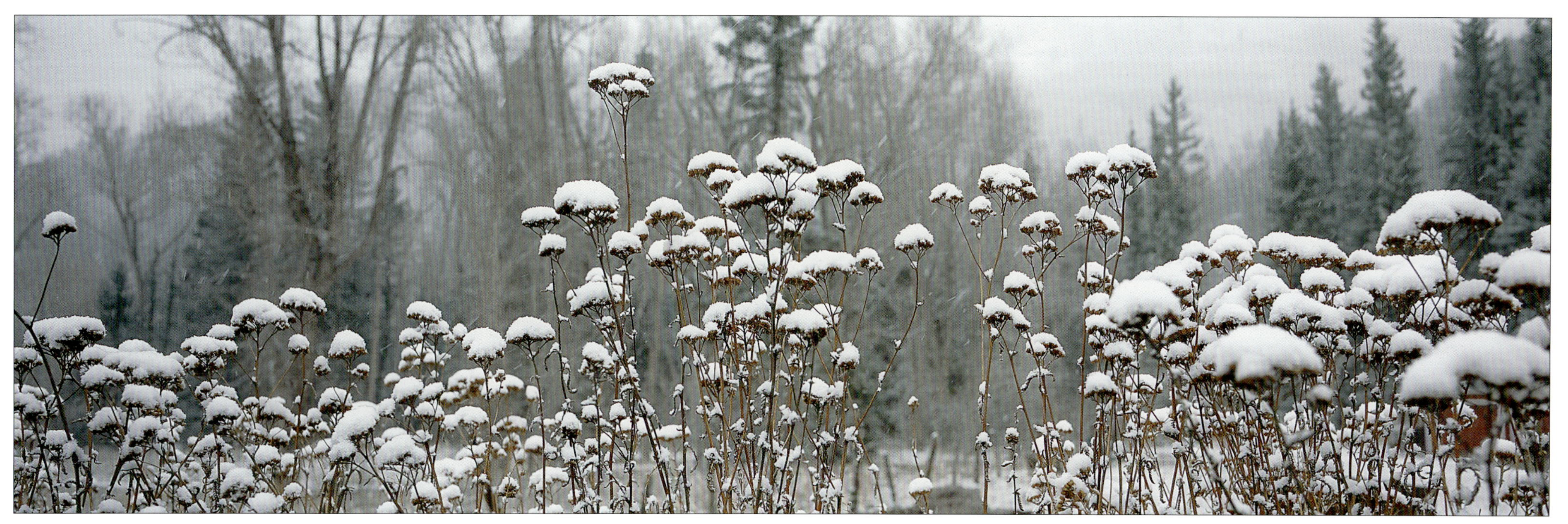

Near Telluride

The first snow of winter gently settles on a pond.

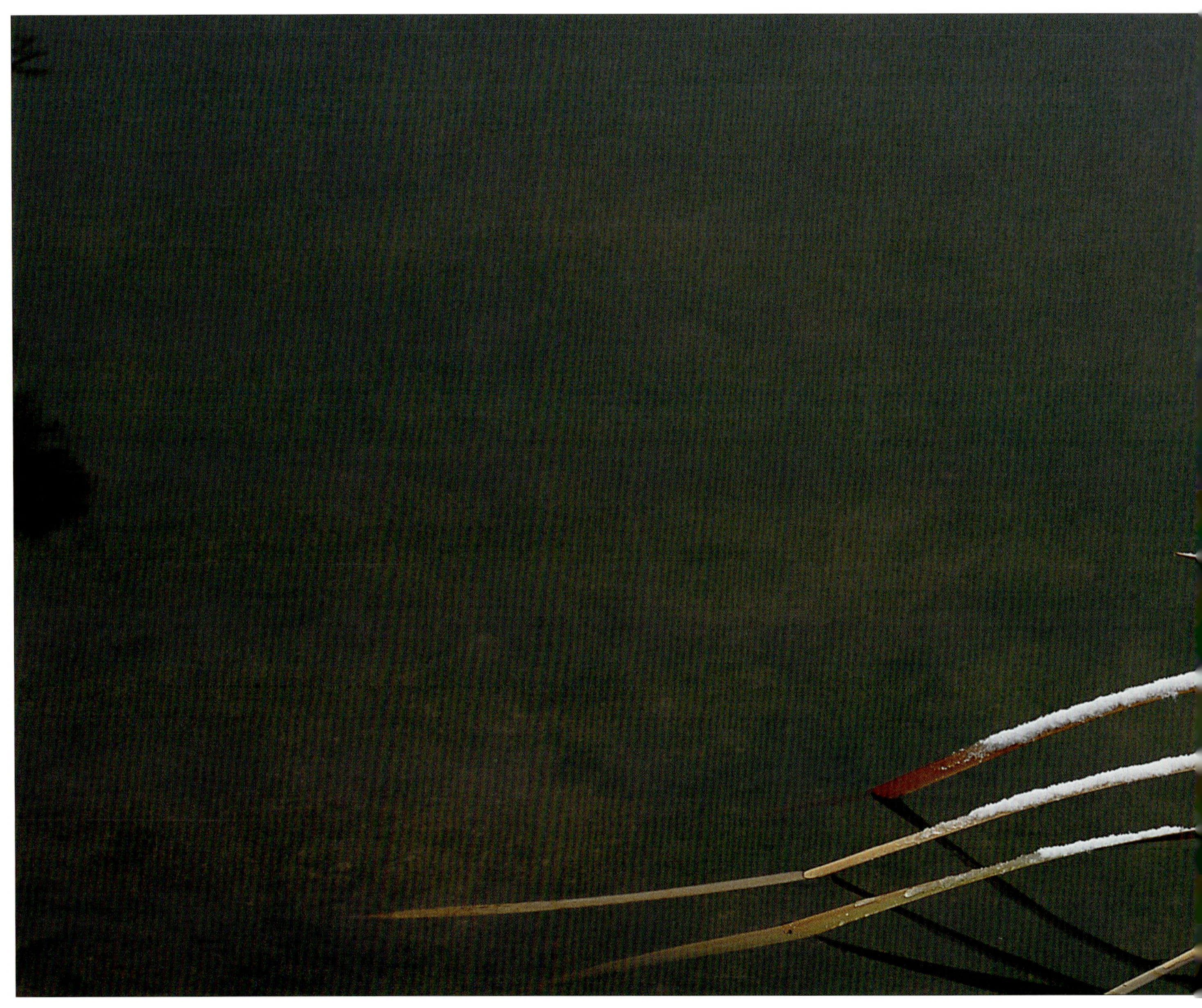

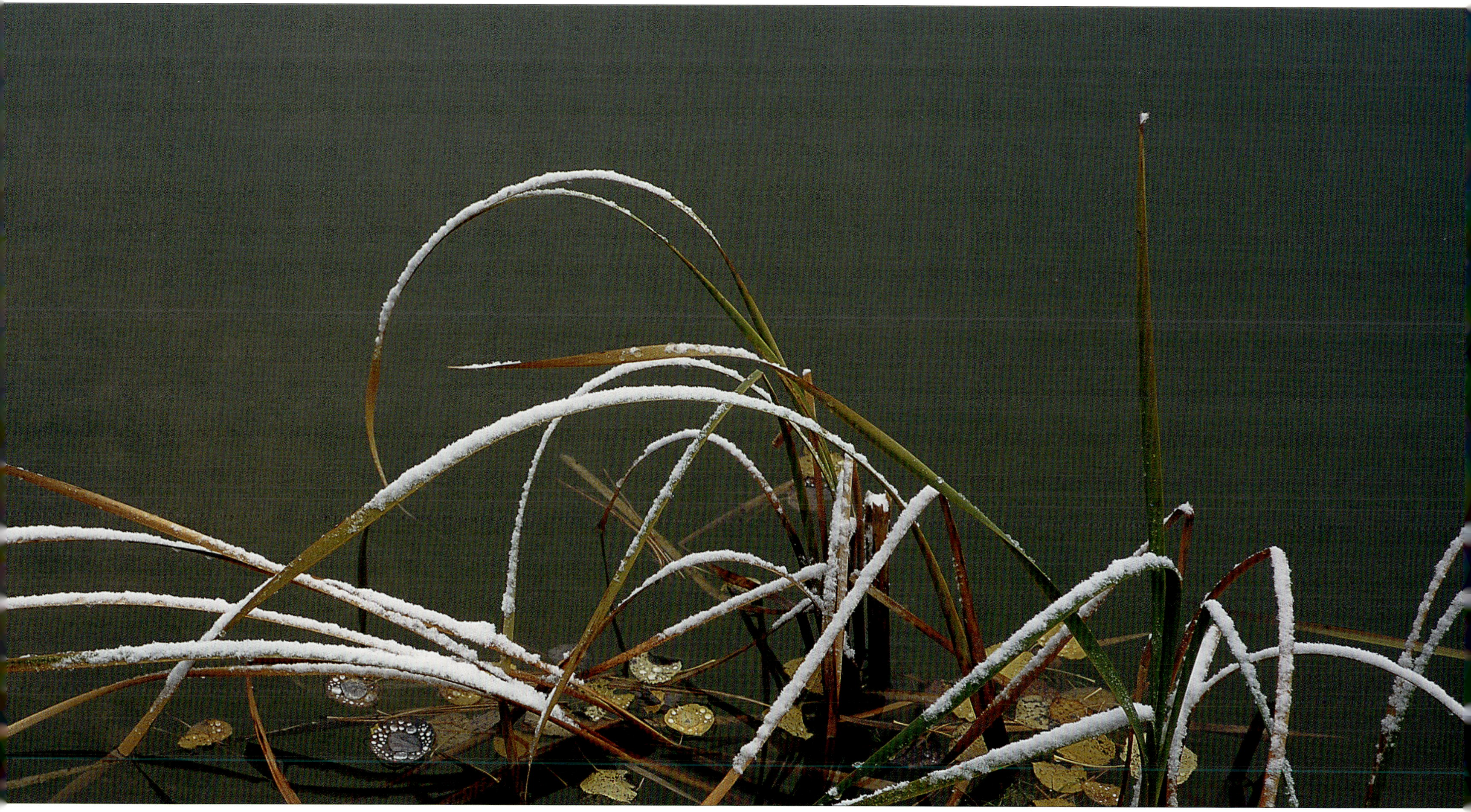

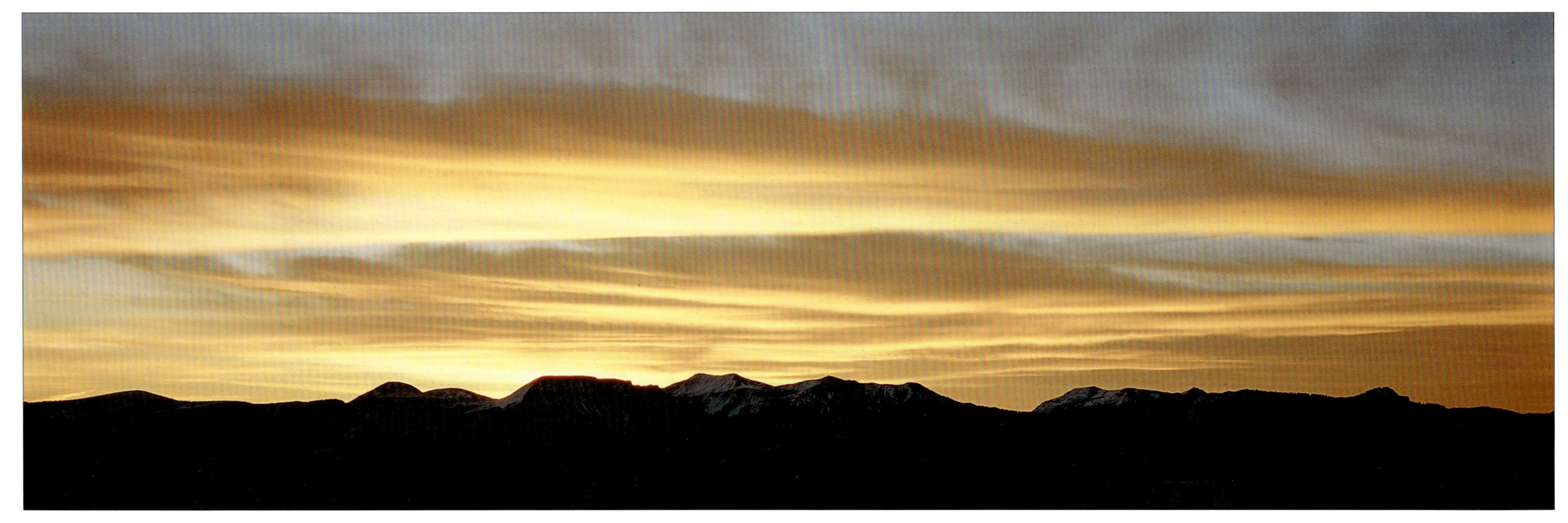

The Wet Mountains

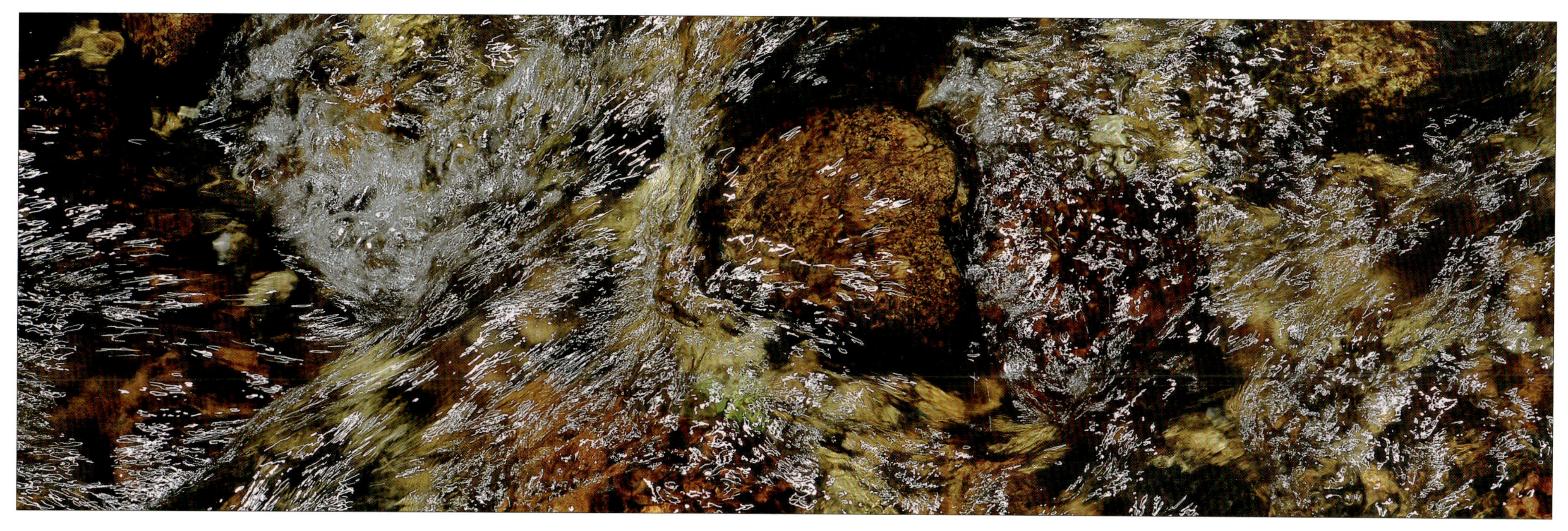

The beginning of spring runoff

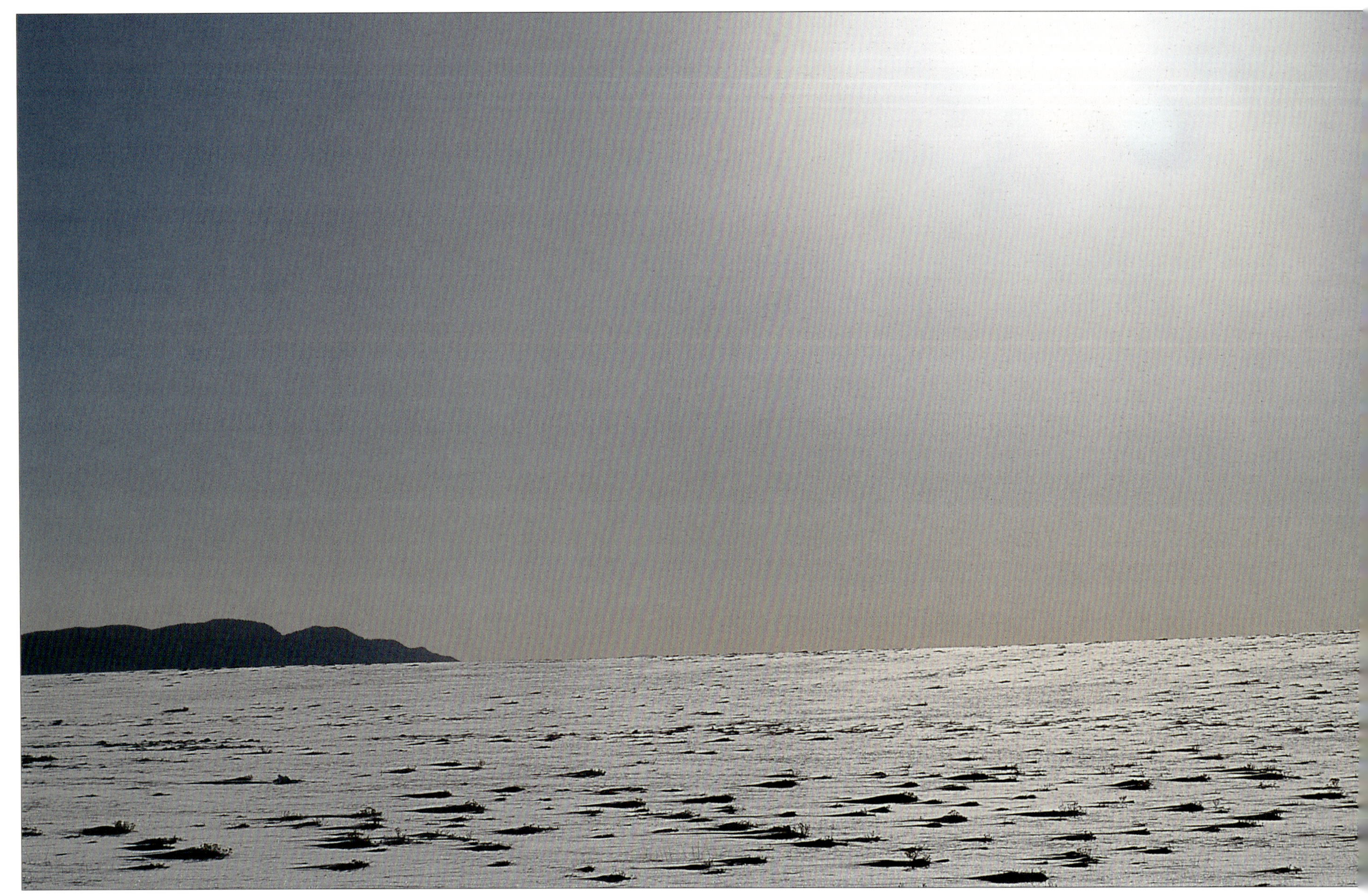

South Park. Still lonely, but the bison are making a comeback.

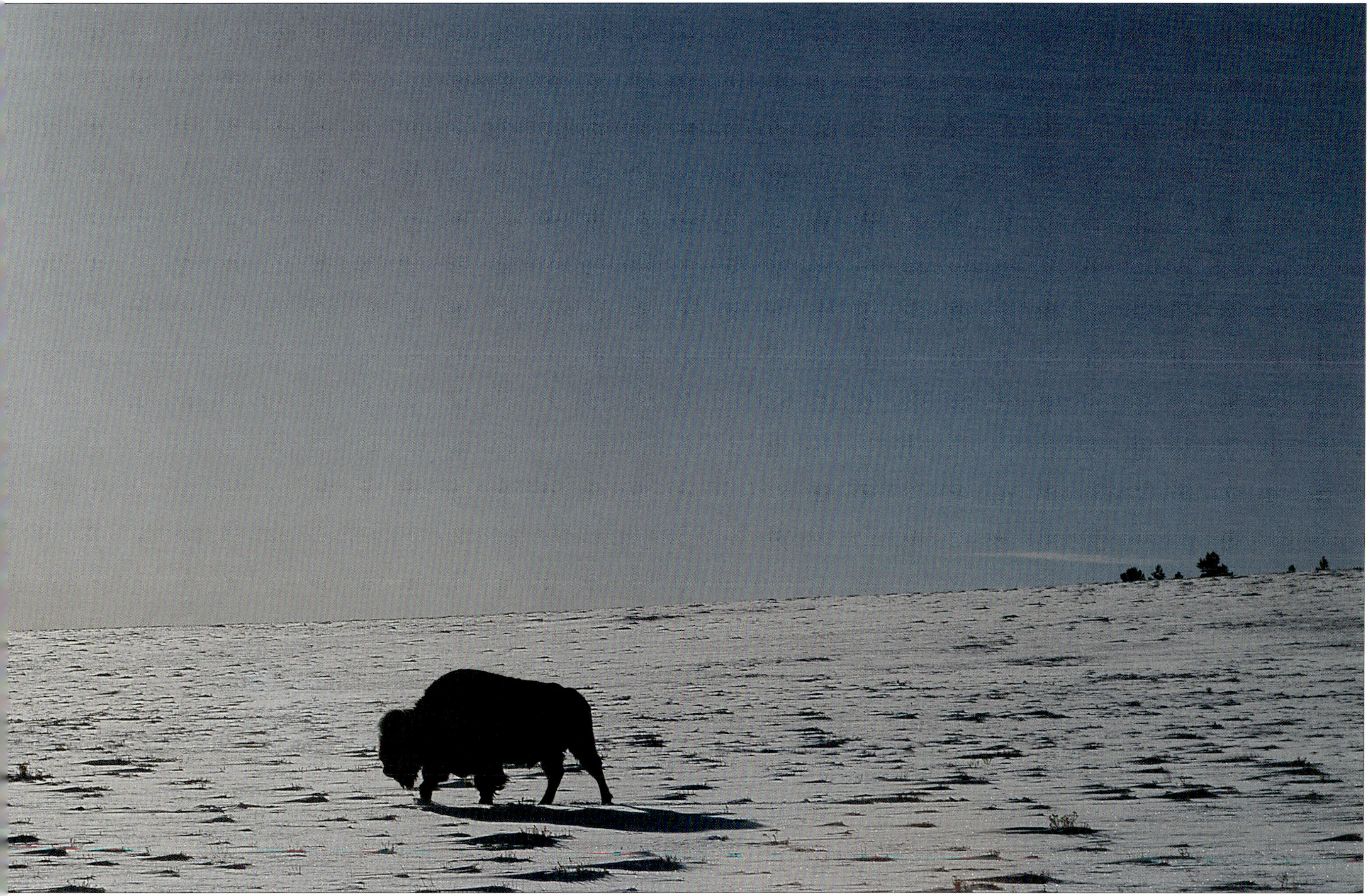

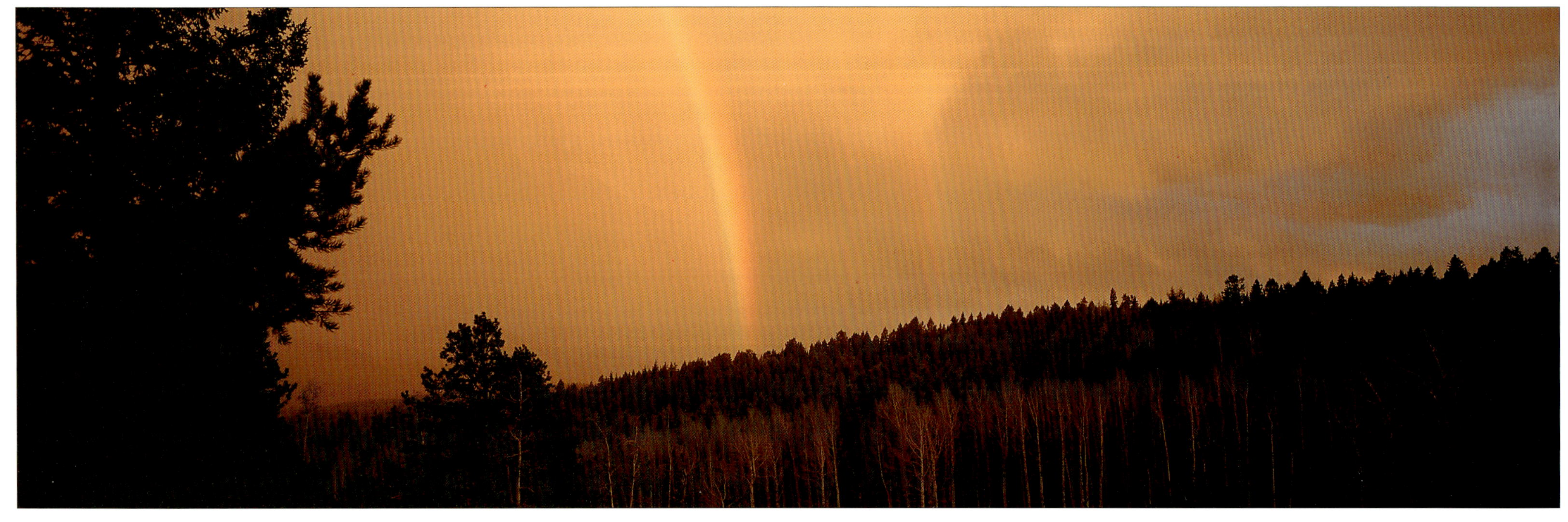

Mueller State Park

The wind was blowing right into the camera lens on the evening this panographic image™ was created. I didn't have my tripod with me, so I leveled the camera with some padding from my camera case, bracing it all on a rock. About six exposures were made at 1/4 of a second, and between each exposure I turned my back to the driving rain to wipe off the lens. This was the only exposure that was sharp enough to keep. It was an invigorating ten minutes.

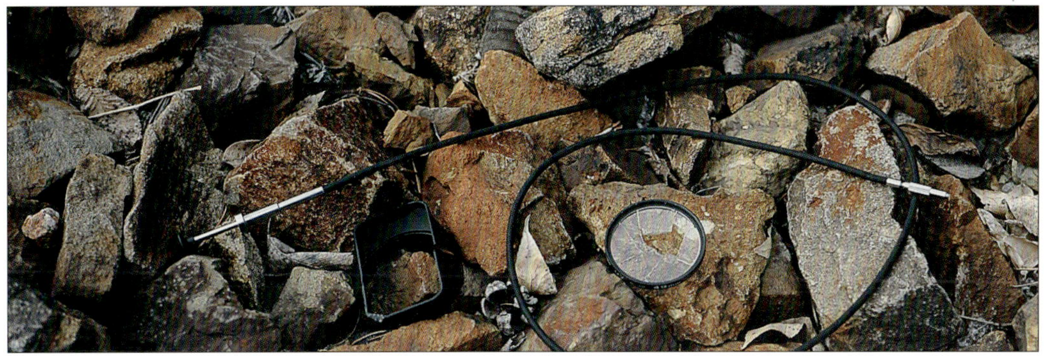

I was in position well before sunrise to make panographic images™ of Wilson Peak. It was less than a half-mile drive off the highway on a snow-covered gravel road. I made a few early dawn images and then clouds diffused the sunlight, eliminating shadows. So what better time to start breakfast than while I waited for the clouds to leave? I put a pot of water on the small stove to make some oatmeal. While looking for my coffee mug, I noticed that the sun was hitting the range to the north. Quickly grabbing the camera and tripod, I ran up a small ridge and made a couple of exposures before running out of film. When I ran back to the car to get more film, I noticed the water boiling away on the stove and took a moment to add the oatmeal, replacing that pan with a pan of milk for hot chocolate. With more film in my fanny pack, I returned to the light-show taking place on the northern range. I made one panographic image™ after another, and slowly began walking back to the car. My stroll was sharply interrupted by the smell of burnt milk back at my outdoor kitchen. In my haste to attend to this mess, my jacket caught on the camera cable release, pulling my camera and tripod crashing to the rocks. The lens hood and filter shattered, with no telling what damage might be done to the camera. Just as I was picking up the camera, the sunlight returned to Wilson Peak. Should I curse, cry or finish breakfast? With nothing to lose, I removed the broken filter and created the image on the next page. I thank God for the light and that the camera was not broken in the fall.

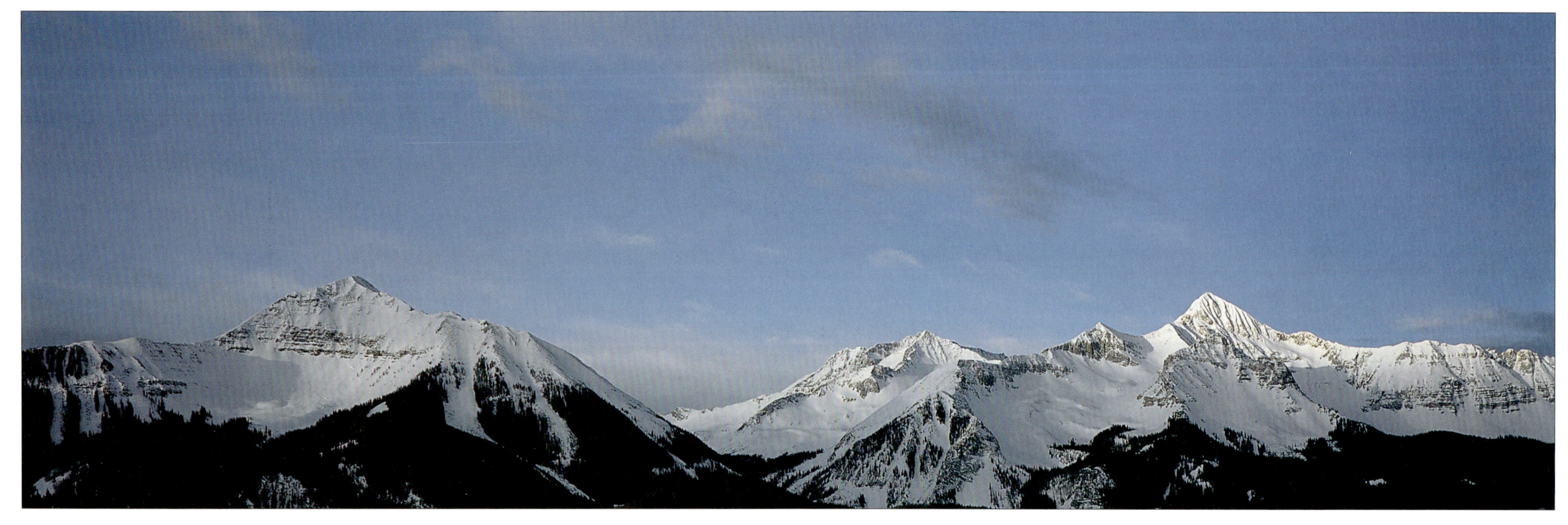

Wilson Peak